Empowering Educators

A Comprehensive Guide to Teaching Grades 3, 4, 5

Julie Kelly ● Andy Moral ● Jenni Lee Groegler Pierson ● Amanda Stessen-Blevins

Center for Responsive Schools, Inc.

ISBN: 978-1-950317-19-6
Library of Congress Control Number: 2021944519

Photographs by Jeff Woodward
Additional photographs by Oliver Scott Photography

Center for Responsive Schools, Inc.
85 Avenue A, P.O. Box 718
Turners Falls, MA 01376-0718

800-360-6332
www.crslearn.org

Third printing 2022

Contents

Publisher's Acknowledgments

Center for Responsive Schools is deeply grateful for the combined talents and expertise of Linda Berger, Kirsten Lee Howard, Julie Kelly, Andy Moral, Emily Parrelli, Jenni Lee Groegler Pierson, Brian Smith, Amanda Stessen-Blevins, Amy Wade, Becky Wanless, Lisa Dewey Wells, and Heather Young. Their hard work, collective wisdom, and collaboration made this series of books valuable resources for other educators.

Center for Responsive Schools would also like to express appreciation to the following people for their involvement in the creation of this book: Michelle Benson, Kevin Bradley, Barbara Findlen, Michelle Gill, Elizabeth Greene, Emily Hemingway, Allison Henry, Cathy Hess, Dr. Lora Hodges, Lindsey Lynch, Jeff Miller, Noelle Serafino, and Anne Sussman.

Introduction

· ·

At Center for Responsive Schools, we believe that educating all children is the most important work in the world. But it's no easy task.

Teachers of upper elementary grades meet their students at a magical moment in their educational journey, a time when children are rapidly growing more independent, more confident, and more aware of the world around them. Students in third, fourth, and fifth grades care deeply, work hard, and delight in a challenge and the chance to make a difference. It takes a special kind of adult guidance to offer upper elementary students the right combination of what they need: both independence and support, a mix of cooperation and competition, and expectations that are high and yet achievable. Developing this balance is just one of the upper elementary teacher's many talents.

Who Should Read This Book?

The goal of this book is to help upper elementary educators do their essential work. Each chapter offers tools, tips, and strategies for building classrooms where all students feel safe, seen, and significant and where educators are empowered to respond to all students' academic, social, emotional, and developmental needs.

To create positive and healthy school and classroom communities, diversity, inclusion, and equity must be at the center of one's pedagogy. Woven throughout these chapters, you will find relevant, impactful practices that can reach every child in every school, every day. All of these practices are based on the *Responsive Classroom* approach, whose six guiding principles form the core of this book. Those principles are:

1. Teaching social and emotional skills is as important as teaching academic content.

2. How we teach is as important as what we teach.

3. Great cognitive growth occurs through social interaction.

4. How we work together as adults to create a safe, joyful, and inclusive school environment is as important as our individual contribution or competence.

5. What we know and believe about our students—individually, culturally, developmentally—informs our expectations, reactions, and attitudes about those students.

6. Partnering with families—knowing them and valuing their contributions—is as important as knowing the children we teach.

Especially in difficult times, these guiding principles remind us of what is most important and motivate us to create classrooms that are inspiring, student centered, and rigorous. All educators, new and veteran ones alike, will find ideas, insights, and innovative approaches in the pages that follow.

How to Use This Book

This book encompasses three different grade levels. We encourage you to read each grade-level section. Equipped with this range of information, educators who teach a single grade level will understand more deeply where their students have come from developmentally, where they are, and where they're going. Educators who teach multiple grade levels, perhaps in multiage classrooms or as special area teachers, will find valuable information on third, fourth, and fifth grades in this book. For ease of use, the book is color coded so you can quickly find the grade you are looking for: yellow for all grades, indigo for third grade, blue for fourth grade, and turquoise for fifth grade.

You can use this book in many ways. You might want to read the book in order, from cover to cover. You might choose to focus on certain chapters or sections based on your needs and interests, or you might refer to different sections throughout the school year. The chapters are organized in the approximate order in which you might approach your school year planning and are filled with information and ideas that are appropriate at any time.

What You'll Find Inside

Most chapters begin with an overview offering background information and general guidance. Following that, you will typically find sections specific to each grade level. Each section contains useful information that is easily applicable to other grade levels with some minor adaptation.

In **Chapter 1**, "Developmentally Responsive Teaching," you will explore your students' developmental ages and stages to understand more about their developmental journey in your year together.

Chapter 2, "Effective Management," leads you through setting up your physical classroom space and considering the consistent schedule, routines, and procedures you will use throughout the year, while **Chapter 3**, "Positive Community," offers tips, strategies, and approaches for building and maintaining positive community in your classroom.

By **Chapter 4**, "Engaging Academics," it's time to delve into academics, with a focus on engaging all learners, setting high expectations, and guiding instruction based on insights from your knowledge and observations of your students.

The final two chapters focus on the adults in your classroom community. **Chapter 5**, "Connecting With Parents," is a guide to partnering with parents to better support your students and their families. **Chapter 6**, "Healthy Teachers, Healthy Classrooms," focuses on you and what you need to be effective, fulfilled, and flourishing as an educator—all year long, not just after a restful school break!

At the end of this book, you will also find a robust appendix with ready-to-use resources you can incorporate into your instruction right away. You can also scan this QR code for access to numerous additional downloadable resources.

Voices in This Book

This book was written collaboratively by four experienced educators. They blended their combined decades of teaching experience to offer advice, strategies, and tips that all educators can learn from. The advice and approaches they describe are backed by evidence and research, but just as important, they are also tried and tested by the authors themselves in real classrooms with real students.

Julie Kelly

Julie Kelly has taught third, fourth, and sixth grades, been a special subject teacher for PK–8, and served as an assistant principal for eight years. She has been using the *Responsive Classroom* approach in her classroom for over ten years. Her favorite thing about teaching nine- and ten-year-olds is their eagerness to learn and experiment with materials. She wrote the chapter overviews.

Andy Moral

Andy Moral is a fourth grade teacher at Sol Feinstone Elementary School in Bucks County, Pennsylvania. He has fifteen years of classroom experience, teaching all subjects in various interme- diate grades. Andy loves teaching and merging academic learning with social and emotional learning for his students. A certified *Responsive Classroom* teacher, Andy contributed the fifth grade sections of this book.

Jenni Lee
Groegler Pierson

Jenni Lee Groegler Pierson has taught first, second, third, and fifth grades as a classroom teacher and is currently a Reading Recovery and literacy support teacher at Barley Sheaf Elementary in Flemington, New Jersey. With over fifteen years using the *Responsive Classroom* approach, she continues to be rewarded by the excitement students demonstrate when they see themselves as learners and accomplish their goals. In addition to being a *Responsive Classroom* consulting teacher, she feels privileged to be able to support third grade educators with her sections in this book.

Amanda Stessen-Blevins

Amanda Stessen-Blevins is a second, third, and fourth grade English as a new language (ENL) teacher at PS 516: Sunset Park Avenues Elementary School in Brooklyn, New York. One of her favorite things about teaching upper elementary grades is students' appreciation for others' perspectives. Specific examples of her love and joy for this age level can be found in the fourth grade sections of this book.

We hope this book will be a helpful resource for you, one that reminds you of the deep value of your work, imparts practical tips and perennial wisdom, and empowers you to teach with hope and joy.

Chapter 1

Developmentally Responsive Teaching

•••••••••••••••••••••••••••••••••

Overview

What Is Developmentally Responsive Teaching?

Whether you are beginning your first year as a teacher, switching grade levels or roles, or approaching the new school year with a fresh start, you may be wondering how you are going to adjust and adapt to meet the strengths and challenges of the students in your room. Successful teachers take a developmental point of view when creating classroom community, planning instruction, and managing the classroom. Developmentally responsive teaching refers to the practices that teachers use to learn about and respond to students' individual, cultural, and developmental needs and strengths. Knowing what students are developmentally capable of doing is the cornerstone of developmentally responsive teaching, as it provides direction on how to nurture and support students and have realistic, developmentally appropriate expectations as they learn and grow over the course of the school year.

What Do Developmentally Responsive Teachers Do, and Why?

Developmentally responsive teachers invest time in observing their students individually and collectively, continuously learning about their students, and paying attention to the students' developmental traits, strengths, and needs. Prior to the start of the school year, spend time with your class list of student birthdays. Chip Wood's book *Yardsticks:*

See the appendix, p. 325, for the Birthday Cluster exercise.

Child and Adolescent Development Ages 4–14 is a useful guide as you gather information for planning for and responding to anticipated developmental needs. During the school year, pay attention to the conversations taking place in your classroom, in the hallway, and on the playground, during both structured and unstructured times of the day. Base your decisions for teaching and discipline on your firsthand research and knowledge of your students' social, emotional, physical, and cognitive development. For example, choosing books about fairness and incorporating role-play into instruction would meet nine-year-olds' increasing awareness of and interest in issues of fairness. Focusing on growth and development to meet our students where they are developmentally enables us to provide an optimal learning environment, one into which students eagerly enter each morning. Consider these ways to become a developmentally responsive teacher:

- **Purposefully select interactive learning structures and student groupings that meet the developmental needs of your students.** Identifying meaningful learning structures and rich opportunities for collaboration is a key part of the planning and implementation of active and interactive teaching practices. For example, nine-year-olds like to work with a partner of their choice. You set students up for success by establishing an inclusive classroom community, providing guidance to students in choosing a work partner, and giving them opportunities to practice and reflect on their experiences of choosing a work partner.

- **Create a classroom environment in which students feel welcome, have ownership, and experience a sense of belonging.** Choose materials that are developmentally appropriate and accommodate a wide variety of student needs. For example, cluster work areas to provide spaces in the classroom for various work arrangements and provide the physical space that students need to move safely. In displaying student work, include examples from every student; this builds a sense of individual and group ownership of the classroom. (See Chapter 2 to take a deeper dive into the physical setup of the classroom and Chapter 3 for community-building suggestions.)

Skillfully using teacher language and visual cues, support students in developing self-control, building a sense of community, and gaining academic skills and knowledge. You can build a foundation of trust with words, both by naming students' strengths and by listening to the voices of your students as they share their thoughts, interests, concerns, and laughter. Establishing this foundation allows a community of learners to develop and grow.

Engage your students in building a community of learners. Together, you and your students create an environment in which all participants are engaged in learning. As the lead learner, you actively research, plan, implement, and observe your students with the goal of getting to know them developmentally, personally, and culturally, using the information to help your students connect the dots of learning. Knowing your students' backgrounds and cultures allows you to include and honor the diverse voices and cultures in your classroom when teaching the curriculum and in building a diverse classroom library. Your students will see themselves in their work, becoming engaged in both their learning and their classroom community.

Understanding that teaching social and emotional skills is as important as teaching academic skills, embed SEL instruction that is developmentally appropriate. It is important for students in this age group to be instructed in the tools needed for managing their emotions. For example, ten-year-olds should be able to seek help when unable to resolve conflict with peers. Incorporate class problem-solving meetings as needed.

What Do We Know About Child and Adolescent Development?

Psychologists and educators such as Jean Piaget, Beatrice and Arnold Gesell, Maria Montessori, James P. Comer, and Sonia Nieto have observed, researched, and documented how children change from age to age and have discovered common patterns of growth. The patterns are seen in physical maturation, language acquisition, social and emotional behavior, cognition, and ways of approaching the world. The information gleaned from the research into these patterns informs our expectations of our students. As teachers, we must constantly ask ourselves, "Are our expectations reasonable?" As we consider this question, we should keep in mind four universally observable maxims (Wood 2017):

1. **Stages of growth and development follow a reasonably predictable pattern.** Children tend to share common patterns of growth and development. For example, the awkwardness we sometimes see in the coordination of eight-year-olds is replaced with better coordination as they become nine-year-olds.

2. **Children and adolescents do not proceed through each stage at the same pace.** Each child is unique. Development is influenced by a variety of factors including but not limited to culture, personality, and environment. While children go through predictable stages, they may not proceed at the same pace. When comparing two students at the same chronological age, you may find that one child is more like a ten-year-old in some developmental aspects, such as cognition, with an increasing ability to think abstractly and concentrate for longer periods of time, whereas the other child may be more like an eight-year-old, with a limited attention span.

3. **Children and adolescents progress through the various aspects of development at their own rate.** Physical, social, emotional, linguistic, and cognitive development do not all take place at the same speed. One student may experience tremendous growth in physical development, with quickly developing large muscles like those of a ten-year-old, yet emotionally the child may be more like a nine-year-old, impatient and easily frustrated.

4. **Growth is uneven.** In the development process, you may see active periods of growth or spurts alternate with quiet periods or a plateau. Nine-year-olds have moods and interests that shift rapidly, compared to ten-year-olds, who are generally happy and whose interests are solidifying. Compare growth to the excitement of learning something new. Once you have grown the new learning, you settle into it.

These maxims show that there is no "average" student, that every student is in a unique developmental place and therefore has different, particular needs that teachers must meet. Using these maxims will enable you to make the best use of the information provided in the relevant grade-level-specific section in order to meet your students where they are and teach them in ways that will help them thrive in your classroom.

As you explore this chapter, you will learn common characteristics of students in your relevant grade level, how to use the developmental information in the classroom, and how child development connects to social and emotional learning. Keep in mind that students in your class-room may fall into a two- to three-year age range. Consider the potential needs of the students on the younger and older ends of the age range and how you might address those needs. By knowing your students' develop-mental capabilities and challenges and utilizing this information in your instruction, you will be able to provide an optimal learning environment for your students.

Grade ❸

"I'm in third grade!" Kellen exclaimed, as he saw a familiar teacher waiting to escort him to his classroom on the first day of school. Hardly able to contain his excitement, he went from topic to topic as they walked down the hallway. "We're going to do cool projects, and I really hope my friends are in my class," he announced. As Kellen neared the door, he asked, "Do you think my new teacher's going to like me?" "Of course she will, Kellen," the teacher reassured him, as she reflected on the changes in students as they leap from second to third grade. "You're going to have an amazing year!"

Kellen embodies the key characteristics of a third grader—excitement for learning and willingness to take on new challenges, interest in peer relations, and of course, eagerness to have the approval of their teacher and classmates. As the year unfolds, Kellen will benefit from working with others and at times will become preoccupied when events are not "just" or "fair" in his mind. He will be willing to take on even more than he can handle some days, as his attention span may be short until he is thoroughly engaged in a task that he is committed to completing. He will benefit from hands-on experiences where he can investigate and manipulate what is in front of him; his increasing hand-eye coordination will aid him in this area.

Take a moment to view the charts at the end of this section to learn more about where Kellen and his third grade peers are developmentally throughout this pivotal year.

Meeting Third Graders' Developmental Needs

As educators, we often ask ourselves, "How can I support the developmental needs of all my students *and* their social and emotional learning?" The challenge is to determine how we can meet so many different needs in one classroom, knowing that students' growth is uneven despite the predictable developmental stages. Keeping in mind that some students may require additional support or additional advancement, the following

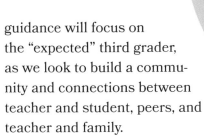

guidance will focus on the "expected" third grader, as we look to build a community and connections between teacher and student, peers, and teacher and family.

Teacher and Student—Forming a Partnership

Think back to reflect on an educator who was significant to you by making you feel valued, known, and safe; this person is someone you felt comfortable talking to and seeking out when you needed help. Your third graders need you to be that person for them, especially as you support their social-emotional growth. When a relationship has been established and they feel you truly know them, they will be responsive to your guidance on everything from academic skills to how to talk about their emotions. We can only hold students accountable for what we know is within their control. You are establishing a culture where they know mistakes will happen, but the trust and rapport you have with them will help challenging moments become valuable learning opportunities. Consider keeping your own informal chart to write down what you know about each student and what they know you are aware of in their life. This can be a set of anecdotal notes to help you foster relationships with all students. In building trust with your students, you are also laying the foundation for a partnership that supports both the social-emotional and academic aspects of their learning. Consider the following scenario describing a teacher preparing students to transition into a small-group activity. Before students move into their groups, she sets the stage by announcing, "Decide which partner will get your materials. Work together to find a spot around the room where your group will be able to do their best work. Remember what it should look and sound like as you move around. I'm excited to watch how successful you'll be and how quickly you'll be able to get started!" The teacher's use of reinforcing, reminding, and envisioning language proactively sets the students up for a successful learning experience. As the students navigate their way, she notices how they open storage bins to get materials, use flexible seating options, and organize their space in a timely and efficient manner.

The success of students during this transition is the result of the teacher's purposeful planning of their classroom space—yes, *their* classroom! She has taken the time to consider furniture placement, think about heavy traffic areas in the room, and position materials so they are easily accessible to students. She has used Interactive Modeling so children know what the expectations, routines, and procedures look and sound like. Through Guided Discovery lessons, students have learned how to care for materials and know expectations for appropriate use. Then, by organizing the space and materials for the small-group activity in partnership with the students, she has taken into account their developmental needs and ownership in their learning. While it takes time to utilize Guided Discovery and Interactive Modeling to set students up for success, the teacher can now meet their emotional, social, cognitive, and physical developmental needs. The environment reflects the students' interests and input, and it empowers them to take on independence and ownership.

Peers—Respectful Relationships

See the appendix, p. 325, for the Birthday Cluster exercise.

"I have a very young class this year," a third grade teacher shared with her colleague. She was referring to the Birthday Cluster exercise developed by Chip Wood, a powerful tool to guide teaching of not only academic content, but also social and emotional skills. As you are planning partnerships and helping students to navigate conflict resolution, birthdates can provide insight into where students are developmentally so you know how to support their problem-solving skills.

"What can you do if you are working with your partner and you do not agree?" a teacher posed to her students. Some hands flew in the air quickly and other students scrunched up their faces as they pondered the possibilities. This question was the start to a role-play scenario to help proactively provide students with problem-solving options. As we see developmental milestones that could cause conflict, they become teachable moments to set students up for success. All learners require active and interactive structures to support academic engagement; we need to equip students with the tools to be successful when we send them off to facilitate each other's learning.

Teacher and Family—Creating Collaborative Connections

"The phone Laura holds is not for playing; it is to make sure her body is staying healthy," a parent explained, as the students looked on and raised their hands to ask questions. This guardian was invited into the class to explain about Laura's diabetes, so the students could learn more and build a network of support and empathy with peers. Whether sharing about medical needs, cultural celebrations, or careers, families are just as much a part of the community as the students we enter the classroom.

Are you comfortable sharing information about your family with someone who is new in your life? Chances are, probably not. If you put yourself in the shoes of a student's family member or caregiver, you can see that there can be a lot of personal information and experiences that they may feel uncomfortable sharing or discussing openly. Building bridges with family members and guardians can help to establish relationships so you can learn more about the students. While we know developmental trends for children, we also need to be mindful of how adverse childhood experiences may impact our students' development. When forming a partnership of empathy and understanding, we need to remember that it is always about everyone wanting to do the best for the child and that all adults involved can work together to set the student up for consistency and success. (See Chapter 5 for further discussion of teacher-family collaboration.)

Pause and Ponder

As you are thinking about your enthusiastic third graders and establishing a foundation that will engage, empower, and enrich their academic, social, emotional, and physical development, consider the following questions:

- How well do I know my students developmentally?

- What do I know about each student—their personal interests, areas of strength, areas to support, and family insights?

- How can role-play support the social and emotional growth of my students and foster strong peer relationships?

- How does the classroom become one that belongs to *all* of us—students and teacher?

- What can I do to foster relationships with families and caregivers?

Third Graders

Common Characteristics	School Implications

Social-Emotional

• Enjoy socializing and working in groups.	• Structure large-group projects, but expect a mix of socializing and work.
• Are generally easygoing.	• Change groupings frequently and use other structures (for instance, whole-group games such as tag and soccer) to stretch children to work across gender lines and with a mix of classmates.
• Adjust well to change.	
• Enjoy larger friendship groups, preferably with same-gender friends.	
• Are willing to take risks; usually recover quickly from mistakes or problems.	• Expect enthusiasm for community-building projects and activities.
• Are concerned with fairness and justice; often have arguments and complaints about fairness issues.	• Be ready to help with arguments and complaints about fairness and justice.

Physical

• Are usually full of energy.	• Give frequent, short movement breaks and incorporate movement into the curriculum throughout the day to boost concentration and productivity.
• Often hurry.	
• May move awkwardly.	
• Can focus visually on both near and far.	• Ask for "best" handwriting only on projects and posters, not daily assignments.
• Tend to play hard and tire quickly.	• Give time to practice handwriting, drawing, and crafts.
• Have improving hand-eye coordination and fine motor skills.	• Allow children to do some copying from the board.

Third Graders

Common Characteristics	School Implications

Cognitive

Common Characteristics	School Implications
• Are industrious and often overzealous, taking on more than they can handle.	• Give many short assignments and activities rather than a few long ones.
• Have limited attention span but can become engrossed in an activity.	• Break assignments down into manageable parts.
• Are better at using manipulatives to explain their thinking and problem-solving.	• Give third graders opportunities to sort and organize, but realize they'll often need your help.
• Usually care about process and product; eager for approval of peers and adults.	• Display students' in-process work as well as their final products.
• Are increasingly interested in logic, classification, and the way things work.	• Include study of various cultures—highly enjoyable for third graders.
	• Craft hands-on math and science lessons that help students grasp abstract concepts.
	• For read-alouds, offer mysteries and other stories involving logic.
	• If children become really engaged in a lesson or discussion, go with it if you can; most third graders can comfortably handle a change in plans.

Language

Common Characteristics	School Implications
• Have quickly growing vocabularies; many love to talk and explain ideas.	• Leverage their love of talking by teaching skills required for conferring in groups, talking with partners, and sharing reflections on their work.
• Tend to exaggerate.	• Keep social and academic conferences short, with bite-size teaching points.
• Tend to listen well, but have so many ideas that they may not remember what they heard.	• Invite them to write tall tales and poems using exaggeration, along with nonfiction about what they're learning in social studies and science.

The information in this chart is based on *Yardsticks: Child and Adolescent Development Ages 4–14*, 4th ed., by Chip Wood (Center for Responsive Schools 2017) and Child Development Guide by Center for Development of Human Services at SUNY Buffalo State (New York State Office of Children and Family Services 2015).

Grade 4

During a midyear Morning Meeting, a share is going around the circle as students express how their identities have evolved over time.

See the appendix, p. 324, for more on Morning Meeting.

"I used to be competitive, but now I'm calm," Zhi Xiang says.

"I used to not be good at games, but because of my determination, now I'm good at games," Azizah shares.

"I used to not like learning on a computer, but now I figured out ways to fix the problems and try again," Sofia remarks. As one student shares, the rest of the class members listen and nod, showing their appreciation for different perspectives or connecting with similarities.

This snapshot demonstrates the students' own reflection about the developmental characteristics of fourth graders. Nine-year-olds can be competitive, self-critical, impatient, and easily frustrated. Ten-year-olds tend to be cooperative, do better with group games and activities, can concentrate for longer periods, and like to problem-solve. Knowing these developmental characteristics is an integral component when planning academic, social, and emotional instruction.

Meeting Fourth Graders' Developmental Needs

The better we know our students, the more effectively we can teach them. Knowing our students personally, culturally, and developmentally informs our instruction as we get to know their strengths. As our relationships grow, trust builds a foundation that allows for students to take risks in their learning. Developmentally responsive teaching is essential to building a classroom environment that represents all students. This section will address ways of planning for the developmental needs of your class.

See the appendix, p. 325, for the Birthday Cluster exercise.

At the beginning of the school year, the Birthday Cluster exercise, developed by Chip Wood, can be helpful in order to plan according to the developmental needs of your class. Students in fourth grade will start out the year as eight-years-olds and turn nine or begin the year as nine-years-olds and turn ten. The chronological list will help you to notice clusters of birthdays and whether most of the class is on the older or younger side. This exercise will also help you to identify outlying students and figure out ways to meet their developmental needs. For example, one year I had a student who was an entire year older than the rest of the class. I noticed a significant increase in his participation when the energizers and activities reflected where he was developmentally.

Organizing the class with the Birthday Cluster exercise can also help you to mentally prepare for the new school year. Remember that by the time you end the school year, your fourth graders have grown a lot and are nearly a whole year older than they were at the beginning of the school year. Using the Birthday Cluster exercise at the beginning of the school year is invaluable for reframing your expectations of the younger, new students you will be greeting on the first day of school. Revisit the Birthday Cluster exercise and Chip Wood's book *Yardsticks* several times a year but especially around the midyear mark. The exercise provides a time to regroup and continue to anticipate the developmental needs of the students you now know so well.

While the Birthday Cluster exercise is a place to start at the beginning of the school year, observing and talking with students every day will inform your practice more deeply. Consider students' strengths and assets. Get to know students' families and caregivers, and allow their expertise and insights to shape your perspective. Any class will showcase a diverse range of learners that makes each class unique and exemplifies the importance of students' feelings of belonging and significance. This diversity allows us to predict a range of developmental needs of both older and younger students, and there are many ways to balance this range of needs.

Offering choice is one way to balance developmentally older and younger students. This might mean students choose to work with a partner or group. Nine-year-olds can thrive with partner choice some of the time, while ten-year-olds do well with group activities. Choice might also include an academic process, such as how students show their work in math: eight-year-olds and nine-year-olds often still need concrete objects and pictorial representations, whereas ten-year-olds are increasingly able to think more abstractly; these distinctions may be reflected in how students prove their math thinking. (See Chapter 4 for additional examples of choice in academics.)

Preparing students for the next developmental stage through explicit teaching can be another way to balance developmentally older and younger students. This might include purposefully choosing energizers and activities that highlight cooperation for the soon-to-be ten-year-olds, while also providing modifications for the possible anxieties of the nine-year-olds in the class. Another example might be noticing that eight- and nine-year-olds have expanding vocabularies and love wordplay, while ten-year-olds are very good at memorizing poetry. With this in mind, consider studying poetry throughout the year rather than in a stand-alone unit for just a few weeks. At the beginning of the year, lessons might focus on exploring poems with sophisticated words and digging into figurative language. By the end of the year, students can recite and perform their own poems.

See the appendix, p. 313, for sample energizers.

Assigning partners to work together for short periods of time is another way you might consider balancing the range of older and younger students. For example, for a science project, you might intentionally pair a student exhibiting anxious nine-year-old behaviors with a student who is demonstrating ten-year-old behaviors of cooperation and flexibility. It's important to change partnerships frequently and allow for choice from time to time, but this is another way to balance developmentally older and younger students. Some interactive learning structures that allow students to change partnerships frequently include Mix and Mingle to Music, Four Corners, and Maître d'. You know your students best, so consider many factors when planning to pair them together.

See the appendix, p. 318, for more on these interactive learning structures.

Noticing how the scope and sequence and curriculum across the school matches (or doesn't match) child development needs is also something to consider. For example, you might notice that fourth grade is finishing a

poetry unit right as the second grade is beginning a poetry unit. Knowing that a developmental characteristic of ten-year-olds is enjoying assisting younger grades, you might consider partnering the two grades together during the second graders' poetry unit. Fourth graders can practice synthesizing what they have learned and have an audience for their poems, while the second graders will also have an audience and role models offering them encouragement.

Child Development and SEL Instruction

We can use what we know about patterns in development to help us consider and proactively plan to incorporate social-emotional learning competencies into our day.

Cooperation

We know that nine-year-olds can be easily frustrated and show signs of impatience. They can also feel worried or anxious. Knowing this, it will be important to explicitly incorporate the social-emotional competency of cooperation into our instruction. Before starting an activity, for example, we might ask, "What are ways we show our support to someone who makes a mistake?" We might use an interactive learning structure to demonstrate what it looks like to resolve differences quickly. We might utilize an activity such as a role-play to model how to cooperate either as a group leader or as a member of a group; for example, students might role-play a meeting with a book club in which they would take turns being a leader and a group member. While these ideas would be proactive in supporting nine-year-olds at the beginning of the academic year, they will continue to support students throughout the year as they transition to demonstrating the developmental characteristics of ten-year-olds, who tend to be cooperative and flexible and are highly sensitive to questions of fairness and issues related to friendship.

Assertiveness

Nine-year-olds have a tendency to say, "This is boring" or "I hate it" when work is repetitive or challenging. Therefore, teaching students how to express strong emotions and opinions and how to persist when facing challenging events will be important. Understanding that nine-year-olds often feel anxious or worried, it's important to teach them how to seek help, reassuring them by showing openness and honesty with lightheartedness and humor. For example, in the middle of the year, an out-of-classroom teacher asked a student if he wanted a drink of water from the water fountain before they got started in their small group. He paused, then nodded yes. He walked partway down the hallway, almost to the drinking fountain alcove, and came back. "Is everything okay?" the teacher asked. "I don't know where the water fountain is," the student mumbled, with his eyes to the floor. "Oh, right, of course! You always bring a water bottle to school! I'll walk with you," the teacher responded. As they walked, the teacher realized if the student didn't know where the water fountain was, he likely had never used the bathroom in this fourth grade hallway, either, since one must walk past the drinking fountain to get to the bathroom. After the student drank some water, the teacher suggested, "While we're walking, let's walk this other way to our small group," and casually pointed out the bathroom along the way. Later that week, the teacher noticed that the student requested to use the bathroom—perhaps for the first time in the middle of the year! This story demonstrates the need to teach students how to ask for help, but it is also a gentle reminder to us all not to assume that showing or telling students something one time is enough. Teaching these assertiveness skills early in the year will support students developmentally as they enjoy engaging in class problem-solving meetings and conducting school surveys.

Responsibility

There is certainly explicit teaching needed within the competency of responsibility. Nine-year-olds can be critical of themselves and others and often complain about fairness issues. Children in this age group also tend to be aware of who is in and out of certain groups in the lunchroom and on the playground, they may be excluded from (or included in) cliques in and out of school, and social media will increasingly play a role in their social lives. These developmental patterns directly relate to accountability for oneself and to demonstrating social, civic, and digital responsibility. This explicit teaching will help to support a foundation in the classroom culture as students start to exhibit developmental patterns characteristic of ten-year-olds: they are able to learn peer mediation or problem-solving and are more interested in community service and tutoring younger students.

Empathy

Nine-year-olds often feel worried, anxious, frustrated, moody, or negative. For these reasons, it will be important to explicitly teach them how to recognize and manage their own emotions and to recognize those emotions in others. There is the possibility of exclusion in the lunchroom or the playground as well as from cliques, making it important to explicitly teach your students how their actions may impact others. It is characteristic of ten-year-olds to begin to show an appreciation for others' perspectives, but it is still necessary to explicitly teach how that looks and sounds.

Self-Control

The ability to recognize emotions is an important factor when working on self-control, as it's helpful to know what you are feeling and why in order to manage those feelings. In this case, nine-year-olds can benefit from explicit instruction about the various influences on their emotional state. Their emotions are influenced by factors such as what is said by teachers or other students, events happening at home, or their own perceptions of academic or social challenges. Students at this age demonstrate a tendency to become easily frustrated, so they should be proactively taught how to show hope and perseverance. This might include using envisioning language for mastering math facts or presenting a project. (See Chapter 3 for more on teacher language). This direct teaching will be useful again later in the year as students exhibit ten-year-old behaviors, when they are quick to anger and to forgive, get better at resolving friendship and fairness issues, and appreciate being noticed and acknowledged for their efforts.

Pause and Ponder

Below are some questions to consider as you plan developmentally responsive teaching with fourth graders:

- How well do I know my students developmentally?

- What do I know about my students personally, academically, and culturally?

- How might I build deeper relationships with students, families, and caregivers?

- How can I be intentional about partnerships?

- How can I incorporate developmentally appropriate structures that support learning in our daily schedule?

- How can academic choices provide opportunities for differentiation and balance developmental ranges in the class?

- How can I explicitly teach social and emotional learning and embed opportunities to practice these skills throughout the day in developmentally responsive ways?

Fourth Graders

Common Characteristics	School Implications

Social-Emotional

- Are individualistic and competitive. May experiment with new ways of dressing and grooming and trying on different personas.

- Are often worried or anxious.

- Complain about fairness and hurt feelings.

- Are critical of self and others.

- Are more aware of social dynamics; often prefer same-gender friends.

- Need lots of encouragement.

- Assign partner work when possible; this minimizes the long debates and arguments that large-group projects may trigger.

- Watch carefully for overcompetitiveness and criticism of peers.

- Use gentle joking and laughter to help keep things light and playful; avoid sarcasm, which wounds fourth graders deeply.

- Lead cooperative and team-building games to build a sense of community and safety.

- Keep assessment low key, concrete, and focused on strengths, not deficits.

Physical

- Push themselves to physical limits.

- Complain about aches, pains, and injuries.

- May twist hair or bite nails to relieve tension.

- Are better coordinated but still working on physical control.

- Can't sit still for long.

- Still need recess and snack.

- Have better fine motor control.

- Keep students moving to reduce wiggles and help with focus and attention.

- Allow students to choose their best working position (sitting, standing, etc.) when possible.

- Keep direct-teaching lessons short.

- If possible, have two shorter recess breaks, rather than one long one.

- Include snack in the daily schedule.

- Practice with a variety of fine motor tools and tasks (weaving, knitting, carving, drawing, etc.) to increase manual dexterity.

Fourth Graders

Common Characteristics	School Implications

Cognitive

• Are industrious and curious; can be impatient and frustrated with work they deem boring. • Are beginning to see "bigger world," including social issues. • Are still very concrete in their thinking. • Can draw information from printed material (they've moved from "learning to read" to "reading to learn"). • May be easily overwhelmed.	• Elicit passionate engagement by embedding discussion of right and wrong, justice and fairness into science and social studies. • Break large projects into bite-size chunks. • Offer hands-on, experiential learning activities.

Language

• Love wordplay, new vocabulary, and descriptive language. • Sometimes revert to baby talk. • Enjoy exaggeration and "dirty" jokes. • Are very verbal—if they think it, they say it!	• Use jokes, limericks, silly poetry, and word games for transition activities (standing in line, waiting for assembly, etc.). • Tap into students' playfulness and sense of humor throughout the day. • Do short skits drawn from their books and stories so they can play with voices. • Expect lots of "verbal observations" ("Ew!" "Cool!" "I hate that!" "Awesome!") during lessons, read-alouds, and projects. • Avoid hypothetical questions—fourth graders frequently answer them aloud!

The information in this chart is based on *Yardsticks: Child and Adolescent Development Ages 4–14*, 4th ed., by Chip Wood (Center for Responsive Schools 2017) and Child Development Guide by Center for Development of Human Services at SUNY Buffalo State (New York State Office of Children and Family Services 2015).

Grade 5

It's writing workshop time in fifth grade. There is a high level of energy and excitement as students engage in an energizer called Choose Sides to debate opinion essay topics. As the workshop period continues, students begin to write their own position statements for student-selected topics. They later work with partners to debate and confer about their ideas. Later in the day, students work through a series of math problems while choosing which strategy to use to solve each problem. The teacher uses this time to check in with students, to reteach skills as needed, and to reinforce students' progress with solving problems accurately. After a brief energizer to refresh and recharge, students are ready to finish the day working in small groups using microscopes to study organisms in science. Throughout the entire school day, there is a constant buzz in the classroom as students engage in academic tasks. Responsibility and autonomy are on display as students contribute to a positive learning community all day long. The teacher reflects at the end of the day on what a well-oiled machine this community of learners has become. The teacher's structure, instruction, and support of students' physical, social, and emotional needs has yielded another day of high-quality learning for this group of fifth graders. It is evident the teacher understands fifth graders' developmental needs and has taken time to teach the skills necessary to be successful.

Some educators may think this scenario is an unattainable dream. Others may see this type of learning environment in their own classroom from time to time. For others, this type of learning community happens almost daily. In order to create a high-functioning and high-achieving learning community like the one described, the teacher must have a keen understanding of child development and use that knowledge to inform how the teacher will support students. Teachers need to know their students in order to best reach them. When we know the students we teach—both individually and collectively based on common developmental milestones—we are better equipped to support their academic and social-emotional learning and create learning communities like the one described above.

Meeting Fifth Graders' Developmental Needs

As with students in any grade level, fifth graders present common, predictable development characteristics as they grow and learn more about the world around them. Physically, fifth graders experience high levels of growth and maturation while exhibiting a substantial need for movement. Socially, fifth graders are stimulated by peer and adult interactions. Emotionally, fifth graders crave reinforcement for their positive attributes and adult empathy when redirections are given. Although there are many other developmental characteristics worthy of consideration, these three are most significant for educators when determining daily classroom tasks—such as how to structure routines and procedures, how to design lessons, and how to respond to misbehavior—in order to best support students with their academic and social-emotional growth.

Physical Considerations

Ten- and eleven-year-olds enter an important phase of physical maturation in their lives. During this time of rapid growth, students have a strong need for movement. Teachers must consider this need during the entire school day. Throughout the school day, teachers should strive to have students move as frequently as possible, ideally multiple times during a given lesson. There are many ways teachers can support fifth graders' need for movement during the school day.

Ensuring students are actively engaged with their learning is one way to support their need for movement. One way to do this is to use hands-on manipulatives. For example, have students complete a science investigation using science tools as opposed to watching or reading about a concept. Physical movement can also be incorporated into daily math tasks by providing students with manipulatives to demonstrate multi-digit multiplication. Also, consider taking an "I do, we do, you do" approach to learning. First, model a new skill through Interactive Modeling, allowing the students to notice the steps needed to carry out the skill. Second, have all students practice the new skill together. During this phase, consider having all students complete the task, perhaps in a copybook or on a dry-erase board, to ensure all students are focused and practicing the skills. Last, have students finish the exercise by trying out the new learn-

See the appendix, p. 323, for more on Interactive Modeling.

ing with active practice. While students have the chance to try out the new skill independently, the teacher can reinforce and reteach it as needed.

Another way to support students' need for physical movement is to incorporate breaks during the day. Energizers, when selected carefully by the teacher, are an effective practice that can be used before, during, or after a lesson. Teachers should plan to use these activities proactively and should schedule them to occur frequently throughout the day based on the students' needs. Teachers can also use energizers reactively; if during a lesson students start to show signs of needing a movement break—squirming in seats, tapping pencils on desks, or frequently getting up out of their seats—consider using an upbeat energizer to provide a movement break. Many fifth graders gravitate toward being outdoors, so consider scheduling some energizers outside if possible. When considering breaks throughout the day, also be sure to provide snack breaks to keep students' energy levels high.

See the appendix, p. 313, for sample energizers.

Playing games is another effective way to support physical movement needs. Games can be a helpful way to review previously taught concepts while ensuring students are actively engaged in content. Many educational board games, for example, allow for physical movement as students use the game board and pieces. Technology devices are effective tools for engaging students with content as well. When students are able to play while engaging with academic content, often their need for physical movement is met while they learn.

Social Considerations

Ten- and eleven-year-olds crave social interaction. Whether working with partners, in small groups, or as a whole class, fifth graders appreciate time to interact. Many teachers may operate under the assumption that a quiet classroom is a productive classroom. This is not the case with fifth graders. Knowing this, fifth grade teachers should provide time for students to interact about academic and social topics throughout the school day. An effective way to do this is by using interactive learning structures.

Interactive learning structures are practices that
allow students to discuss
and listen to ideas in a
clearly defined manner.
The structures can be
ones that students
engage in individually,
with partners, in small
groups, or with the entire
class. For interactive
learning structures to be
effective, teachers need to
teach and model how to follow
the directions for the activity.
Many teachers find it helpful to
introduce new interactive learning struc-
tures around social topics first. For example, if a teacher plans on using a
structure like turn and talk during an upcoming reading workshop, it is
helpful to introduce this structure around a social topic. This could happen during a Morning Meeting as students talk about what they did the
previous weekend. Interactive learning structures are an effective way to
support fifth graders' need for social interaction while addressing their
academic and social-emotional needs.

See the appendix,
p. 324, for more on
Morning Meetings.

Although many fifth graders developmentally crave social interaction, it
is important to caution that some students, particularly fifth graders who
are young for their grade or those who are more introverted, may experience interactive learning structures as a struggle. To support these
students, teachers should make sure that a wide range of interactive
learning structures are being used. For example, if you plan to have
students engage in a turn and talk, it is helpful to make sure that think
time is also provided. Consider giving students time to think about what
they will share. It may also be helpful to provide students with an index
card so they can write down their thoughts. Doing so can allow students
to listen more carefully to their partner, instead of focusing on what they

will share when it is their turn. Another way to support introverts is to include interactive learning structures that incorporate writing or drawing pictures to share. To best utilize interactive learning structures, it is important that teachers know their students and use a wide variety of types. Using interactive learning structures to support student learning will be discussed more in Chapter 4.

Emotional Considerations

Fifth graders appreciate reinforcement, as well as empathy, when redirections are given. Reinforcement goes beyond awarding a grade; it should include recognizing and validating students' academic and social behaviors. One way fifth graders appreciate recognition is with check-ins at the beginning and end of the day. During these times of transition, informal conversations that take place between the teacher and students can help support students' emotional needs. These conversations go a long way in solidifying trusting classroom relationships. Another effective way to provide meaningful recognition for students is to use positivity notes. These are short messages, written by the teacher on a sticky note or a notecard, that highlight something the teacher noticed the student doing well. When redirections or consequences are needed, teachers should be cognizant of their teacher language. For example, when the teacher observes the student playing a game, they may say, "Jessica, use the laptop to research facts about the American Revolution." Or a teacher may say, "Brett, our rules say we include others; make sure everyone has a turn with the microscope during today's science investigation." Using a calm, nonjudgmental tone, with a predictable reactive strategy, helps to support fifth graders' emotional needs. When responding to misbehavior, keep in mind the importance of teacher empathy as well; adult empathy, humor, and sensitivity are helpful tools to maintain a positive student-teacher relationship. Supporting students' emotional needs will be discussed further in Chapter 2.

Skills Needed to Be Successful

In addition to having a strong knowledge base of child development, teachers must take actions to support students' developmental needs. Time must be spent explicitly teaching and modeling social and emotional skills throughout the school day, and all year long, to best support students' learning. Fifth graders gravitate toward working with partners and small groups. In order to be successful, students need instruction and time to practice cooperating as leaders and members of groups. Listening and speaking skills, along with learning how to agree and disagree, must be taught, modeled, and reinforced all year long. Additionally, fifth graders need to learn how to be assertive. Time dedicated to teaching students how to persist through challenges and work toward goals is essential. Lastly, fifth graders need teaching and reinforcement about how to be responsible learners. Learning how to be accountable will benefit students during their fifth grade school year, as well as in their future. When teachers combine their knowledge of child development characteristics with explicit teaching of social and emotional skills, students are set up for tremendous academic and social-emotional learning gains.

Pause and Ponder

As you plan to apply the standards of developmentally responsive teaching to your work with your fifth graders, here are some questions to consider:

- How well do I know my students developmentally?

- What do I know about my students personally, academically, and culturally?

- How can I include more movement throughout the school day to meet some of fifth graders' physical needs?

- What are some upcoming academic and social topics for which I can incorporate more interactive learning structures to meet some of fifth graders' social needs?

- What are some ways I can reinforce fifth graders' academic and social efforts throughout the school day to meet fifth graders' emotional needs?

Fifth Graders

Common Characteristics	School Implications

Social-Emotional

- Are generally happy; enjoy family, peers, and teachers.

- Work well in groups.

- Are usually truthful; are developing a more mature sense of right and wrong.

- Are sensitive to and able to resolve issues of fairness.

- Are able to enjoy cooperative and competitive games.

- Build group work into lessons, activities, and projects. (Flexible groups can work well; students can work with lots of different people, including adults and peers.)

- Expect arguments (and that they will tend to end quickly).

- Encourage their developing sense of fairness and of right and wrong. (Their awareness of these can lead to lively class debates and discussions.)

- Provide opportunities for peer tutoring, book buddies, and development of conflict resolution and other interpersonal skills.

Physical

- Are quickly developing large muscles.

- Are drawn to the outdoors and physical challenges.

- May have handwriting that is messier than in fourth grade.

- Due to growth spurts, are frequently hungry and can tire easily.

- Set up schedules to include sufficient time for recess and other outdoor play, energizers and other movement breaks, snacks, and lunch.

- Consider a snack option that enables students to eat and work in the classroom.

- Provide instruction and practice for use of tools such as rulers, compasses, and computers.

Fifth Graders	
Common Characteristics	**School Implications**

Cognitive

Common Characteristics	School Implications
• Are good at memorizing facts. • Are increasingly able to think abstractly; good at solving problems. • Enjoy rules and logic. • Enjoy collecting, classifying, and organizing. • Take pride in schoolwork and conscientious with homework. • Are able to concentrate for longer periods of time.	• Structure complex projects with proper scaffolding and guidance to build on their abilities to be highly productive with schoolwork. • Give ongoing encouragement and reinforcement for both effort and results. • Include lessons that help build students' memory skills (for example, practicing math facts and learning facts about geography, history, and world records). • Support classification and other organizational skills with hands-on science work and math projects.

Language

Common Characteristics	School Implications
• Are expressive and talkative. • Like to explain things. • Are able to listen well. • Show stronger interest in reading independently.	• Encourage students to verbalize their thinking to help make discussions, debates, book groups, writing conferences, math groups, and so on more productive. • Provide opportunities for choral reading, singing, reciting poetry, and performing skits and plays. • Include time for independent reading and writing.

The information in this chart is based on *Yardsticks: Child and Adolescent Development Ages 4–14*, 4th ed., by Chip Wood (Center for Responsive Schools 2017) and Child Development Guide by Center for Development of Human Services at SUNY Buffalo State (New York State Office of Children and Family Services 2015).

Final Thought

"To reach their fullest potential, students need teachers who know and understand them."

—Chip Wood, *Yardsticks*

Chapter 2
Effective Management

. . . .

Overview

Let's turn to the management of the classroom and consider all of the small decisions that a teacher makes to create a classroom environment that is welcoming and organized, that conveys a sense of purpose, and that sets the stage for a day of learning characterized by respectful and kind behaviors. Where does one start in creating such a community? Start by imagining a classroom that conveys the following message: *You belong here. This space was created for you, with your needs in mind. Because you matter. Because your learning matters. Because our community matters.*

Join us as we outline key practices of effective management, from advice on classroom arrangement and organization, to suggestions for creating schedules and teaching routines and procedures, to guidance on how teacher leadership and teacher language impact the classroom.

Classroom Organization

While the size and layout of the physical classroom varies from school to school and from classroom to classroom, the goals remain the same. We aim to have a classroom space that:

- Welcomes all students

- Values everyone's ideas and work

- Supports active and engaged learning

- Supports multiple developmental levels and learning styles

- Fosters independence, responsibility, and cooperation

- Cultivates care of materials and equipment

Classroom arrangement and organization are key practices in creating a calm, orderly environment that promotes autonomy and allows students to focus on learning. Prior to arranging the furniture and space, spend time sitting and breathing in the classroom. What vibe does it emit? Take inventory of permanent fixtures in the classroom space, such as windows, doors, closets, whiteboards, built-in bookcases, and lighting. Give thoughtful consideration to your classroom library. Whether you are inheriting a classroom library that was left by the previous teacher or unpacking your library for the new year, think of the classroom library as a garden. Take time to cultivate, grow, and weed the book garden so that it is welcoming for all students. As you learn about your students' interests, you will grow

See the appendix, p. 334, for a list of recommended books.

The Classroom Library

The classroom library is a powerful place to showcase what many call windows, mirrors, and sliding glass doors (Style 1988; Bishop 1990). The library should include books that reflect, as do mirrors, the lives of readers in the classroom, but they should also offer a view into reality, as windows do (Style 1988). Books, like sliding glass doors, allow readers to enter the world the author created (Bishop 1990). Published student writing can be one way to feature windows, mirrors, and sliding glass doors. As Toni Morrison famously said in a 1981 speech, "If there's a book you want to read, but it hasn't been written yet, then you must write it" (as quoted in Brown 1981). This is a call to action we use frequently in the classroom because major publishers are not yet keeping up. Data on books by and about Black people, Indigenous people, and people of color published for children and teens is compiled annually by the Cooperative Children's Book Center, part of the School of Education at the University of Wisconsin–Madison. In 2019, their research shows that about 12 percent of books were about Black/African characters, 1.6 percent were about Indigenous characters, 8.8 percent were about Asian characters, 5.9 percent were about Latino/Latina characters, 0.1 percent were about Pacific Islander characters, and 0.9 percent were about Arab characters. Given these statistics, it's clear that having windows, mirrors, and sliding glass doors in our classroom libraries can be a challenge.

your collection to meet their needs. Consider furniture items that can be repurposed or easily moved around, such as desks, chairs, and tables, and materials that require student access. How will students safely navigate the classroom space? How can the space be organized so that it provides at least one personal space for each student in the classroom? How can the space be structured to provide consistency and predictability while promoting student autonomy and fostering student responsibility? Measure, sketch, and identify the ebbs and flows of movement in the classroom as you arrange and organize the classroom space to meet the students' developmental needs. Teachers effectively manage classrooms when they organize the classroom for safety and autonomy and arrange the classroom environment for maximum learning.

Here are five important questions to ask yourself as you set up the classroom space:

1. "How should I arrange the furniture and plan for the areas we will need in the room?"

2. "What supplies do I need, and how can I arrange them?"

3. "How am I going to fill the wall space before the students enter the first day of school?"

4. "What am I going to do with all the books in my classroom library?"

5. "How will I plan for the use of technology with students?"

Teaching Routines and Procedures

Once the classroom has been arranged and organized, students need to know how to navigate the space. How will students transition from their desks to the meeting area? What are the expectations for writing workshop time? For signing out and returning technology? Create a list of routines and procedures to establish and reinforce them with your students. Interactive Modeling is a key practice to set students up for success in completing routines and procedures independently. It provides a visual hook for students to understand that routines and procedures establish a sense of order and predictability in the classroom, making it a better place to be. Interactive Modeling is a direct, simple, and nonnegotiable way to teach the routines that will help keep the classroom running smoothly and safely. When you explain the *why* for the routine that you will model, giving students the task of actively observing *what* you're modeling— and then giving them multiple opportunities to practice while you provide feedback—they are more likely to be invested in the routines and to take responsibility for their behavior. Teachers effectively manage classrooms when they establish and reinforce clear routines and procedures.

See the appendix, p. 323, for more on Interactive Modeling.

Revisiting Routines

There will be times throughout the year when you will want to be proactive and revisit routines with students. Here are a few important ones:

- After the first six weeks of school
- After a long weekend
- After a long break or holiday
- When a routine does not meet the expectation

Impact of Teacher Leadership Style and Teacher Language

Teacher leadership style and teacher language are the tools that we carry with us, as we utilize them in every interaction that we are a part of in the classroom and they collectively impact the management of the classroom. Teachers who lead with authority establish clear expectations for behavior and actively teach students how to live up to those expectations. Note, though, that acting with authority does not mean being autocratic or uncaring. Authoritative teachers strive to be firm, kind, and consistent, preserving the dignity of each child while they learn, develop, and practice the social and emotional skills needed to be successful in the classroom.

Teacher language is used to communicate our belief in students' ability to meet our expectations. Brief, matter-of-fact, and direct, teacher language is delivered in a calm and neutral tone of voice. Teacher language includes verbal and nonverbal messages, such as body language and facial expressions, sent to students. Mindfully using teacher language, an authoritative teacher cultivates a warm, welcoming, and positive learning environment. Teachers effectively manage classrooms when they communicate clear behavior expectations and respond to misbehavior respectfully.

As you explore this chapter, you will learn the practices of classroom arrangement and organization; schedules, routines, and procedures; and classroom management. These practices, when ingrained in the learning environment, form the baseline for a safe and predictable environment where students can learn and take care of themselves and each other.

Grade ❸

See the appendix, p. 324, for more on Morning Meeting.

Ding! As the teacher returned the mallet to the chime, she heard the buzz of conversation lessen and saw eyes and bodies pivot in her direction. When the students were silent and paying full attention, the teacher gave the words all were waiting for: "It's time for Morning Meeting! Remember what it should look like and sound like in our classroom. I'll be watching to see how you get ready for our special time." Turning to one student, she made a request: "Skylar, will you start our song for today?" As Skylar went over to press play on the iPad, the class sprang into action. The teacher observed students returning materials to their bins and carefully placing books on the bookshelf. She noted, as well, a few students finishing unpacking after a delay in their bus arrival. She saw chairs being pushed in and bodies navigating the room safely and efficiently. As the song neared the end, she observed some students, who were already sitting in the circle for the Morning Meeting, get up to help those who were still organizing their space. When the musical transition came to an end, she was the last to take her place in the circle. She remarked, "I wish I had a video to show what I saw this morning. I saw books being returned to the bookshelf with care. I observed chairs being pushed in and students walking carefully to stay safe. I even noticed some of you going over to help others. We are so lucky to be in such a kind and caring community together. We are definitely ready to begin Morning Meeting, as soon as we revisit our expectations for this time together."

The snapshot of this third grade morning was the result of careful planning, consistent use of practices and strategies that empower students to be independent, and daily reflection to reinforce desired behaviors and revisit areas for growth. Throughout this section, we will revisit this Morning Meeting experience as we focus on how to effectively manage third graders.

Classroom Arrangement and Organization

When planning for a new school year, you can lay the groundwork for a positive learning experience by transforming your outlook as a teacher from one that thinks of *my* classroom to one that understands the possibilities of *our* classroom. Such an approach requires fully understanding who your students are, starting from the very first day of school. As you prepare the classroom space to meet the developmental needs of third graders, carefully consider how it will support the hallmarks of this age group—a high level of energy and a desire for social interactions and spending time with peers. In order for students to feel a sense of belonging and significance, and to be able to have fun and learn together, they need to feel invested in their environment. It is the educator's responsibility to make sure students understand that it is *our* area in which to learn and work together.

Setting Up the Space

Setting up the classroom space with a view toward supporting students' sense of engagement and ownership allows them to take responsibility for their education. It will nurture their confidence in following classroom routines, working independently and with others, and managing their own participation in classroom activities, from joining in Morning Meeting to selecting a book from the class library.

As you empower your students to assert themselves to take care of their own needs as learners, prepare some locations where students may choose to relocate themselves as they work. Some educators will have a table or extra desk in the room where students can move if they feel a change in setting would support their learning. Some provide flexible seating options around the room or the use of a standing desk, to meet each child's needs. You might be someone who needs to move furniture around to get a feel for the amount of space and structure within the room. For others, drawing it out is a preferred option.

Finally, and perhaps most important, think about how to make the classroom feel like home! Plants, seasonal decorations, lamps, air diffusers, and even curtains can give students an added touch of comfort and security. (It is always important to check with your specific district protocols for safety guidelines.)

Furniture and Seating Arrangements

To build community, for both Morning Meeting time and instructional time when you need to bring the class together, a whole-group area is essential. Preparing for students to sit in a circle fosters a sense of community, inclusion, and equity among everyone. If your space makes this a challenge, consider arranging tables and desk groups in the middle of the room, so students can be in a circle around the perimeter of the room.

Students will need to have individual desk space. Remembering the gregarious nature of third graders, though, desks should be arranged in groups of two or three so students can immediately have a partner to turn to and talk with throughout the day. Plan the spacing between table groups to allow for ease of traffic flow. As you are determining where students will sit, take into consideration their individual needs. If you have a student who is easily distracted, a seat near the door would not be as conducive to learning as a location with less activity.

Also, plan to change groups on a monthly basis. By regularly varying seating arrangements in this way, you will provide students with the opportunity to form connections, while also ensuring they will get to know and work with everyone in the room. When you form new groups, build in time for brief activities that will allow the students to get acquainted. For instance, having students in each group come up with a team name gives them a group identity, while also making it easy for you to call them to the circle space, to line up, or to get materials.

Supplies and Materials

There are three keys to classroom supplies: variety, quality, and quantity. Think about how you will change out materials throughout the year to maintain variety. For example, the craft sticks might be utilized before

you switch them out for toothpicks. You will bring the craft sticks out again, but providing this variety will reinvigorate your students' enthusiasm. The quality of the materials is important. Take time to check that the scissors still cut, the markers have not dried up, and the glue is still sticky. Investing students in this process of helping to go through materials, perhaps during indoor recess or on a Friday afternoon, will make them feel ownership, and they will enjoy categorizing and classifying the materials. Also, be sure that you have enough materials for everyone. Whether you opt for the materials to be located in a bin for each table group or one large bin for the whole class to use, making sure everyone has high-quality items only sets them up for success.

Think as well about which materials students will have of their own, which they will have for use within their table group, and which will be available for whole-group access. The use of Guided Discovery will help students to explore and model appropriate usage and care of materials, while reinforcing the classroom expectations. This proactive practice will also help you to maintain the quality and quantity of your classroom's supplies. For example, allow students to make labels for the storage bins after you have introduced a new item during Guided Discovery. Taking a picture of a student using the item the right way or what it should look like when it gets returned will further help to build community. Each student will enjoy having their photo in the classroom space too!

See the appendix, p. 317, for more on Guided Discovery.

Knowing that third graders often have big ideas and can bite off more than they can chew, it is important to limit the supplies you are making available to them at any given time. Consider keeping the materials you want them to use within reach, while relocating the items that are not daily options. For example, the glitter containers might be an added touch for some projects, but they are not something you want them to use regularly. Keeping it out of sight keeps it out of mind.

Classroom Displays

While many companies expect educators to spend their hard-earned money on birthday charts, alphabet charts, writing process charts, and more, those items prevent students from feeling valued and known in the space. Purchased displays do not reflect students' experience, effort, and enthusiasm. Instead, consider how you and your students can create displays together. So as you are preparing the walls for instructional displays, create them together with your students. To begin with, invite your students to make suggestions about what might be included in the displays. Anchor charts, word walls, routine charts, math charts, reading and writing charts, and reminder displays are more meaningful when students are involved in discussions during their creation. Consider, too, when students can participate in designing and constructing instructional displays.

As you and your students slowly add displays to your classroom, think about having some bulletin boards that focus on the process, not the product. While a final project is important to display, students also need

Birthday Chart Activity

You want to create a birthday display—and you want your students to participate. What better way to do so than by integrating the activity with a Guided Discovery lesson that models how to use and take care of the materials that students will need for this craft project? First, decide which materials you want students to use. Then allow them to create a design for their own birthday hat, drawing it on plain paper. Finally, give them plenty of time to create their hats, using the supplies they've been introduced to during the Guided Discovery lesson. Once they've finished their projects, take a picture of each student wearing their hat. Consider having students line up in order of their birthdays. While your students are lined up, you can hang their pictures and hats on the wall in birthday order while the students view their work being displayed.

to value a growth mindset by seeing that work takes time. Displaying work in progress also allows students to reflect on what they are learning and how they are going to achieve their goals. To encourage students to develop this outlook, one teacher created a bulletin board with the title "#WorkInProgress." As part of the process, the students decided what they wanted to display. When students are invited to make choices about what work they will share, it offers them the opportunity to reflect on why they are choosing that piece, supporting their social and emotional skills.

Keep displays current and relevant, and refer to them often so students understand how to use them to support their learning. When you change units and topics, consider taking photos of the charts that have been posted in your classroom and putting the pictures in a binder for each subject area. This will be a powerful resource students can consult when they need a reminder about a previous unit or topic, while also ensuring the most important academic content is being displayed.

Control Clutter!

Walls cluttered with charts and papers can appear messy and add to stress levels in the room.

Leave ample blank wall space around bulletin boards, anchor charts, and student display spaces. The blank spaces make it easier to focus on individual pieces of work.

Classroom Library

The students walked into the classroom to see the bookshelf covered with colored fabric. Their curiosity sparked, the students whispered and wondered about what they saw. During language arts time, the teacher invited ideas about what the children thought might be hidden behind the fabric, before asking one student to unveil it. Of course, the students then found books the teacher had carefully selected, representing many different genres. As a class, the children brainstormed all the ways the books could be organized, and before long there were piles of books around the room, with sticky notes on them identifying the genres. As the students worked, they debated where some books should go because they could fit into multiple categories. The students eagerly noticed that there were books about many different people, cultures, countries, and animals, and even many topics they had never read about before. The teacher had taken great care to ensure that the interests and background of each child were represented within the book options, and the children were noticing that as they worked. After pausing and coming back to their bookshelf project, the students eventually organized the books in a meaningful way. They modeled and practiced what it looked like to take a book off the shelf to read and how to put it back. They even prepared for what to do at those times when they might have difficulty remembering where a book should go.

The classroom example above shows how the teacher was investing students in the classroom library. Because all the students had participated in planning for the management and organization of the library, there was now a buzz about books, including from even the most reluctant reader in the room.

Technology

Many third graders view technology as being as important as water and shelter in their lives. While we know technology can be utilized to engage students, we also need to proactively establish our online community as well as our in-person community. Students need to understand the importance of consistently following the classroom expectations when they are working on a device. Routines and procedures for appropriate care, storage, and use of charging stations need to be established and modeled.

Learning needs to be active and interactive. While technology has an important role, we also want our students to learn how to manage relationships and interactions in person.

See the appendix, p. 327, for sample schedules.

Schedules, Routines, and Procedures

Establishing a predictable schedule and clear routines and procedures will provide third graders with a sense of stability they need to feel comfortable and confident in their environment.

Schedules

Think about a time when you were not given a schedule. Maybe it was before teaching a new grade level or when an agenda was not shared before a meeting. It can make us feel uneasy not to know what is coming next, and it can impact our ability to focus on the content at hand when we are unsure what to expect next. In the scene described at the beginning of this chapter, we saw how the students were excited to begin their day with Morning Meeting and clearly knew the plan for the activity. As do many of us, third graders thrive when there is a sense of structure and predictability. Our responsibility, as teachers, is to proactively prepare for the inevitable question, "What do I do next?"

When planning for the daily schedule, it is important to remember some of the key characteristics of this age group, starting with their stamina levels. As discussed earlier, third graders can have short bursts of energy and will often bite off more than they can chew. Keeping lessons to a thirty-minute time span will support them. For longer blocks of learning, building in energizers and interactive learning structures will keep them engaged and refreshed. In fact, we will have students move in the middle of a lesson when we see they need to be rejuvenated.

Consider displaying a visual schedule, using magnetic strips or sentence strips, to list each activity item for the day. This technique allows you to quickly and easily manipulate the display when scheduling changes occur—and as we know in education, changes can occur at any moment! Displaying the schedule this way not only supports the students, but also will help you as you are looking at the day. Remember to include energizers, bathroom breaks, and snack breaks on the visual schedule. Having set breaks listed also helps students to develop their personal decision-making skills. If a student sees a bathroom break is a few minutes away, they may be less likely to take one as you are giving the final directions for an activity.

Finally, it is important to note that many school districts provide schedules for educators, while others allow individual teachers or teams to decide how to organize their day. Consider what is outside of your control (usually arrival, specials, lunch, and dismissal), and then set your sights on making the most of the time inside your classroom.

See the appendix,
p. 323, for more
on Interactive
Modeling.

The Power of Interactive Modeling

The secrets to Interactive Modeling are planning and reinforcement. We can only know what we want students to do when we have thought through and envisioned exactly what we want it to look like on a daily basis. Interactive Modeling provides you with the opportunity to set high expectations for your students, build their independence, and foster trust and empowerment. You are also proactively supporting students because when they know exactly what is expected and have practiced repeatedly, the chances of misbehavior dramatically decrease. Remember to plan the correct way to follow the routine or procedure you are going to model. Our brains have an inherent knack for remembering the negative, so the more we show, practice, and hear the correct way, the chances for success and making these routines and procedures a habit will increase. When we have students do the noticing, we are engaging them and they are hearing from others what the teacher did in modeling the routine or procedure. Students need the guided practice in order to be successful, beyond just hearing what our expectations are for them.

Routines and Procedures

As the students prepared for Morning Meeting, they moved effortlessly because the teacher had set them up for success from the beginning by planning for the routines and procedures students would need. She also trusted a powerful teaching practice: Interactive Modeling.

Third graders have prior knowledge about school. From kindergarten through second grade, they have put materials away, they have transitioned from recess to academics, and they have packed and unpacked their backpacks more times than they can count. Still, each year their teachers have offered them a unique experience. Reflect for a moment on your own schooling experience and the routine of unpacking to begin the day. While each teacher had routines specific to them, the end result was the same: unpacking was part of the process of transitioning from home to school and preparing for a day of learning. The specific structure of the Interactive Modeling strategy ensures students know why each procedure is important, observe and notice what you as the teacher are doing, have an opportunity to practice, and receive reinforcing feedback.

At this point, you might ask, "There are so many routines and procedures: where should I begin?" This is a frequent question, and even for a veteran teacher, the start of a class is a reminder of how much your previous students learned over the course of the prior year and all the routines and procedures they became proficient at completing in a timely manner. It can be tempting to want to hurry this process to start on the academic instruction; however, teaching routines and procedures is the first step in ensuring your students will maximize their learning during the year. Here are a few key routines and procedures to prepare at the beginning of the year:

- **Signals for attention.** Think about what signals you will use with your students, and practice them from the get-go. An auditory signal will help students when you are not in direct eyesight or when they have their heads down while working. Whether a chime, bell, instrument, or rain stick, the auditory signal you use should sound pleasant and should be easy to hear even if students are in the middle of an energizer. Prepare a visual signal; this could be a raised hand, or it could be a unique signal used only in your classroom. Whether you use a visual or an auditory signal, practice using it with your students so they know what it will look like. As part of this practice, show students how to finish a conversation within a few seconds, and encourage them to do this with their classmates. Politely ending a conversation is a way

Effective Use of Signals

Keep it simple. Signals should be easy to use in a variety of settings and easy to respond to. Complex signals, or multiple signals used simultaneously, can be confusing for third graders.

Demand a quick but not immediate response. Give students fifteen seconds or so to get to a stopping point in their work or conversations before responding. This allows them to better focus on the next set of directions. It's also more respectful. Wait until everyone has responded to the signal before you proceed.

Be consistent. Students need to know that you will hold them accountable for responding correctly to signals. If your requirement is that everyone stops and looks at you but you let things slide when children don't do this, students won't know for sure how they should respond.

for them to show respect to each other, and it will help to foster positive relationships among all the students in the class. Also, consider the signals you want students to use to get *your* attention. This can be a traditional hand raise, a peace sign, or a thumbs-up. It can also be a way to incorporate sign language into your room.

- **Bathroom procedures.** As third graders, unless they are new, your students will have had experiences with bathrooms in the school. Remember, their second grade teachers will have done things differently, and even if those routines sound similar to your plan, you want to make sure students know the expectations for your classroom. Consider whether you will prefer to take students for whole-class bathroom breaks. Some third grade teachers find a stop at the restrooms after recess ensures fewer visits during instruction later in the afternoon. What you do one year may look different the next year, as we must always be responsive to the specific needs of the students in front of us. Even if you take whole-class breaks, it is inevitable that students will need to use the bathroom at other times of the day. Consider whether you will have students sign out or take a bathroom pass. The use of a magnet or clip near the door can be a helpful visual to see who is out, especially if students are working around the room. If there is an emergency, teachers can grab the magnets or clips to let safety teams and administration know who is not with the class. As you think through your specific routine, remember to address timing with students and empower their decision-making. Encourage your students to ask themselves, "Is this the best time for me to step out, or can I wait until the directions are finished?"

- **Lining up and walking in the hall.** How will students line up? What should it look like and sound like in the hallway? Walking as a group is something your third graders have already experienced, and teaching this procedure will not require as much time as it will for your colleagues who teach younger learners; however, your procedures need to be planned and prepared.

- **Classroom transitions.** What will it look like and sound like as students navigate the room? In this chapter's opening description of students getting ready for Morning Meeting, we could see the routines and procedures of students putting away materials, pushing in chairs, and walking safely. In that scenario, students were transitioning with music, which provided a parameter for how much time the transition should take. If students are moving to the whole-group space, what will that look like? If they are transitioning back to their desks, what is expected of them when they arrive?

- **Whole-group meeting.** Whether students are coming to the circle for Morning Meeting and are expected to sit around the outside edge or they are coming to the carpet for direct instruction or a read-aloud, your procedures may involve students arriving with empty hands, finding their personal space, and being ready to listen and participate. Having consistent expectations for students each time they come to the circle can help them to learn the expectations quickly and provide greater consistency.

- **Emergency procedures.** Emergencies can happen at any time with no notice, from the fire alarm sounding to a tornado coming to the area. These procedures are likely prescribed by your state and district, thus requiring less planning on your behalf; however, they need to be strictly modeled and reinforced. Reminding students that the purpose is to remain safe at all times can help to pacify the wonderings and "what-ifs" they might raise.

- **Snacks and food.** Third graders' appetites are growing right along with their height! What will snack time look like in your classroom? Remember to consider the need for breaks and social interactions. Allowing your students to enjoy a five-minute snack break can support their social and emotional skills far more than forcing them to finish math problems while they munch. Having the time to connect and share with others will free them up for learning when the wrappers have been put in the garbage and the remaining snack is packed away. With a consideration of allergies, you may need to put additional procedures in place as advised by your school nurse. Regardless, remember handwashing before snack is a must for any Interactive Modeling plan you are incorporating for this time.

- **Other routines and procedures.** You will use Interactive Modeling for many routines and procedures, as well as for academic and social skills. Take time to generate your list of routines and procedures. Remember other topics, including these:

  ○ Using respectful behavior during assemblies

  ○ Packing and unpacking

  ○ Taking care of supplies and materials

  ○ Finding a partner

  ○ Knowing how to give and receive feedback

  ○ Behaving appropriately at recess

  ○ Participating in indoor recess time

Classroom Management and Responding to Misbehavior

The secret to classroom management is teacher language. Take a moment to reread the teacher's comments to the class in this chapter's opening scenario. She was using empowering and reminding language before students began the activity, and she reinforced all the positive observations at the end. The tone, brevity, specificity, and uplifting nature of her comments demonstrated for the students that she believed in them and that she was ensuring their safety and success.

As third graders are concerned about fairness, it will help them to see that their teacher is looking out for them and applying the expectations consistently for everyone. In Chapter 1, we thought about the social and emotional competencies of this age group and how we can build relationships and support how they cooperate, assert themselves, and become more responsible and empathetic, while they build stamina and self-control. It is not only the words we use that convey a message of faith and respect for our students; it is also what we do not say—our silence, body language, facial expressions, and tone.

Teacher language will be discussed in upcoming chapters; you might consider recording yourself to see how your verbal and nonverbal communications are supporting your students. Consider using the following reinforcing and reminding language stems too. You will be modeling for students how they can begin partner conversations at the same time. These can be posted on an anchor chart in the room and modeled during Morning Meeting. You may also place a sticky note with a few ideas on your computer that you can use the next time you are sending an email or teaching online.

Reinforcing Language Practice

Characteristics	Replace With
Names concrete, specific behaviors	"I noticed . . ."
Applies to all students	"You paid attention to . . ."
Emphasizes description over personal approval	"You remembered . . ."
	"You all helped . . ."
Reflects important goals and values	"Did you notice . . .?"
	"You followed our rule by . . ."

Reminding Language Practice

Characteristics	Replace With
Reflects clearly established expectations	"Who can remember . . .?"
	"Remind me . . ."
Question or statement	"Let's remember . . ."
Proactive or reactive	"Think back to yesterday . . ."
Used when teacher and child feel calm	"How might we follow our class rules as we . . .?"
	"How will you . . .?"
Brief	"Let's review . . ."
	"What can you do if . . .?"

Pause and Ponder

As you think about your third graders and establishing an environment where they are empowered and excited to be in *their* classroom, consider the following questions:

- How am I going to arrange my space?

- How will materials and supplies be organized and taught for success?

- What displays will I be creating with my students?

- How will my classroom library and technology meet their needs?

- What will my schedule be, and how will I display it?

- How am I going to plan for all the routines and procedures?

- How can my teacher language positively contribute to effectively managing the class?

Final Thought

"From day one, we need to convey the message that in this classroom, respect, kindness, and learning will prevail. Students need to know with certainty that the teacher is in control and that the standards for behavior are high. This knowledge gives students a sense of physical and emotional security and frees them to participate in all classroom activities in a meaningful way."

—*Teaching Self-Discipline*

Grade 4

On the first day of school, the teacher looks around the classroom before students arrive. There are blank bulletin boards with labels that say, "Coming Soon." Libraries and tools are covered with labels that say, "Opening Soon." There are blank index cards placed at each individual table spot so that students can create name tags. The teacher smiles, thinking about how the day's read-aloud will launch students to fill this blank canvas in the upcoming days, weeks, and months of the year. The teacher will use Guided Discovery to help students learn about different art tools as they create borders for the bulletin boards. Students will explore book bins and sort books into different categories, shaping the library around their interests. They will organize their desks and learn which hook to use for their backpacks and coats. Students will be able to locate their designated spot in the meeting area. In the first weeks, students will identify their hopes and dreams, which will be displayed and revisited and revised throughout the year as they meet their goals and set new goals. But on the first day of school, the classroom is a blank slate of opportunity for all that will be discovered throughout the year, representing the communal ownership of the space and the learning.

See the appendix, p. 317, for more on Guided Discovery.

Classroom Arrangement and Organization

Think of a store where you like to shop. Put yourself there. What about the space makes it enjoyable? When you think about this place, you might imagine that it was designed with you and your specific needs in mind. The same is true for students when they think about the classroom environment. We want our students to walk in and think, "This room was created for me with my specific needs in mind because I am important and my learning is important." It sends the message that this space is ours.

Furniture and Seating Arrangements

- **Arrange desks in table groups of four or five students.** This setup enables students to interact and collaborate throughout the day. Change these groups frequently—every four to six weeks—to meet the developmental needs of students.

- **Make sure the furniture and the space fit the children's growing bodies.** Attention and behavior problems can occur when furniture is too small or space is too crowded. When possible, choose desks, tables, and chairs that fit nine- and ten-year-olds. Any furniture taller than students should be placed on the perimeter of the classroom. Shorter furniture, such as freestanding bookshelves, can be used to create boundaries for different areas in the classroom, but keep in mind that students should be able to see and be seen from all areas.

- **Plan the amount of space needed for class gatherings, such as lessons and meetings.** Create a space so everyone can sit comfortably in a circle, with about three inches between each student. If your students are sitting on the floor, they may find it useful to have something to lean against, such as a wall or the back of a freestanding bookcase. Or your fourth graders may benefit from sitting on chairs, which will need to be moved into the circle. It's also important to have space between the meeting area and other areas of the classroom, to avoid any distractions. When tables or chairs need to be moved—either to bring chairs in and out of the circle or to clear away distractions—use Interactive Modeling to show students how and where to move the furniture safely, quickly, and quietly around the room. Moving potentially distracting furniture away from the meeting area might be a job for a student who sits at a nearby desk. Shelves of classroom materials facing into the meeting can be a distraction to students, so if it's not possible to move them, consider solutions like covering the shelves with curtains. Also, as issues do arise, collaborative problem-solving methods, such as role-plays or problem-solving conferences, allow students to name their needs and brainstorm solutions.

See the appendix, p. 323, for more on Interactive Modeling.

- **Envision the flow of traffic.** Passageways in the classroom should allow two students to walk past each other comfortably. It might be helpful to draw out the space and consider where everything is located using the diagram tool. It can be helpful to talk through these ideas with a colleague before students enter the space and even act it out to get an idea of what it might look like with nine- and ten-year-old bodies in the room. Also consider where students will line up inside the classroom.

- **Keep in mind that the classroom is a shared space that will grow to fit the personalities and learning of the entire community.** It should be jointly constructed with students. Begin the school year with read-alouds to launch conversations about how students, especially now that they are in fourth grade, will have a voice in creating the look, feel, and sounds of the space. At the end of the year, you can return to those same read-alouds to reflect on all the learning and growing that took place in the space and work together to begin to pack up the space so that it will be ready for the next year's fourth graders. Fourth graders can be included in community conversations around what the classroom looks like, from bulletin boards to featured book displays. If you're thinking about making major changes to the layout, students can also be involved in that conversation and can help to prepare by moving books off of shelves on Thursday afternoon in anticipation of Friday's changes. Then students will have a day to get used to the changes before the weekend.

See the appendix, p. 334, for recommended read-alouds.

- **Consider thinking flexibly about student work spaces.** A math group might come to the meeting area to work on a problem. Students might sit at different desks during reading workshop in order to meet in book clubs. Students might switch between desk groups for lab rotations. This approach allows students to work with different partners throughout the day and take ownership of the entire classroom.

Supplies and Materials

Fourth graders should have two distinct places for their belongings, one for their personal items and one for their schoolwork and supplies. They should each have a clearly identified spot, such as a locker, cubbyhole, or wall hook, located within or just outside the classroom, for their coats, backpacks, and lunch boxes. They will also need storage space, such as a desk or seat sack, for their classroom materials and tools. Consider what they may have used in the younger grades and how what they will now use in the fourth grade will represent "stepping up" in some form. For example, if your students have used seat sacks in younger grades, how might they use them differently in fourth grade? How will you reintroduce this same tool in a way that supports students? How will you communicate that they now have more autonomy and individual responsibility for organizing their materials?

Fourth graders will frequently be working with notebooks, folders, and writing tools that they will keep in their desks. Consider how you will teach the use of these materials throughout the year. For example, a reading notebook may need tabs to identify mini anchor charts, a reading log, read-aloud responses, and written responses to independent reading. You may need to remind students what section they need to use for a task or to open up to the next clean page and write the date so that the notebook stays organized.

Additional supplies should be available in communal spaces around the classroom, clearly labeled so students know where to find and return them. Materials students may use frequently include math tools, such as manipulatives and calculators, and writing tools, such as highlighters, colored pencils, markers, sticky notes, wide-ruled paper, and scrap paper. Materials used less frequently can be kept in storage until needed in order to keep the space organized and avoid distractions.

Get creative with storage options. Many classrooms have limited storage space. Perhaps cabinets, bins, or ottomans can be used for tabletops or flexible seating in addition to storage. Utilize space under counters or tables to store bins. Maybe some boxes can be stored high on bookshelves if you need them infrequently. Consider the possibility of sectioning off a storage area with a curtain rod and curtain. Keeping the space organized and areas clearly defined will go a long way in maintaining a purposeful classroom.

Classroom Displays

Displays and bulletin boards are an important component of the classroom environment. They can be used to exhibit many different items that support the class's interests and learning, such as student artwork, charts marking student growth, anchor charts, and focused teaching tools. Here are some guidelines to consider when developing and using this important part of your classroom:

- Keep displays at your students' eye level whenever possible.

- Allow students to create or cocreate displays to help them build pride and ownership in the classroom space.

- Reference teaching tools such as anchor charts frequently.

- Use Interactive Modeling to show students how to use displayed teaching tools effectively from various work spaces.

- Be sure that these visuals are purposeful, with a clear focus, and leave sufficient space between items in each display so students can view them easily.

At the beginning of the year, when many students are around nine years old, displays might showcase student growth and self-evaluation in order to direct their competitive tendencies. For example, you might create "before" and "after" displays that students could use to show growth in their writing. Or you might invite students to post their math work on a bulletin board, and to use sticky notes to highlight something of which they are proud and one way they might stretch themselves next time. Displays might also be used to reflect the nine-year-old's characteristic appreciation for in-depth study and quality end products. Posters and signs created by students might also add humor to the space by recognizing the tendency of nine-year-olds to worry or say something negative. You might, for example, post a playful chart of idioms focusing on phrases like "one step at a time" or "get the ball rolling." Later in the year, as many students turn ten, displays might show finished products that showcase individual and group efforts. They might also highlight ten-year-olds' aptitude in memory and interest in collections.

When it comes to displays, be sure that all students in the class are represented and celebrated. Sometimes it is useful to include premade displays or printouts. When you think about using these displays, ask yourself the following questions: Who is represented in our classroom, school, and community, and who is not? How might displays be used as an opportunity to highlight individuals who might not usually be represented?

Classroom Library

The classroom library is an important and inviting space that should encourage students to discover treasures, explore the familiar and unfamiliar, and build excitement for a rich reading life. Therefore, the library should be developmentally appropriate and reflect students' interests. Consider starting the year with students having access only to a few bins or shelves with high-interest books in the first days of school. As you unveil the library, get students involved in sorting books. They can begin to explore, getting enticed by book covers, blurbs, and books they find fit together. Students can work together to categorize the books, placing them in bins according to genre. They can create labels and be part of opening the library for everyone to use. As a result, the library will reflect student interests and give you ideas about how your students think about different topics and genres.

As your students develop over the year, their reading interests will too. At the beginning of the year, when most of the students are developmentally around nine years old, biographies, mysteries and other fiction, poetry, nonfiction, and resources for research tasks would be great books to feature. Because nine-year-olds are also competitive, consider ways of organizing classroom libraries around topics, authors, series, and so on, rather than around guided reading levels. As students turn ten during the year, consider including books that reflect their changing interests: books centered on themes, series books, comic books, and graphic novels.

See the appendix, p. 333, for resources for building a diverse classroom library.

Be sure that the books in the library allow students to expand their interests and view of the world. As discussed in the overview of this chapter, use your library to provide a wide selection of windows, mirrors, and sliding glass doors for students.

Technology

Fourth graders can incorporate more technology into their schoolwork than can students in younger grades, where it's still helpful for children to write by hand and use print and other manual materials. By fourth grade, students are able to write using word processing apps and to create slideshows. They can learn to safely search the internet and write emails. With so many students having more access to more technology, this tool can more seamlessly be used between school and home, complementing what's being taught in the classroom, from online libraries, to math games, to writing poems. Students can blog, demonstrate digital citizenship, and connect to class rules. With technology playing a greater role in students' lives in and outside of the classroom, we must think more flexibly about effective management. We cannot always monitor what goes on with technology, so it's important to frequently reference class rules. Role-plays predicting common online behaviors may also be useful. Frequently reinforcing for students' safety and positive use of technology will be invaluable.

Schedules, Routines, and Procedures

Schedules and routines for fourth graders should be as consistent and predictable as possible. Since fourth graders sometimes struggle with change, being able to rely on consistent procedures will provide a sense of stability and help them thrive.

Schedules

See the appendix, p. 327, for sample schedules.

See the appendix, p. 312, for more on closing circles.

When schedules are predictable, students feel safe taking risks. Predictability eases the transition from home to school, the transition between subjects, lunch, and specialty areas, and the transition from school to home. Structures that support learning, such as Morning Meeting and closing circle, create predictable bookends to the day and support the home-to-school and school-to-home transitions. Quiet time after lunch eases the transition from lunchtime, when energy can be very high, back to the classroom.

Nine-year-olds can be restless, so consider adding in frequent energizers throughout the day. They can be used to transition students between subject areas or to take a break from extended work periods. Ten-year-olds are growing quickly, so frequent snack breaks and rest periods are beneficial. Often, fourth grade lunches are scheduled later in the day, so consider one or even two short snack periods in the morning, depending on how late lunch is scheduled at your school. If possible, schedule outdoor time for bigger movement. It can make an incredible difference. High energy without adequate exercise can affect learning in the classroom. It is amazing to see the change to more focused attention on learning and engagement after a midmorning outdoor time. The outdoor time provides an opportunity for students to recharge, but also a chance to learn inclusion, kindness, and cooperation.

We might receive a specialty schedule or a lunch schedule that is not ideal or developmentally responsive. Working within those parameters requires creativity on our part. For example, here is one way that I have seen a teacher get creative when a specialty class was the last period of the day: she skipped the scheduled five-minute transition times between subjects in the morning. Students transitioned from subject to subject quickly, and the time that was saved with those quick transitions allowed for a twenty-minute outdoor break in the middle of the morning. The students came back in the room recharged and ready for another subject before a late lunch. Then students packed their backpacks and had a closing circle before ending the day in their PE class.

One final consideration when it comes to schedules is how to work with out-of-classroom providers and coteachers. Your colleagues will be grateful if you prioritize their often less flexible schedule, especially if they are working with many classes. For example, if you will be working with an ENL (English as a New Language) coteacher for reading, be willing to move your reading block according to your coteacher's availability. It can be a complex puzzle to figure out coteaching schedules, and adapting your schedule is a meaningful, equitable gesture that supports your relationship as coteachers. It also models the fourth guiding principle this book is based on: "How we work together as adults to create a safe, joyful, and inclusive school environment is as important as our individual contribution or competence."

Routines and Procedures

Interactive Modeling is a powerful strategy to use when teaching routines and procedures. As you plan for the new year, you may wish to make a list of these. Some of the most common include:

- Arrival

- Dismissal

- Responding to signals (chime or raised hand)

- Whole-class transitions from the meeting area to working spaces at tables or desks and vice versa

- Lining up in the classroom, lunchroom, specialty class, and so on

- Walking in the hallway

- Walking to and from lunch, recess, or outdoor time

- Emergency routines

At the beginning of the year, start with only one or a few students transitioning at a time. As the year proceeds, build up to everyone transitioning safely at the same time. Use reinforcing language and envisioning language, as these transitions can be challenging. Consider what is developmentally appropriate: if you find yourself giving a lot of reminders or redirections during transitions, ask yourself, "Is this request developmentally appropriate? Was the modeling clear?" For example, it's not a realistic, developmentally appropriate expectation to have students pack or unpack their backpacks in complete silence. It's challenging for adults to do this! It's natural to want to greet a person you haven't seen or to want to wish them a good afternoon. But it would be realistic for students to transition quietly and in under ten minutes.

It's important to practice these routines and procedures in advance of when you need them. It can even be fun! For example, when assigning new places in line in the middle of the year, a teacher used Interactive Modeling to show students how to go to their new line spots. Once everyone was lined up, students waved at the person in front of and behind them. Students noticed an identifying marker nearby (a desk, the rug, a chart on the wall, a window, and so on) and pointed to it. Then the teacher sent the students back to the meeting area, and on her signal, they practiced lining up. When they were standing quietly in their new places in line, she used reinforcing language to support their success in performing the changed routine: "Wow, you were safe as you walked to your line spot, and you tried your best remembering your line spot. Some of you helped each other out with a quiet smile and pointing, which was so kind, while still staying quiet. That only took four minutes! I wonder . . . do you think our whole class could line up again in . . . *three* minutes while still being safe?" The competitive students nodded eagerly and beamed at the challenge. The teacher sent them back to the meeting area, and on the signal, students quickly and safely moved to their new line spots in even less time. Later, when it was time to actually go outdoors for the midmorning break, students were sitting at their desks. "Earlier we practiced going to our new line spots from the meeting area," the teacher said. "I wonder . . . are you ready for the *challenge* of going to your new line spot from your desks?" The teacher's eyes playfully looked around the room to see students vigorously nodding their heads that yes, they were ready for the challenge. "Okay, make a movie in your mind. Think, 'Where is my new line spot?' (Pause.) 'How am I going to get there safely from my desk?' (Pause.) 'What else do I need to remember along the way?'" The teacher then looked at the class and asked, "Who can show us what this looks and sounds like?" The teacher silently pointed to a student whose hand was raised. The student carefully stood up and lifted the chair to push it in as the class had practiced on so many transitions before. The student carefully walked directly to their new line spot, in the middle of the line, and faced forward, ready to go. "Wow, fourth graders. What did you notice?" The teacher continued with the modified Interactive Modeling, encouraging students to share their observations.

Visual Cues for Routines and Procedures

Visual cues aid in the establishment and continued implementation of routines and procedures. During arrival, a morning routine photo could be posted on the document camera. A similar visual cue can be used for packing up at the end of the day. These photos can be taken when routines and procedures are first taught to use as reminders later on; students will love seeing themselves as the focus of these positive images. Other routines and procedures that work well with visual cues include:

1. Take down your chair carefully.

2. Unpack your backpack.

3. Check your folder and hand in notes or homework to the bin.

4. Hang up your backpack and coat.

5. Read and respond to the morning message.

6. Choice: take out a book to read, practice your math facts, or write in your journal.

Classroom Management and Responding to Misbehavior

Positive teacher language is an important strategy that can have a powerful impact on students. Our tone, body language, and facial expressions convey to students that they are safe and cared for, a necessary condition for them to build trust with you and each other and to take risks in their learning.

Envisioning language is powerful for all students, but particularly for nine-year-olds, who tend toward feeling worried, anxious, or competitive. Picturing themselves as successful learners can help ease these challenging feelings and give them confidence that they can be successful. For example, you might say, "As we play Sparkle, we will take care of each other by smiling and waving our hands when someone makes a mistake. That will make it more fun for people to take risks while playing the game."

Reinforcing language tells students what they are doing well. Ten-year-olds appreciate being noticed, so throughout the year, this can be a positive management strategy. This approach takes stepping back and observing. After I have had a challenging day that feels more reactive than proactive, I often reflect and realize I was using a lot more reactive language. The next day, I get a checklist ready and make sure that by the end of the week I have noticed something that each student is doing well and tell them one-on-one. For example, "Immanuel, you wrote a beginning that hooked your readers! You started with a question and then introduced your topic. That will get your reader interested right from the start." I am also more aware of increasing the number of my whole-class reinforcing statements: "I notice that we are using that think time to make a plan about what we will share with our partners. That makes our partner conversations more engaging, and we can go deeper with our learning when we already have a plan." I see these changes make a huge difference, and I go home feeling energized.

Proactive reminding language supports students to stay on track. This language can concern common predictable challenges, such as transitions: "How can we move from the meeting area to our desks safely and respectfully?" It can also be based on an experience of something that was recently challenging, either for the whole class or for an individual student. For example, if on one day Nelson took a long time cleaning up his materials after math class, early the next day you might ask him, "Nelson, what can you do to put away the math materials today quickly and safely?"

Reactive discipline strategies help students get back on track when they need it. Misbehavior will happen, and it's our job as teachers to create a safe and predictable environment that addresses off-task behavior and misbehavior in a way that supports student growth, preserves dignity, and reduces problem behaviors.

There are typical misbehaviors in fourth grade that you will likely need to address reactively at some point. While more will be included in Chapter 3, some common misbehaviors in fourth grade are included in the table below.

Off-Track Behavior	Possible Response
Ahmed starts to run down the hall on the way to the bathroom.	• **Redirecting language:** "Ahmed, come back. We walk to the bathroom. Show me how we move safely in the hall." • **Loss of privilege:** "For the next two days, you will be escorted to the bathroom by me or a buddy. At the end of the day tomorrow we will check in."
As students are writing, Ashley gets up to get a stapler.	• **Nonverbal cue:** Shake head and motion to sit back down. • **Redirecting language:** "Ashley, you can use the stapler at the end of writing. This is your time to write."
As students are lining up, Isabella pushes a student who stepped on her toe.	• **Redirecting language and teacher proximity:** "Isabella, come and walk next to me. I know your energy is high, but we use kind words and safe touches here."

Pause and Ponder

When you plan for building a community and environment with your fourth graders, consider the following questions:

- How should I plan the space so that it is safe and developmentally appropriate?

- How can I set up students for success through Interactive Modeling?

- How might I introduce materials and tools for students to explore in a purposeful way?

- How will students be involved in creating displays, and how will the displays exemplify inclusivity?

- How might the classroom library and technology be used to support windows, mirrors, and sliding glass doors for students? How can they represent diversity and inclusion?

- How can I build the schedule to be developmentally responsive? How might I need to think flexibly around specialty and lunch schedules?

- How can teacher language be used proactively and reactively to create a safe space?

- How can proactive collaborative problem-solving support student growth and autonomy?

Final Thought

"We encourage you to take as many opportunities as you can to listen, to watch, and to engage with children so that you can get to know them in all their rich diversity—their learning styles, strengths and struggles, turn-offs and passions—everything that makes each child shine. Finding those glimmers of gold will help you create learning environments that engage and nurture all the children you teach."

—*The Joyful Classroom*

Grade ⑤

Many fifth graders strive for greater levels of independence as they near the beginning of their young adolescent years. Some ten- and eleven-year-olds are in the final year or two of their elementary school years; others have already embarked on the beginning of their middle school years. Regardless of where fifth graders' school year is taking place, educators need effective management strategies to support students' developmental desire for independence and to support their learning. Teachers need to create welcoming, orderly classrooms that have a safe and predictable environment where students can learn. Simple matters like how to arrange the room and organize supplies must be considered by teachers to set students up for success. More complex tasks, such as developing the daily schedule and establishing routines and procedures, also need careful attention from the teacher. With purposeful and developmentally appropriate classroom management strategies in place, teachers are able to establish learning environments conducive to student success.

Classroom Arrangement and Organization

For many veteran as well as novice teachers, setting up a classroom may sound like a simple task: position students' desks so that they face a marker board or interactive whiteboard, put supplies in a centralized location, prepare some bulletin boards with engaging displays, and organize print and technology resources for students' use. However, there are many subtle nuances that need the teacher's careful attention in order to create a learning environment that supports fifth graders and their learning.

Setting Up the Space

When you lay out your learning space, it is helpful to ask yourself how you envision the classroom looking, sounding, and feeling in order to create an environment that is calm and welcoming and that encourages learning. A classroom that supports fifth graders' needs, allows for good flow, and is neat and organized sends the message that this is *our* classroom and each individual belongs.

Furniture and Seating Arrangements

In thinking about how you will arrange the classroom furniture, take into account how your fifth graders will change and grow over the year. Ensure that students are working in desks and chairs that support their physical needs. Communicate with your maintenance department or administrator about securing furniture that is physically appropriate for fifth graders, and raise or lower the height of the furniture as needed. As you plan the classroom space, consider its overall layout, so that it includes areas where the whole class can meet and where students can work at their desks individually and in small groups. Be sure to leave enough space so that students are able to move throughout the room easily.

See the appendix, p. 312, for more on closing circles.

The whole-group meeting space should be a place where students can gather comfortably in a circle, either seated on the floor or in chairs. Fifth graders appreciate using chairs for the whole-group meeting space, although this is not always possible in smaller classrooms. The whole-group meeting space will be used frequently during the school day for Morning Meeting, whole-group lessons, class meetings, and closing circles. It is also a space where students can spread out while doing independent work.

"I Don't Have Room for a Circle!"

The whole-group meeting circle is the heart of classroom life. Sitting in a circle, everyone can see and be seen by everyone else. By the very nature of its design, the meeting circle invites group participation and fosters inclusion. If you don't have room for an ongoing circle area, here are some possible solutions:

- **Create a temporary meeting area.** At meeting time, students move desks and other furniture to open up a large space for a circle. After the meeting, the students return the furniture to its original place. With adequate teaching and practice, children will be able to do this setup and takedown in just a few minutes. Three keys to creating a temporary meeting area: Choose carefully. Choose a spot with as little furniture as possible. Any furniture should be easy for students to move.

- **Use props to define the area.** An easel pad typically works well. Ideally, the easel pad would stay put and serve as the point from which the meeting circle grows.

- **Teach furniture moving.** Use Interactive Modeling to teach and practice how to move the furniture carefully, cooperatively, and quickly.

- **Create it once, use it twice.** At the end of the day, have students move furniture to make room for a circle, and gather the class for a closing circle, in which the children reflect on their day, share about their work, or plan together for the following day. After the meeting, leave the space as is. The next morning, the space is ready for a meeting that welcomes the children, affirms the strength of the community, and warms them up for the day ahead. Once Morning Meeting is completed, the children move the furniture back.

- **Use a space outside the classroom.** Go to the cafeteria, library, gym, or other space in the school that's large enough to accommodate a circle. This solution works best when you can use the same space at the same time every day, limit distractions, and teach and model transition routines and expectations for behavior outside the classroom.

Position student desks in groups of four or five students. This layout supports fifth graders' need for social interaction and allows for collaboration throughout the day. Here are some guidelines for using table groups effectively:

- **Consider having students create a name and table tent for their group.** When possible, make connections to the curriculum. For example, when your class is studying explorers as part of a social studies unit, have table groups name their group using the last name of an explorer. This keeps the group names fresh while reinforcing new content. Creating group names during Morning Meeting after a new seating arrangement is established is a fun way for students to work collaboratively and build community.

- **Change the seating assignments frequently based on classroom needs.** Switching group partnerships at a minimum every three to four weeks works well.

- **Be flexible with seating assignments, if possible.** Although students will have "their" desk, they might sit in this seat only during homeroom and a few other activities, as well as use it to store personal supplies and materials. Throughout the day, students might sit in other students' desks as the teacher assigns math groups, reading groups, and science teams to work together. Using flexible seating arrangements like this supports fifth graders' developmental needs for interaction and allows the teacher to create homogeneous and heterogeneous grouping formats with ease. Flexible seating also provides practice for switching classes, which students will experience in later schooling years, and minimizes cliques from forming, while promoting an inclusive learning environment.

- **Make sure there is at least one personal space for each student in the classroom.** Typically this is the student's individual desk, which can serve as a place for independent work. Additionally, as noted above, the student's desk can serve as an area to store materials. Often, students will have multiple classroom spaces designated for just their belongings and work. In some districts, fifth graders use lockers for storing personal items. Consider using some of the following storage ideas as well:

- Numbered hooks for backpacks and jackets

- Cubbies or lockers for work in progress

- Mailboxes for efficient distribution of materials

- Organizers that hang on the back of student chairs

- **Add homey touches.** Consider ways you can support the five senses and create an environment that looks, sounds, and feels calm and welcoming. The following are helpful items:

  - *Audio player*—Use a streaming service or device to play calming music when students work independently as well as during periods of transition.

  - *Oil diffusers or air fresheners*—Place these around the classroom. Use scents that are calming and refreshing such as peppermint, lavender, or eucalyptus. Use these items sparingly to ensure they meet the goal of being calming and not overbearing. Check with your district guidelines if you plan to use these items.

  - *Small plants*—Items such as plants, a small garden water fountain, or even a small aquarium with fish set a comfortable, welcoming tone.

  - *Snacks*—Schedule snack breaks for students throughout the day. If allowable, have some small snacks available for students when needed.

  - *Space heater and fans*—If these items are allowed, use them to control the climate. Open and close windows and doors as needed. Talk with your building's maintenance department to ensure heating and cooling units are working properly or to solicit help when needed to maintain a comfortable working environment.

Supplies and Materials

In the fifth grade, as the curriculum expands, students will need access to more and more supplies, materials, and other tools. Students may begin to use separate notebooks for different classes. They may use microscopes for science, and in math they may need calculators and protractors. They will be using tablets and laptops more regularly for writing and research. And they will still need standard classroom supplies such as art materials, markers, pencils, and paper.

Because fifth graders appreciate structure and organization, it is important to store all these community supplies in a way that will support your students. As teachers, we may often feel like there is never enough room for storage. But with some careful thought and creativity, space in the classroom can be maximized to efficiently store materials while ensuring they are readily available for student use. Keep the following in mind:

See the appendix, p. 317, for more on Guided Discovery.

If Supplies Can't Be Shared

If sharing community supplies is not permitted by a health and safety plan, create small, individual caddies or pencil case containers that have the essential supplies students need— pencils, erasers, art supplies, and so on. Create a checklist label that students can put inside the container to keep inventory of what supplies should be in their individual container.

- **Ensure supplies that are currently being used are readily available to students.** For example, if your class is using microscopes to study microorganisms in science, store these materials in a space that is easy for students to access. On the other hand, if you are not currently studying angles in math, store the protractors in a space that is out of sight. Keeping relevant supplies available allows the classroom to stay organized, avoids clutter, and empowers fifth graders to care for their learning community.

- **Consider keeping materials covered at the beginning of the school year.** As they are needed, introduce new materials with Guided Discovery and Interactive Modeling and give students the opportunity to practice using them and receive feedback. Then uncover the materials and make them available for student use.

- **After introducing supplies to students, place the supplies in bins and label them so students can successfully retrieve, use, and store them on their own.** You may find it helpful to store supplies individually in bins labeled with the name of the item they contain.

You might, for example, have one bin for calculators, one for markers, and another for magnifying glasses. On the other hand, some teachers prefer to group related supplies together. For example, if you plan to have a science investigation that requires groups to use calculators, markers, and magnifying glasses at the same time, you can store these materials in a group caddy that is labeled with the group name or number. Doing so allows for quick retrieval and storage of the materials. Regardless of whether supplies are grouped together or stored separately, labeling the supplies builds responsibility for fifth graders as they use and care for the supplies.

- **Designate a bin in the classroom where students can place materials that are no longer in working condition.** If a student finds that a marker has dried up, the marker can be placed in the "Needs to Be Replaced" bin so that it is no longer in circulation. The teacher should monitor the supplies in this bin and decide whether the supplies are in fact no longer in good condition; this will help in keeping an inventory of what supplies need to be replaced throughout the year. The teacher could designate this responsibility as a classroom job. Creating a storage space like this empowers students to take ownership of the materials and ensures students have the supplies needed to successfully carry out a task. You may also want to check with your district about recycling worn-out materials.

- **Be creative.** Use storage containers such as filing cabinets on wheels. Use clear tote boxes that are easy to see through. Or store boxes under community tables covered with tablecloths. Creative ideas like these help teachers to maximize their storage space while keeping the classroom looking neat and orderly.

Many teachers face challenges with having quality materials on hand in the classroom. In situations like these, discuss your needs with your Parent Teacher Organization. You may also consider contacting local businesses for support, reaching out to families of students in your class for donations, or setting up an online wishlist or fundraising page.

Classroom Displays

It is important to remember that developmentally, fifth graders appreciate being recognized. Display boards are an effective way to meet this need and to build inclusive learning communities. Here are some tips to keep in mind:

- Include examples of work from all students, not just high-achieving students.

- Display both in-progress and finished products.

- Allow students to help choose items that can be displayed to recognize their independence and provide ownership of their learning.

- Consider using hallway space to showcase student work, especially for displays that may distract students' focus in the classroom.

- Use a variety of display boards throughout the classroom, while keeping things simple and uncluttered. Here are some types of displays for fifth grade:

  - *Hopes and dreams, classroom rules*—Designate a space in the classroom for students to display their hopes and dreams. Also display the class rules close to the hopes and dreams display, as a reminder of the connection between these two practices. Hopes and dreams and classroom rules creation will be discussed further in Chapter 3.

  - *Community news board*—Use a board for announcements, birthday charts, lunch options, music lesson schedules, or other news that is helpful for all community members.

  - *Quote of the day*—Designate a space in the room to post an inspirational quote each day. Quotes can help motivate students and build community. Use quotes that represent diverse cultures to promote inclusiveness.

  - *Photo board*—As the year progresses, print out pictures of students working on various projects from throughout the year. Fifth graders love seeing pictures of themselves hanging on the wall, and photo boards can also encourage reflection.

- *Interactive displays*—Think of ways you can encourage students to interact with display boards. Use structures like a question of the day board, a question box, a community brainstorming board, or an interactive exploration display. For example, if students are writing opinion essays about wearing school uniforms, create a display board where students can write pros or cons for the topic throughout the school day.

- *Content area boards*—Display word walls, content inquiry charts, or other class-created charts that summarize key ideas from the subject areas students are learning about. For example, if you are teaching formulas for finding area in math, you and your students can create a chart that can be displayed in the classroom during that unit. Creating a chart along with students, as opposed to using a store-bought one, helps to strengthen students' understanding of the concept being learned.

Classroom Library

An important part of any classroom is an organized classroom library that catches readers' attention. For fifth grade readers, it is important to set up a library that has a balance between fiction and nonfiction selections. When choosing specific books to include, look for titles that reflect a wide range of cultures and that match a wide range of abilities, ensuring

See the appendix, p. 334, for a list of recommended books.

that readers of all levels can find books that fit their reading levels. Use testing results and consult with a literacy specialist to determine appropriate leveled books. Model a diverse range of cultures and interests with read-aloud books to use throughout the school year as well. To create an efficient and useful library for students, organize the books into fiction and nonfiction selections. It is also helpful to organize the books in bins or sections by genre, culture, or author's last name to keep the library organized. As with other supplies, label the sets of books to make the library easy for students to navigate. Implement a checkout system that allows fifth graders to be responsible for the organization and care of the classroom library resources. Lastly, consider participating in a discount book club or creating an online wish list for affordable ways to create and maintain a classroom library.

Technology

In many schools, technology resources are readily available for students' use. A critical piece with using technology is teaching fifth graders digital citizenship. Time must be dedicated to teaching students how to act responsibly and safely, particularly when interacting with others. Fifth graders must learn about their digital footprint so that they can navigate online learning appropriately.

Many teachers also use online learning management systems. When using these systems, it is important to model for students how to carry out necessary tasks. Some of these routines in fifth grade may include signing on and off of the device, checking email, opening and saving files, collaborating with peers using an interactive whiteboard, creating movies or podcasts, making slide deck presentations, turning in digital assignments, and much more. Although fifth graders often have experience with technology tools, and at times may be better versed in using the tools than the classroom teacher, it is important that time is dedicated to teaching the

THINK
BEFORE YOU SPEAK

T is it **TRUE?**
H is it **HELPFUL?**
I is it INSPIRING?
N is it **NECESSARY?**
K is it **KIND?**

skills necessary to create a common, even foundation for the learning community.

Lastly, as with any learning tool, it is important that teachers monitor students' technology use. Ensure that students are following the class guidelines and school requirements when using technology devices. Although many fifth graders have highly developed technology skills, close monitoring, frequent practice, and continual reinforcement are paramount to ensuring that technology enhances the learning experience, rather than detracts from it.

Schedules, Routines, and Procedures

Fifth graders' desire for greater independence also carries over into the flow of the school day. As teachers, we must thoughtfully consider this developmental need of fifth graders, along with their many other developmental needs, when structuring the school day. With careful attention to planning the daily schedule and establishing effective routines and procedures, we can prepare our fifth graders to act in a responsible and autonomous manner, which will support their learning.

Schedules

As mentioned in Chapter 1, fifth graders have many developmental needs that should be considered when determining an academic schedule. The needs for physical movement, social interaction, and periods of recognition can be addressed with a well-thought-out schedule. If you are a teacher who has flexibility in determining the daily schedule, begin the day with Morning Meeting. Then focus the morning block on rigorous academic subjects such as literacy, writing, and math. After a break for recess, lunch, and quiet time, students can then move into content-rich subjects like science and social studies, as well as special area classes. The day can then conclude with time for reinforcement and reflection with a closing circle.

In other instances, teachers have little control over determining the complete daily schedule. For example, rigorous academic blocks, such as literacy, writing, and math, are often predetermined for fifth grade teachers based on building needs. Sometimes students who receive itinerant enrichment or intervention have schedules that are set as well. In these

See the appendix, p. 327, for sample schedules.

instances, it is still important to keep in mind the developmental needs of fifth graders, including movement, interaction, and recognition.

Regardless of whether you have control over your students' daily schedule or not, use your knowledge of child development to provide input with school leaders to find a balance that is realistic for fifth graders. Then put structures in place throughout the daily schedule to ensure students' developmental needs are supported. Even if the daily schedule is largely predetermined, begin the day with Morning Meeting to allow students to interact and practice new learning. Next, as students move through their academic learning, balance interactive and independent periods. Alternating between independent, partner, and small-group work is beneficial for fifth graders. Also, be sure to include energizers and frequent breaks throughout the day. Additionally, schedule snack breaks throughout the day as needed. These structures can be incorporated into predetermined or teacher-selected schedules to support fifth graders and their learning.

See the appendix, p. 313, for sample energizers.

Lastly, if you teach in a school with multiple fifth grade classes, talk with your colleagues and administrators about the possibility of departmentalizing. Many fifth graders benefit from switching classes. For this approach to be effective, teachers must work closely together, use similar rules and structures for students' learning, and communicate frequently. Ideally, if having fifth graders change classes, allow them to adjust to this new format by introducing it for only one or two class periods.

Routines and Procedures

Teachers may assume that because fifth graders have been in school for a few years, routines and procedures should be natural for them. Teachers may be tempted to not explicitly teach these skills throughout the school year. However, time must be dedicated to teaching routines and procedures to effectively manage fifth graders and their learning. Academic and social and emotional skills must be taught at the beginning, middle, and end of the school year. See the following chart for routines that should be taught all throughout the school year.

To teach fifth graders routines and procedures, use these effective strategies:

- **Interactive Modeling.** Interactive Modeling is a straightforward, seven-step process through which students gain a clear understanding of what a skill should look like. It is an effective way to teach fifth graders because it empowers them to notice what the skill should look like, sound like, and feel like, and gives them the chance to gain expertise in using it. Interactive Modeling empowers students to take responsibility for their actions, and it meets fifth graders' desire for greater independence. Some specific routines and procedures that fifth graders need in order to be successful are morning arrival, transitions, testing sessions, recess and lunch, quiet time, and dismissal. In each of these circumstances, Interactive Modeling is useful for teaching the skill.

See the appendix, p. 323, for more on Interactive Modeling.

- **Visual cues.** Visual cues, such as hand signals or anchor charts, are effective ways to remind students of previously modeled skills. These teaching tools can serve as verbal or nonverbal reminders for students and are developmentally appropriate for fifth graders and their desire for greater independence. Fifth grade teachers can use visual cues or anchor charts for individual students or for the whole group.

Morning Routine

- Go to desk and completely empty backpack
- Place backpack on your hook
- Place snack in desk and lunch in bin
- Sign up for lunch (skip if not buying)
- Read "Morning Message"
- Make sure you have two sharpened pencils
- Copy homework from "Homework Chart"
- Work on assignment found on the Do Now board

Reflection. Teachers should give students ownership over routines and procedures by having students reflect on the success with which they used the skill. For example, the teacher might ask, "How has our class been following our expectations during testing sessions? What improvements could be made?" When teachers ask open-ended questions like these, it encourages students to reflect and to come up with solutions for any trouble areas. During these periods of reflection, encourage students to help one another, while reminding them that helping others is a class goal.

As the school year progresses, routines and procedures will serve as a strong foundation for an effectively managed classroom. Recognizing fifth graders' desire for greater independence, teachers should gradually release responsibility for the use and care of supplies and materials. Interactive Modeling helps students gain expertise with materials. However, it is important to remember that students will not be perfect and that old routines, as well as new ones, will have to be modeled, practiced, and reinforced to keep the classroom running efficiently. Often in fifth grade, students need reteaching of skills. These instances may occur after an extended break, before an exciting activity, or during a typical school day. In moments like these, teachers may condense the steps of Interactive Modeling or simply refer to a visual cue in order to review the skills in a timely manner. As your fifth graders become successful with meeting the expectations of routines and procedures, reinforce and celebrate their achievement.

Here are a few key routines and procedures to teach and practice with fifth graders:

- Routines (student-led recess games, bathroom, lunch, reading/ writing workshops, individual projects, group projects, homework, leadership roles)

- Transitions (arrival and dismissal, from instruction to independent work, during workshops and project time, walking to and from classes without supervision to move towards independence)

- Using and caring for materials (textbooks, folders/binders, technology)

- Social skills (asking questions, making empathetic comments, apologizing, giving and receiving compliments, making formal presentations, paraphrasing what others said, respectfully disagreeing)

- Academic skills (giving feedback to a partner, locating/highlighting important information in a text, content area skills, taking notes, using graphic organizers, study skills)

Classroom Management and Responding to Misbehavior

In addition to the tangible strategies that we use to create welcoming, calm classrooms, teachers also use techniques that cannot be physically observed by students but that are significant in effectively managing a learning environment. The careful use of teacher language, along with a thoughtfully implemented leadership style, are as important as the other effective management strategies discussed in this chapter. Teacher language and teacher leadership are two foundational means by which we ensure the emotional setup of the classroom will match the physical layout and organization of the learning environment.

The Importance of Teacher Language

Fifth graders are at a pivotal point in their development. They are beginning to develop a strong understanding of the world around them and are able to think and act with empathy in socially ethical ways. With this in mind, it is important that teachers use their teacher language to support these developmental traits. Communicating in this manner ensures a calm, welcoming environment.

Teachers can effectively manage their classroom by showing empathy when using verbal and nonverbal communication with fifth graders. Students are empowered to take responsibility for their actions when teachers use neutral tones and intentions.

Teacher Leadership

Like teacher language, a teacher's leadership style lays a strong foundation in establishing a positive learning community. Teachers need to be firm, kind, and consistent in order to effectively manage a classroom. Students need to see that rules apply to all and are enforced fairly. Teachers should plan responses to misbehavior that are developmentally appropriate for fifth graders and maintain a positive learning community. Throughout the school day, teachers should incorporate the teaching of social and emotional skills to strengthen fifth graders' sense of independence, empathy, and responsibility. Creating rules and responding to misbehavior in a way that meets these goals helps maintain the physical and emotional learning community. These strategies will be discussed in Chapter 3. An authoritative leadership style that is assertive and approachable is an effective management strategy that supports fifth graders in all aspects of the classroom.

Pause and Ponder

As older elementary students, fifth graders will sometimes seek ways to test limits in the classroom, but most of these ten- and eleven-year-olds are generally excited about the academic and social learning they encounter during fifth grade. With purposeful strategies in place, teachers are able to create inclusive, calm, and welcoming classroom environments that support these students as they grow. Learning communities that implement the strategies discussed in this chapter help to support fifth graders' desire for greater independence and need for empathy while continuing to support their individual and collective development throughout the school year.

Final Thought

"From day one, we can send students the message that the classroom is an inclusive and respectful space, that the teacher is in control, and that standards for behavior are high."

—*Seeing the Good in Students*

Chapter 3
Positive Community

● ●

Overview

When we take the time to know and understand our students, we can provide a safe and supportive learning environment and build a positive community in which students learn to care for themselves, their classmates, their environment, and their work. Teachers develop, cultivate, and maintain a positive community when they meet students' needs for belonging and significance, interact respectfully with students, approach discipline proactively, preserve students' dignity when disciplinary measures are needed, and provide opportunities for success that are equitable, fair, and just. We'll consider these practices in the following pages.

Meeting the Need for Belonging and Significance

When students feel known and supported by those around them, they learn and behave at their best. Our students, as well as teachers, come to school with a need for belonging, significance, and fun. The small interactions we share throughout the school day, such as greeting students, learning their interests, and asking questions, are opportunities to strengthen relationships by building belonging and significance. Starting the day with Morning Meeting is an effective way to meet students' needs for belonging, significance, and fun, right off the bat. The components of Morning Meeting (greeting, sharing, group activity, and morning message) strengthen our relationships with our students and the connections between the students. Getting to know students—knowing their personal goals, unique interests, culture, and latest happenings—benefits the overall classroom community.

The routines and procedures outlined in Chapter 2 also help nurture a sense of belonging in our students. When we are able to meet their needs for belonging and significance, students are more focused and display respectful behavior, which leads to increased academic engagement and learning. Teacher and peer relationships are strengthened, which in turn supports social and emotional growth for all.

Interacting Respectfully

Students look to their teachers to be the calm. Teacher language is the tool we carry with us to be the calm in the sea of interactions in the classroom—teacher to student and student to student. The messages we send to students with teacher language, both verbal and nonverbal, set the tone for all interactions and impact the classroom community. Our words, tone, and body language can build an atmosphere of warmth, safety, inclusiveness, and caring grounded in our belief in our students. Purposeful and intentional, the use of teacher language helps to build relationships, communicate expectations with students in a respectful way, and create positive learning communities built on trust, responsibility, accountability, and positive interactions.

Positive teacher language includes the same characteristics, regardless of age level: it's always direct, encouraging, action oriented, and to the point—and it incorporates thoughtful silence as well as the spoken word. Keep in mind the following guidelines when communicating with students:

- **Be direct and genuine.** Friendly and respectful words and tone build a positive community—a community in which students learn to trust their teachers because the teachers say what they mean and mean what they say. Directions are clear, simple, and direct.

- **Convey faith in children's abilities and intentions.** Assume that everyone is operating from the best of intentions. By noticing and commenting on what students are doing well, you create a positive common ground for the classroom community.

- **Focus on action.** Using language that connects abstract terms with concrete behaviors and centers on specific attributes of children's work, effort, and behavior enables students to understand the *how*. For example, "Everyone got their materials out quickly today. What helped you do that?"

- **Keep it brief.** Enough said.

- **Know when to be silent.** Provide wait time. The silence provides time for students to think and rehearse what to say. Students may also need the time to gather the courage to speak.

There are four types of teacher language:

- **Envisioning language.** We use envisioning language to establish a positive tone for learning, set the stage for possibilities, generate interest in a topic, and build a community of learners, scholars, readers, scientists, mathematicians, and so on.

- **Reinforcing language.** This type of teacher language is used to acknowledge what students are doing well in meeting individual goals and classroom expectations.

- **Reminding language.** We can use reminding language in two ways: it can be used proactively to set students up for success prior to beginning a task, or it can be used reactively when we notice a student is just starting to go off track.

- **Redirecting language.** This is a respectful way to stop misbehavior and get students back on track in a timely way.

Approaching Discipline Proactively

Interacting with students in a respectful manner leads us to approach discipline in a proactive way and builds a positive community. A proactive approach to discipline uses teacher language and classroom rules as a foundation for the classroom community. A positive community supports student growth and encourages students to identify hopes and set realistic goals for the school year. The process of creating classroom rules with students begins with identifying, sharing, and reviewing everyone's hopes and dreams, which then opens the door to brainstorming about guidelines or rules that would support everyone's learning on all levels—oneself, one another, and the community. The possible guidelines are categorized and reworded to be positive, concise, and few in number. The foundation is built on the assumption of positive intentions—that students want to become knowledgeable, competent, and autonomous learners. The agreed-upon rules shape the classroom community and become the cornerstone on which the positive community is built.

Support Students During Teacher Absences

There are times during the year when you will need to be absent. Although you will not be present, the community will still be together. It is helpful for the students and the guest teacher to have structures in place before a teacher absence occurs. Plan a Morning Meeting that the guest teacher can use to start the day off with students by using the following:

- **Greeting.** Have students introduce themselves. If you have classroom name tags, use a name tag greeting. For this greeting, place all student name tags in the middle of the circle. One at a time, each student will retrieve another person's name tag, greet the student whom the name tag belongs to, and give that student the tag. After each student receives their name tag, students can wear the name tag throughout the day to support the guest teacher.

- **Sharing.** Have students go around the circle and answer the following prompt: "What is one way you can follow our classroom rules while [guest teacher's name] is with our class today?"

- **Group Activity.** Have students show the guest teacher how they can engage in a collaborative activity that follows the rules.

- **Morning Message.** Use a prewritten message (or slide) that the guest teacher can project for students. Include a list of the classroom rules and the daily schedule on this message to remind students of classroom expectations and routines.

Plan this Morning Meeting and practice it with students *before* an expected or unexpected absence occurs. It sets the tone for a productive day.

At the end of the day, the guest teacher should have the students use the closing circle to identify how they helped to follow the classroom rules to make it a productive day. Encourage the guest teacher to prepare notes during the closing circle that can be shared with you when you return.

Discipline is a subject that can be taught using Interactive Modeling and role-play. Interactive Modeling of social and emotional skills and academic skills needed for purposeful, supportive interactions provides an atmosphere of safety and fosters the development of a positive community. When routines and procedures are established through the use of Interactive Modeling, the classroom develops a predictability that makes students feel safe. A safe environment sets students up for success and helps to reduce misbehavior.

These routines and procedures become a positive habit that helps sustain a positive and safe learning environment. Role-play is a strategy used proactively to teach a variety of appropriate responses that students can use in complex social situations, enabling them to live by the rules. In role-play, teachers and students discuss the situation, brainstorm possible responses to handle the situation, and then act out the positive possibilities. Role-play helps children to envision appropriate responses and practice positive behaviors. The effective use of teacher language supports the implementation of Interactive Modeling and role-playing.

Preserving Dignity

We model empathy and self-control for our students when we respond to misbehavior in ways that preserve their dignity. Misbehavior consists of behaviors that are disruptive to the learning and the agreed-upon classroom rules. Misbehaviors are missteps and are also opportunities for learning. When we respond with empathy, students feel heard. For instance, with off-task behaviors such as daydreaming or doodling during independent reading, teachers can help students by using proximity, visual cues, and reminding language.

All students want to fulfill their potential. There are times when students may need support to express and identify what is keeping them from achieving their potential. Misbehavior, such as acting out to gain a sense of power, might be a result of a student's need for belonging or significance not being met. One of the most effective ways to teach empathy is for the teacher to model empathy in responding to misbehavior. Stopping student misbehavior and then addressing it in a respectful, firm, and calm manner allows students to learn from, correct, and repair their mistakes.

When it's time for students to repair their mistakes, use logical consequences. These strategies help in building and maintaining a positive community—one where students feel physically, socially, and emotionally safe, where students know the limits, and where the behavior, not the student, is the problem. Logical consequences help children learn how their behavior affects themselves and others and give them dignified ways to repair any damage or harm that their behavior may have caused.

A Calming Strategy

- Place one hand in front of you and spread fingers apart.

- Use the pointer finger of the opposite hand and place it at the base of the thumb.

- Begin to trace the outside of the thumb as you inhale.

- Trace the inside of the thumb as you exhale.

- Repeat the inhale/exhale cycle for the remaining fingers. (As you trace up, inhale. As you trace down, exhale.)

Consequences are logical when they are respectful, related, and realistic. *Respectful* consequences stop the misbehavior while preserving the dignity of the student; teachers apply them using a firm and calm tone, facial expression, and body language. Consequences are *related* when they allow students to see the connection between the mistake or action and the class rules. When consequences are *realistic*, the student can successfully accomplish the associated tasks or goals, and the teacher can successfully follow through in implementing them.

There are three types of logical consequences to consider using:

1. **Loss of privilege.** As members of a positive community, students are expected to act responsibly. Students practice responsibility throughout the school day as they navigate school life and take care of themselves, each other, and their space and materials. When a student acts irresponsibly, by, for example, using scissors in an unsafe manner, the privilege of using the scissors is temporarily revoked. Then we reteach and remind them of the skill that they need, in this instance holding and using scissors to cut paper, in order for the student to be successful the next time.

2. **Break it, fix it.** Used in cases when a student is able to fix a mistake independently by making amends and taking responsibility for their actions, break it, fix it is an appropriate tool for connecting actions and consequences. For example, if a student is moving too quickly in the classroom and knocks over a bin of art supplies, they can repair what is broken by cleaning up the mess.

3. **Positive time-out.** When a student needs to take a pause to regain self-control, they are temporarily removed from the situation. A positive time-out gives the student space and time to practice calming-down strategies, such as the five-finger calming breath, so that they can regain self-control and return to the work that they were doing.

Providing Equitable Opportunities for Success

Mutual respect and trust between the teacher and students form the basis of an equitable, fair, and just classroom. Students know that the teacher and their peers see, hear, and know them. The information we know about our students is used to set high expectations and provide opportunities for students to take ownership of their learning—both individually and as a community. The teacher must provide opportunities for all students to show their best selves. How do you begin? Begin with what you know about your students, developmentally and culturally, while keeping in mind their interests, strengths, and academic learning goals. Use a fair and friendly tone with all students. Teacher language and the subtle messages sent through tone and body language, such as a warm welcome, being present, and positioning oneself at a student's eye level, all communicate inclusivity. Consistently model, guide, and reinforce that the expectations are for everyone through the practices of Interactive Modeling, role-play, and responding equitably to misbehavior. When the teacher and students work together to establish a positive community, students see themselves as a valuable part of their classroom.

In the following pages, we'll look further into teacher language; strategies for getting to know and connect with students; the process of establishing rules and getting students invested in the rules; a proactive approach to discipline, including responses to misbehavior that preserve the dignity of students; and methods for maintaining a strong community. You will find specific and age-appropriate ideas for creating a safe, predictable, joyful, and inclusive environment where all students have a sense of belonging and significance.

Grade 3

"These will be our group guidelines," the teacher overhears a student sharing one March afternoon. The third graders are not only buzzing about books; they are buzzing about their new book clubs, especially after the teacher explained that he is participating in a book club with colleagues. He observes several groups gathered around the room with materials in hand. Bending down near the group seated at their desks, he listens further to the guidelines being shared. Everyone is so engaged that he moves to the next group without the students even noticing.

In this group, the students are trying to navigate the roles of each member. One student turns to him, asking, "Should each person have the same role for each meeting, or should we take turns?" In a reassuring voice, the teacher replies, "This is something you need to decide together. You all will make the best decision for your group." Navigating to the next group, the teacher sees that there seems to be more tension, and one student is visibly becoming more upset. "Steven is not helping us at all," one student declares.

The teacher decides to take Steven aside for a private discussion. "Steven, tell me more about what is happening with your group." Immediately, Steven shares that he does not care about this project because he is thinking about his mom and dad getting divorced, and now his group is mad at him and they don't understand. "I'm so sorry to hear that, Steven," the teacher whispers. "I appreciate you telling me, and I know that your group will understand that everyone has rough days. You will be able to contribute when you are able to focus. It can be hard when you have something on your mind." The teacher makes a mental note to monitor Steven. He had noticed that Steven had been more withdrawn lately and quicker to anger; now it all made sense.

During closing circle that day, as students are seated around the outside of the rug, the teacher invites students to share a success, apology, or aha moment from the day. The fast-paced sharing comes to a halt when the talking piece reaches Steven. "I want to apologize to everyone. I am not

See the appendix, p. 312, for more on closing circles.

being a good friend because I'm sad about something at home." Steven immediately looks to the teacher, as he gives a comforting smile and slight nod to Steven. Despite the rule that the one holding the ball is the speaker, students erupt with empathy. "It's okay, Steven." "I'm not happy about things at my house sometimes too." "Tomorrow will be better." As Steven's bus is called, the teacher meets him at the door. "Steven, you should be really proud of yourself. It took a lot of courage to share with us today. You can come to me anytime you want to talk." "Thank you," Steven whispers as he leaves for his bus.

These events on this particular Wednesday in March illustrate what it means to establish a positive community in which the social and emotional well-being of each member of the classroom takes priority. All of the interactions that took place—including Steven's willingness to confide in his teacher and the eagerness of the other children to support him—were the result of the work of a teacher who laid the groundwork for students from the first day of school, fostering cooperation, assertiveness, responsibility, empathy, and self-control. The teacher not only developed trusting relationships with the students, he also empowered their relationships with one another. Throughout this section, we will be revisiting this scenario to learn more about the process that was taken so this third grade class could reach this point of independence and support for one another.

Teacher Tone and Demeanor

> "Effective teacher language can be used to help students visualize positive outcomes for themselves, to recognize their efforts, and to help them get back on task when they make mistakes."
>
> —*Teaching Self-Discipline*

In the chapter overview, the five characteristics of teacher language were described in detail. Take a moment to see how each one was present within the scenario described above.

1. **Be direct and genuine.** The teacher displayed empathy toward Steven.

2. **Convey faith in children's abilities and intentions.** The teacher said to the group that they would make the right decision.

3. **Focus on action.** The teacher told Steven why he should be proud of himself.

4. **Keep it brief.** Each time the teacher spoke, he kept it short, sweet, and to the point.

5. **Know when to be silent.** The teacher observed the first group without providing any comments, empowering them to take ownership of their work.

As we delve deeper into the types of teacher language and examples of their use with third graders, continue to revisit these five characteristics to see how they echo across the types of language. What we say and how we say it supports the social, emotional, and academic success of our students, and enhances a community where students feel they belong, are significant and safe, and can have fun learning together.

Reinforcing Language

The most powerful of the four types of teacher language, reinforcing language is often the least used, as we often notice what is not going well instead of offering specific praise to help students develop patterns of success. The more positive reinforcement we can verbalize, the more likely students will be to continue to demonstrate these desired behaviors. Students become more independent as a result. And as teachers, we spend less time responding to misbehavior when students are continuously noticing how their actions are supporting the classroom expectations.

In the examples of teacher language that follow, note the boldfaced sentence stems, each of which is completed with an illustration of how these sentences can be used when addressing students. Consider generating an anchor chart in the classroom with these prompts listed. Not only will a chart be a visual reminder for you, but you'll be amazed at how quickly the students start to change their language when speaking with each other. These clear options for use in peer-to-peer discussions will promote positive communication and working relationships among the students in your class. Consider how the sentence stems in the following sentences reinforce positive behavior:

- **I noticed** that you walked to line up so we can stay safe.

- **I see that** everyone is working quietly so we can focus on our reading.

- **You remembered to** put your eyes on the speaker to show you're listening.

- **You all helped to** respect our classroom space by putting materials away.

- **You paid attention to** the mini-lesson by trying this strategy as you worked.

- **You followed our rule by** having your materials out and getting started quickly.

- **Did you notice** how it felt to help your partner?

- **One of the reasons your group was successful today was** that you made sure everyone was included and worked together.

- **Because you** took your time, **your work** was easy to read.

Reminding Language

This type of language is unique as it can be used proactively, prior to students beginning a task, or it can be used reactively, when we observe students starting to get off task. The more we proactively remind students, the more they have positive experiences. Reminding language promotes positive behaviors and is particularly beneficial for students who need to hear directions more than once. Consider when you will offer the reminder and when you will encourage a peer to restate the expectations. Students feel empowered when they can restate the directions, and students benefit from hearing expectations from their peers. Remember to focus on the boldfaced words that could be used for an anchor chart in the classroom, while also reflecting on the presence of the five characteristics for this type of language. Here are some examples of sentence stems that provide proactive reminders:

- **Think about** the steps you need to follow so you're ready to get started.

- **Show us how** it will look when you turn and talk to your partner.

- **Remind everyone how** to put the books back on the bookshelf carefully.

- **What if you** are unsure what to do next? What can you do?

- **What might help you** if you and your partner disagree about the solution?

- **How can you** decide which choice is better for you?

- **How do you** walk in the hallway?

- **Who can tell us** where to find the assignment in Google Classroom?

Redirecting Language

Everyone makes mistakes! We proactively set our students up for success, but it is unrealistic to think they will never make a mistake or require redirection. Redirecting language is a respectful way to help students regain safety and ensure they get back on track in a timely manner. The rest of the class is always watching us; we model for our students and convey messages of trust and faith as they see our interactions with others. The sooner we provide a redirecting language stem, the sooner the students know they can trust us to keep them safe. Remember, our third graders are very concerned about fairness, so we model for them that the expectations are the same for everyone. Consistency leads to trust, and trust leads to a classroom where students feel safe to take risks. That is when learning is at its peak!

Continue to think about the boldfaced sentence stems and how they can support your quest to use language to benefit you and your students:

- **Stop. Put away the** scissors to stay safe.

- **Pause. Get started on** the next math problem.

- **Stop and think. Then raise your hand if** you can remind us what quiet time should sound like.

- **It's time to** get back to work and finish the discussion later.

- **Clean up the** markers.

- **Sit at another desk where you can** focus on your reading.

- **Focus on** what you were asked to do on this activity.

- **Right now you need to** listen to the directions.

Envisioning Language

Envisioning language inspires students to be ready to put forth effort and persistence in the unit or lesson to come. In addition to building a positive tone and excitement for learning, it generates a feeling of community and sense of belonging. We will all be doing this together!

We provide students with hope and the expectation of success when we engage them with sentences that begin with the following stems. These are also powerful ideas to include in the morning message for the day.

- **I hope that** you are ready to become scientists today for our experiment!

- **Imagine that you** are a famous author. You have so many strategies to use for the next writing unit.

- **What needs to happen so everyone can** feel they reached their goals for the week?

- **You're going to be** a team today. **How will you do that successfully?**

- **Think about what you would be doing if you were a professional** meteorologist.

- **What will make our** Morning Meeting successful today?

Getting to Know One Another

"Before we get out our familiar reads, we are going to greet each other and ask, 'What's the news?' Remember, pick the most important thing you'd like us to know," the literacy support teacher shared with her small group of four students, all coming from different homerooms.

"Good morning, Weston. What's the news?" Payton asks.

"Good morning, Payton. Today is my brother's first day of preschool."

"I hope he has fun," Payton replies.

The combined greeting and sharing go around the circle, with the teacher being greeted at the end. She includes envisioning language in her sharing to set up the thirty-minute support lesson. "We are going to be veterinarians today with our new nonfiction book. We will gain so much knowledge about animals!"

The Importance of Knowing One Another

Maybe you are just starting at a new school, or perhaps you can reflect back to your first day. You have a principal who is new to you, and you need to learn what they expect from their staff. There are a lot of new faces and names to learn. You may have a new colleague or mentor who has reached out to you. You have a lot to learn and questions to ask. You are excited about the opportunity and awaiting the feeling of comfort that will come a few weeks later, when you know more names, have found a few colleagues with similar interests, and feel your principal knows you. This is how your students feel at the beginning of the year too!

By third grade, many students will know one another already, with the exception of those new to the school. On one hand, the familiarity with many is a positive. On the other hand, we want each student's year to

start with a fresh, clean slate, especially for the child who may have had a challenging second grade year for one reason or another. When we know each other's names and personal facts, it provides a connection that will guide academic goal setting, conversations, comfort, and trust. When students are in an environment where they feel socially and emotionally safe, they are more apt to take risks. That is when real learning takes place. The following ideas can help you create this type of environment:

- **Learn names.** Whether you are a classroom teacher, special area teacher, specialist, or teacher assistant, it is important that you know each student's name, including the correct pronunciation and spelling, and that students know each other's names. Consider using name tags for the first days of school and having names posted around the classroom. Posting student photos in the room (with permission) helps everyone learn names while also representing students in the classroom. During Morning Meeting, there are greetings, shares, and activities that can be used to support learning names.

- **Start the year with greeting activities.** At the beginning of the school year, a straightforward greeting allows students to feel valued and known by their classmates. They learn one another's names and develop key conversational skills that empower academic conversations throughout the day. Greeting each other with a smile, making eye contact, and experiencing a positive interaction develops relationships so all students get to know one another and develop working relationships. Each group activity, whether you are a classroom teacher or work with small groups of students, must start with greetings that allow all students to participate and to be successful. Low-risk greetings, with minimal physical contact, allow a level of comfort to develop. There is no magic formula for when to increase the complexity of greetings. You need to use your professional judgment and power of observation as you get to know each student and plan for the needs of your group. The use of Interactive Modeling anytime you are introducing a new greeting will proactively set students up for success, along with your use of reinforcing language to promote the desired actions and expectations.

See the appendix, p. 323, for more on Interactive Modeling.

- **Be present at the door.** You have a lot to prepare for each day. However, it is important to be at the classroom door when students arrive so that you can greet each student individually. They feel known as you ask them how they are doing, inquire about the soccer game the night before, and check in about how they did with their homework. This daily greeting also offers you the opportunity to take an emotional temperature reading of each student, too. The child who looks upset may need your reassurance and a few minutes to talk so they are set up for a positive day. Third graders are old enough that some of them may be getting themselves up and out of the house in the morning. You might be the first friendly face to say good morning to them!

- **Hold a daily Morning Meeting.** Whether you do a full four-component Morning Meeting in the classroom or modify it to meet your time constraints, the predictable structure of starting each day the same way helps students to develop a routine. Transitioning from home to school, students are building their connections to their peers and teachers, while also integrating academics and social and emotional skills that will provide a strong foundation for the learning to come that day. The four components of Morning Meeting include greeting, sharing, group activity, and morning message.

- **Build regular sharing into the school day.** Sharing helps to develop a collaborative and supportive tone in the classroom. Third graders thrive on social interactions, and they want to share their personal experiences. They are also developing their conversational skills and are eager to ask follow-up questions. By teaching children how to interact with others, we are preparing them for the academic conversations that are sure to follow throughout the day.

Keeping Sharing Safe for Everyone

The following suggestions will help you set up sharings that are appropriate and successful for all students:

- **Brainstorm appropriate topics.** Before students start sharing, have the class brainstorm a list of suitable topics: pets, friends, trips, hobbies, family events, and so on. Hang this list in the circle area for easy reference.

- **Model only appropriate topics.** As you model sharing, make sure the topics are simple and interesting. Make them the stuff of everyday life, so students see that they don't need to impress people with really exciting stories.

- **Preview sharings.** At the beginning of the year, when you're still getting to know the students, have them quietly tell you what they want to share ahead of time to make sure it's appropriate. This can be a great way to coach children on how to share while also checking to make sure the content is appropriate.

- **Set the expectation that sharings will be appropriate.** Say something like this to the class: "If you think anyone would be embarrassed or upset by something that you're thinking of sharing, tell it to me privately first to see if it's okay to share."

- **Be ready to cut off inappropriate sharings.** When a sharing is sounding inappropriate, quickly but respectfully cut the student off. You might say something like, "Alex, hold on for a moment. I'd like to check in with you later about that sharing to make sure it's okay for the class. Let's move on to Sam's sharing for now."

Consider how you want to structure your sharing. You may have a predetermined schedule for who will share each day. This could include a topic for the week. If you are focusing on character traits in reading, for example, you might ask students to prepare to share three character traits about themselves. If a patriotic holiday is approaching, you might invite students to share a photo and information about someone they know who served in the military. Another option is to have students sign up during Morning Meeting if they would like to share. Maintaining a list of who has shared ensures everyone has an opportunity. You may also notice students who never share; this can spark a personal conversation to learn more about their apprehension and provide the chance to support their sharing through rehearsal or knowing the topic in advance. Some students may need a modification of being able to share through writing or inviting a friend or teacher to share on their behalf.

At the beginning of the year, having every student share incorporates all voices and allows students to build connections with peers. Remember to use low-risk questions, which will enable all students to be successful. Category shares, such as favorite food, animal, color, season, book, hobby, and so on, will also provide information you need to learn about student interests in order to engage them in their learning. (More on that in Chapter 4.)

- **Consider the power of closing circle.** Think back to Steven's closing circle apology. The teacher in that scenario ended each day with the same predictable structure for students. The predictability and trust built throughout the year allowed Steven to take the risk to share something so vulnerable without the teacher suggesting or prompting him. Closing circle allows teachers to correct any misunderstandings from the day, take an emotional temperature reading of the class and individual students, and check for academic success, by asking students what they learned or what goal they achieved. Incorporating an element of reflection and celebration helps foster a community atmosphere until students walk out the door. Some teachers will use a poem or song that helps students transition into a closing circle. While the same core elements should be present each day, as the year progresses, continue to vary the closing circle reflections. Maybe you will practice an interactive learning structure to get students talking about their day, or maybe a few students will share out. As dismissal begins, being at the door whenever possible to say goodbye to students makes them feel known, valued, and excited to return the next day.

Special Projects and Activities

Sharing during Morning Meeting is an important time for you to get to know the students and for them to get to know each other. You may ask students to bring in pictures to share or invite students to sign up if they have interests or personal experiences around particular topics, such as traditions at Thanksgiving time or ways that families celebrate New Year's Day. Projects and activities that bring the class together offer mutual experiences and shared memories, too.

- **Field trips.** Depending on your school guidelines, you may be able to take a field trip to a museum, theater, local business, or park. These activities connect to your academic content while building excitement and providing a new experience. If you are unable to take your students off school property, get creative! Virtual field trips can give students unique experiences, especially if you make the classroom environment come alive to enhance the experience. One third grade teacher told her students, "Get your clipboards, books, and pencils ready. Today we are getting on the 'bus' for a field trip outside." While they were actually lining up to work outside, the term "field trip" made it feel like an exciting change for the students. "It's a beautiful day," Avery said the day after working outside. "I wonder if we'll be taking another field trip!"

- **Class singing.** Consider the importance of music and singing throughout history. It is a common source of enjoyment and bonding. Develop a list of common songs everyone enjoys. You might consider creating songs around academic content and skills, sung to common tunes. Not only does singing produce a positive sense of well-being and community, but the songs can also be used during classroom transitions.

- **Student-generated activities.** Throughout the year, some projects and activities will be generated through curricular units. You may also have students think of ideas. "We have been working hard on our poems. Be thinking about what we could do to share them with others," one teacher suggested at the end of writing. By the next day, several students had come up with the idea of going to the kindergarten classes to read the poems to them during their Morning Meeting. Students feel vested in the community when they feel ownership over the ideas and activities too.

Inclusive and Purposeful Classroom Celebrations

When it comes to classroom celebrations, from birthdays to holidays, how we go about observing them depends on knowing the students we teach. When you send home a survey to families and caregivers at the beginning of the year, in addition to gathering information about the hobbies, strengths, and areas of growth that the adults in the third grader's life want to share, you can also ask if there are holidays or special events in the child's life that they would like to have acknowledged in the classroom. You might even include a question about whether someone would be interested in coming in to share about this tradition. Some teachers will also include the curricular topics for the year and ask if there is anyone with a job, interest, or expertise in a related field.

See the appendix, p. 329, for a sample survey.

Birthday celebrations in schools can vary, based upon food allergies and healthy food guidelines. Some teachers will have students sign a book and then leave a message for the student as a third grade birthday keepsake, while others provide the birthday student special privileges such as working at the teacher desk for the day or getting to select the energizer or Morning Meeting activity.

Planning for Noninstructional Times

Third graders are growing so quickly, and they love to engage with one another—lunchtime and recess are of the utmost importance! While these times should be a break in the day filled with laughter and food, it can also be a challenging time for students and a source of anxiety, frustration, and isolation. We specifically model and plan for classroom structures; the same care needs to be put into lunch and recess too. A few minutes of reminding and reinforcing language can support students in successfully transitioning into an afternoon of learning and help to uphold the positive community.

- **Lunchtime.** Students need to have cafeteria procedures modeled and explicitly taught. With the exception of new students to the school, most will know what to do; however, some students may also forget some things from year to year as they get older and receive additional privileges. Consider assigning students to a seat, especially at the beginning of the year when they need to get to know one another. Generate conversation topics that can be used to build common interests with others. The use of role-play can allow students to practice dealing with common challenges that can arise during lunch. Ensure students have a countdown or visual to know how much time they have left. Providing a five-minute warning before cleanup time ensures that tummies are full and food is not wasted when it is time to leave.

Key Cafeteria Procedures to Model

- Lining up for food
- Paying or using a ticket system
- Finding a seat
- Responding to the signal for attention
- Using the bathroom
- Throwing away trash
- Lining up for dismissal
- Cleaning tables and floors
- Using an appropriate voice level

- **Recess.** As with lunchtime, you can set students up for a safe and inclusive recess period by using Interactive Modeling and role-play strategies. Each element of the playground should be modeled for students. Consider going over some of the following with students early in the year:

  - How to use the slides, swings, and so on

- Where to get equipment

- How to get an adult's attention

- What to do if someone is hurt

- How to respond to the signal for lining up

- How to ask to join a game

- How to come back into the building

- How to be a good sport whether your team is winning or losing

The use of reminding language before students start recess will ensure a fun period of fresh air, exercise, and social interaction. The adults who are supervising should be walking around as students play, providing reinforcing language. For example, you might say, "I saw you invite Sara to join you, when you saw her on the buddy bench. That is being a kind friend." If a student is demonstrating unsafe behavior, it should be addressed immediately: "Stop. Go down the slide feetfirst only."

Prepare students with some structured activities they can use when outside. Teaching your class some games will give options for the unstructured recess time. Remember, those third graders have big ideas. Sometimes they take a long time planning a complicated game only to find it is time to return to class. Generating this list and sharing it with the adults who will be outside gives everyone a recess toolbox of inclusiveness and fun for everyone.

- **Quiet time.** "As you enter the room, hang up your coat, and get settled, think about which quiet time option you would like to enjoy today. When the music stops, everyone should be ready for quiet time to begin. Noah, then you can start our quiet time timer." As the students enter the room, the teacher plays a calming song, which students have come to associate with this transition. As they hang up their coats, some get books and read at various locations around the room, others are getting out their desk folder to catch up on work, one student has chosen blank paper and is beginning to sketch, and another student has his head down on his desk. The teacher used

Interactive Modeling to allow the students to practice what each choice looks like, and everyone has practiced all the choices, empowering them to decide for themselves on a daily basis. With the song ending, Noah goes over to the laptop and selects the digital timer that is being projected on the board. The classroom is peaceful—quiet time has begun.

Consider what it would feel like to have a jovial lunch with friends and then be asked to sit, read, and focus on academic content. It would be challenging and could result in you being mentally distracted, finding reasons to get up, or going through the motions of learning without digesting the content. Quiet time, usually ten to fifteen minutes, allows students the chance to reset. When initially introducing quiet time, begin with five minutes and allow students to build up stamina. Time is of utmost importance; however, investing a few minutes in this structure will dramatically increase productivity in the afternoon.

Establishing Rules and Investing Students in the Rules

It's a few days into the school year. The teacher has worked with students on establishing routines and procedures such as how to sit during instruction and how to respond to the quiet signal. She has used Interactive Modeling to reinforce the turn and talk structure. The students are eager for read-aloud time and listen attentively to the stories the teacher has chosen. As she closes the last book, she reminds the students about everything they have been learning so far and what it means to be a reader, mathematician, writer, and scientist in third grade. Then she leans in close; the class leans in toward her as she whispers, "What will you do with your chance as a third grader?"

She is silent as a few hands start to raise and a few puzzled faces are formed. Then she says, "You have learned what we will be learning about this year. I want to know what your hopes are for this year." Knowing that some students will need guidance in forming realistic goals that are attainable in the coming months, she shares her own goal for the year: "My hope is that we are a kind community where we encourage and support one another. I also hope you learn to love our independent reading time." Sending them back to their desks with a piece of paper, she instructs, "I'm going to set a timer for five minutes. Start making a list or sketching your goals."

As the students jot and draft, she looks over shoulders. A few students are running out of space, while others have blank papers. As the timer sounds, she encourages students to look over their list and circle their top two goals, prompting them to look for academic and social and emotional ideas. The next morning, the papers are waiting on their desks. She has taken note of which students have identified their goals and which ones she will prompt for more information as she greets them at the door. During Morning Meeting, the around-the-circle share focuses on what each student thinks their goal will be. Throughout the day, students work on writing their goal and creating an illustration to accompany it, the teacher encouraging them to be inspired by one of the growth mindset books they read. The teacher has each student's photo already posted on the bulletin board, just waiting to have their goal displayed next to it.

With the goals created and displayed, students are ready to begin generating the classroom expectations. The teacher prompts them by asking, "We have so many goals and opportunities for success this year. In order for everyone to 'take their chance,' what can we do to support each other? What guidelines can we have so everyone can be successful?" So begins the rules-creation process. As students share ideas, the teacher jots them on sticky notes and ends up filling her easel. Students work together to put the sticky notes in groups, categorizing them (which we know third graders love to do) and developing them. These become the rules for the year. With student help, the teacher combines them on a chart, and each student signs that they promise to do their best each day. Now comes the hardest part—breathing life into the rules each day, so they become a chart to live by and not a poster that blends into the walls. Students need to know what it looks like, feels like, and sounds like for each of the expectations to be upheld.

Third Grade Expectations

- Respect others and materials
- Offer encouraging words
- Be an active listener and learner
- Try your best

Beginning each day by revisiting the rules and linking them to the goals will keep them alive. The language you use will support students: "I notice you are being respectful to others by working quietly. That will help those who want to get better at their math facts right now." "Remember, you are going to get started quickly so those around you can concentrate."

Proactive Approach to Discipline

When children's needs for belonging, significance, and fun are met, their energy is more available for learning. Think about all of the proactive strategies that will support students and set them up for success, as you establish a strong community. Consider how Interactive Modeling will be at the forefront of establishing proactive discipline, as students know and practice the expectations for both instructional and noninstructional time. The rules-creation process ensures that everyone who enters the classroom knows what to expect and how to act. Boundaries have been established and students learn how to safely navigate through these group norms.

Maintaining a Strong Community

While the curriculum is generally the same from year to year, one of the greatest joys is recognizing that each class has a different identity. One year, you might have a class that thrives on whole-group activities, while another year the class loves anything involving music or art. As you get to know the interests of each class, you will be able to select the Morning Meeting activities, energizers, and special events that meet their needs.

The goal should always be to maintain the strength of the community and to continue building interpersonal relationships so students are developing their social, emotional, and academic skills. In Chapter 1, we looked at the developmental trends of third graders. As the year progresses and relationships strengthen, students will be growing and maturing. Reflect for a moment on the story of Steven that began this section. The teacher's hard work, consistency, and fidelity in implementing developmentally appropriate practices and strategies resulted in a student feeling courageous enough to show his vulnerability and share something so personal.

For students to feel safe physically, socially, and emotionally, they need to know what the boundaries are and that the rules are being applied consistently. They also need to take comfort in the idea that everyone makes mistakes. Consider how the following logical consequences can help to maintain a strong community, while encouraging students to reflect and learn from their mistakes. These logical consequences can be successfully implemented only when students have a strong connection to the classroom expectations. They should also adhere to the guidelines mentioned in the overview to this chapter: they need to be respectful, related, and realistic. Here are some suggestions about how to implement logical consequences with third graders:

See the appendix, p. 318, for this and other interactive learning structures.

- **Break it, fix it.** Third graders have an understanding of cause and effect, which is the basis of break it, fix it. During Morning Meeting, one third grade teacher used the Inside-Outside Circles interactive learning structure to practice this logical consequence, which should be introduced only when students know the expectations and have had time to practice what fulfilling each expectation should look like, sound like, and feel like in the classroom. The teacher announced, "I'm going to tell you about a common mistake that can happen; talk with your partner about the best way to fix it. Here is the first one: you walk by someone's desk and accidentally knock something off." The students quickly whispered about picking up the item. The teacher had the outside partner take a rotation to the right before sharing the next problem: "You get up to leave the lunchroom and there is still food at your spot." As the students progressed, the teacher increased the difficulty level of the scenarios, until finally she said, "You're at recess and say something that hurts your friend's feelings." By giving students the opportunity to practice these logical consequences, she empowered students to correct mistakes independently, while also gathering information about topics to role-play and revisit.

- **Loss of privilege.** Our goal is to ensure students are safe and acting responsibly in the community. Throughout our day, providing third graders with privileges makes it easy to navigate a loss of privilege. It is important to remember that students need a chance to redeem themselves to make better choices. This may mean loss of privilege for a few minutes, with the ability to try again, or a loss for the day with a new chance tomorrow. Here are a few examples of a loss of privilege for third grade:

  - Students are allowed to work anywhere around the room, but the volume becomes louder than expected. Loss of privilege—everyone returns to their desk for the day.

  - Students use markers for an activity, and they are not put back as modeled. Loss of privilege—the markers are not available the next day.

○ Students are playing soccer and the game gets out of hand. Loss of privilege—soccer is stopped for that day.

○ A student is using a computer at their desk and decides to go to another website outside of the directed options. Loss of privilege—they stop using the laptop for that period or need to sit next to the teacher to complete the assignment.

- **Positive time-out.** Students need to learn that being able to regain self-control is paramount to their success. They need to have strategies for when they become frustrated, which can proactively help them calm down before a situation escalates. With a positive time-out, a student goes to a designated location in the classroom when they need a break. Keep in mind that this location is separate from the various workstations around the room where students can go if they need a change of location to complete their work. At the beginning of the year, all students should try using this positive time-out area after the teacher models how to quietly get up, sit in the location, take a few calming breaths, and quietly return to the work they were doing. You will need to vary the expectations for this area from class to class and from month to month as you get to know your students and as they grow and mature. In September, when the classroom rules have been modeled and practiced, you might send a child to this area to collect their thoughts and focus. Later in the year, you will want students to recognize when they are becoming distracted and encourage them to be proactive, using this space to regain self-control before a minor situation escalates.

As the school year cycles through, continue to focus on the progress students have made. Proactively remind them of expectations and use reinforcing language on a consistent basis. When a routine falls short of your expectations, revisit the Interactive Modeling practice. Keep in mind that there will be some key times in the school year when you will need to set students up for success by cycling back to the initial expectations: after long weekends, after winter break, around holidays, in the springtime, before special events, and so on. When you are consistent, students are much less likely to try to push limits; they will know the expectations so well that living up to them will become second nature.

Pause and Ponder

- Which of the characteristics of teacher language will you focus on?

- How will you incorporate reinforcing, reminding, redirecting, and envisioning language into your vocabulary and the classroom environment?

- Which "getting to know you" strategies are at the top of your list?

- How will you prepare for classroom celebrations and projects?

- How will you structure the goal-setting and rules-creation process?

- Which of the proactive approaches to discipline are at the top of your list to implement?

- How will you maintain a strong community and support mistakes by using logical consequences?

Final Thought

"Experimenting with rules and testing limits is a normal part of children's development. . . . In the process of doing this testing and experimenting, students will make lots of mistakes. Just as with learning an academic subject such as math or reading or science, students need regular practice to solidify their learning about positive behavior expectations."

—*Teaching Self-Discipline*

Grade ④

A fourth grade class gathered in a circle in the meeting area. The teacher asked, "What about today's math task made you proud?" As students took turns answering, they looked from speaker to speaker. Students made "me too" connections with each other by using an agreed-upon hand signal. Students took interest in the different perspectives that were shared and asked purposeful questions to better understand one another. When the discussion was over, students worked together to safely put away the materials from the math stations. Students then put their own materials away and stood behind their desks, ready for an energizer to transition them to the next subject of the day.

This classroom exemplifies a strong foundation of a positive community. Though it may not be obvious from this short snapshot, this class had spent a lot of time building this foundation. This section will demonstrate some of the ways to get started and maintain a safe and caring community of fourth grade learners.

Teacher Tone and Demeanor

There is so much more to communication than the words that we say. We rely so much on the way something is said. According to *The Power of Our Words* by Paula Denton, language "molds our sense of who we are; helps us understand how we think, work, and play; and influences the nature of our relationships" (2015, 3). Teacher language is the use of words, tone, pace, and even body language to promote a positive community of learners. While we refer to this as "teacher" language, it should be noted that this positive language is used by *all* school adults, not just classroom teachers. As noted in the overview to this chapter, positive teacher language has five important characteristics:

- **Be direct and genuine.** Nine-year-olds often use coded language, saying, "I'm bored" when a task is too challenging. Ten-year-olds are known to be sensitive. Saying what we mean and showing that we mean what we say can support students in building trust and helping

them to be willing to take risks in their learning, especially for nine-year-olds, who love to negotiate. It also conveys exactly what is meant rather than asking students to make guesses about other forms of coded language. When we model being direct and genuine for students, they learn to be assertive and say what they really mean as their trust grows. Because we are the adults, it is important that we do our best to remain calm. Meeting a moody or sullen attitude with a positive and calm response can allow students to reset and get back on track.

To be genuine, ensure your body language matches what you are saying. For example, if an unexpected fire alarm sounds right when students have settled in their seats for the last day of the writing unit, you might say, "Move quickly and quietly to your line spots. I trust we remember what to do." Your shoulders are squared and relaxed, your tone is calm and clear, and your facial expression exudes confidence and trust to match the message you are conveying (even if this is not how you feel on the inside). All students notice when there is a mismatch between our words and our body language, but fourth graders are particularly sensitive and notice these discrepancies.

- **Convey faith in children's abilities and intentions.** Many nine-year-olds can be critical of themselves and other students, while ten-year-olds appreciate being noticed. As the teacher, your language can support students in seeing the strengths in themselves and others. Another aspect to be aware of is that we can sometimes use different language patterns with different students in a way that shows bias. It is not our intention, but our unconscious biases can be performed through our language. To raise your awareness, invite a trusted colleague to observe your interactions with students of different genders, races and ethnicities, and socioeconomic status, or for whom English is a new language or who have other possible perceived differences. If a colleague isn't available, you can also make a video of yourself teaching. For example, a colleague might notice that you call on boys more often than girls in science or that you invite more native Chinese-speaking students to demonstrate a math problem on the board. Watching a video of yourself, you might notice you use more redirecting language with a Black student and more reminding language with a white student. We all need to reflect upon our own experiences and potential biases, and being aware is the first step. Remember that students notice these subtle differences in communication, and this implicitly informs how they think and act.

- **Focus on action.** By the time they are ten, children are increasingly able to think in more abstract terms, but it is important to continue to help them translate abstract terms like "be respectful" into concrete actions. Focus on the action, not character or attitude, especially for nine-year-olds, who tend to be critical of themselves and frequently shift between various moods.

- **Keep it brief.** "The more you say, the less they hear" has been some of the best (life) advice I have received. When we talk at length during announcements, lessons, reminders, and so on, we often see students lose focus and fidget. Keeping it short and to the point is a proactive discipline strategy. Leave out any threats and warnings, as fourth graders are particularly sensitive and susceptible to lowered self-confidence.

- **Know when to be silent.** Providing wait time for students to think deeply can raise the quality of conversation. Avoid repeating all or part of what a student said or repeating yourself, as it conveys the message that what has been said is not really important. When students know we will repeat directions, questions, or comments, it gives the message that they don't need to listen the first time because we'll restate it anyway. Allow a student's voice (and your own) to stand on its own. Finally, silence allows us to listen. It leaves space for students to talk, and that allows us to get to know students, building trust and relationships within the classroom.

Reinforcing, proactive reminding, and envisioning language should be used most often. These convey faith and set a positive tone. Reactive reminding and redirecting language will be used least often because having established a strong foundation of proactive strategies, you will not often get to the point of needing these reactive tools. When reflecting on a day that feels "off," set an intention for yourself the next day to use more reinforcing language. You might develop a checklist to remind yourself to use proactive language or display a few prompts to use throughout the day. This small change can have a huge impact.

At the beginning of the year, positive proactive language can help set the tone for nine-year-olds who are anxious and moody. Our language is a powerful tool to support students to trust, take risks, and build relationships with us and each other. As the year goes on and students turn ten, this strong foundation in positive teacher language will go far as students work cooperatively and build on those positive relationships in the classroom and beyond.

Type of Teacher Language	When to Use It	How It Might Sound	Sentence Stems
Reinforcing language	To coach, to help a group or an individual move past a stuck point, and to point out individual growth.	• "You found repeating words to help you summarize the main idea of that passage." • "I notice you asked purposeful questions in your small groups. What are some other things you noticed that made this activity go well?" • "I see you taking the time to put away your materials inside your desk so you can get to them easily in the future." • "Remember when you thought adding fractions was really hard? Today during work time, you went to the bin to get extra fraction problems!"	• "You . . ." • "This helps . . ." • "I notice you . . ." • "I see you . . ."
Reminding language	To remind students of previously taught expectations, either proactively or reactively.	• "Daniela, show me your plan for writing today." • "Fourth graders, remind us how we will keep everyone safe while we move between stations with our materials." • "How do we disagree honestly and respectfully?"	• "Remind us . . ." • "Show me . . ." • "How do we . . .?" • "How can we . . .?"
Redirecting language	To help redirect students to change direction, figuratively and often physically.	• Specific, direct, and clear. • "Sit in a different space where you can pay attention." • "Stop. It is time to clean up your work area."	• "Do _____, now. • "Stop." (State desired behavior.) • "You need to . . ."

Type of Teacher Language	When to Use It	How It Might Sound	Sentence Stems
Envisioning language	To set a positive tone or vision for future work and to engage students in problem-solving.	• "As we play Sparkle, we will take care of each other by smiling and waving our hands when someone makes a mistake. That will make it more fun for people to take risks when playing the game." • "When you have put your books away, then we will begin." • "Stop and think. Then raise a thumb if you have something you want to add on."	• "We will . . ." • "When you/ we . . . then . . ."

Getting to Know One Another

Community connections are not just for the beginning of the school year. We must maintain these connections throughout the year as students' identities evolve and they explore different interests. Here we explore some ways to keep these connections strong throughout the year.

See the appendix, p. 318, for these and other interactive learning structures.

- **Meetings, greetings, and sharing.** Fourth grade is a time for solidifying likes and dislikes, so it's important that students get a chance to share these with a variety of partners. This can prevent the tendency for cliques to form and will support the practice of inclusivity. Interactive learning structures like Inside-Outside Circles and Mix and Mingle can encourage students to find random partners quickly. Using a variety of topics and ways to share can support students in making connections: around-the-circle discussions, partner share, and dialogue around topics like "special news" can be revisited multiple times throughout the year. Greetings and opportunities to share help to meet students' needs for belonging and significance, which will aid in building a positive classroom community.

Tips for Special Area Teachers

For those teachers who are not the primary classroom teacher—art, PE, music, STEAM, media, English as a New Language (ENL), intervention supports, school aides, and so on—consider ways of building connections with your students even with the limited time you have. At the beginning of each meeting time together, you might invite students to share about their day or special news they have from home. This could even relate to your specialized work with students. A music teacher might begin class by inviting students to share: "Where have you heard music lately?" An ENL teacher might begin a small group by building on the previous day's lesson: "We have been talking about past-tense irregular verbs: let's use those to share what we did yesterday afternoon. Here is our word bank to help us." While students are standing in line as they wait to enter the lunchroom, school aides might ask, "What do you plan to eat for lunch today?" Invite special area teachers to participate in occasional classroom Morning Meetings so they can get to observe students in their homeroom environment. Likewise, special area teachers can invite classroom teachers to pick up their class a little early to see another side of students during dance, music, drama, or other special areas. This can also be an opportunity for students to see adults working together.

● **Closing circles.** Fourth graders can still be anxious with the end-of-day-to-home transition. Closing circles support students in reflecting on their day and their learning, and acknowledge the class's efforts throughout the day in a purposeful way. Students can make connections with each other about their learning and what they look forward to after school or the next day. What is said at closing circle will often be the last thing they remember from the day, so when asked by a caregiver later, "How was your day?" they will likely answer with the reflections that were shared at closing circle.

Special Projects and Activities

Activities and energizers support students in building connections with each other and with teachers. The Tree of Life project is an activity for students to get to know you and each other. Many of our students have endured adverse childhood experiences (ACEs), such as divorce, child abuse, child neglect, or substance use or alcohol dependency by their parents or other household members. ACEs can cause toxic stress, and questions about a student's background or home life can be triggering. The Tree of Life project was purposefully designed as an inclusive, student-led activity for people who have experienced trauma. Each student labels parts of a tree with information such as background, skills, hopes and dreams, and important people in their lives. At the end of the activity, all of the trees can be displayed together to show the "forest," demonstrating that the classroom community is stronger together.

Fourth graders love reaching out to others. A community service project or partnering with a younger grade classroom is another opportunity for students to get to know their own strengths and learn from one another. These opportunities could also integrate academic skills such as writing for a certain audience, identifying character traits by preparing a read-aloud for a younger grade buddy, or constructing a science project for a library display.

Be sensitive to projects and activities that invite students to "write about your culture or family." This can be a difficult question for a lot of students for a number of reasons, including but not limited to a fear of feeling different, having been adopted, being in foster care, the experience of forced home evacuation, or the belief that they don't have a culture. Consider asking students to share "traditions." For example, one fourth grade class shared "everyday traditions." Some students shared that they liked to make their bed as soon as they woke up, another said they liked to brush their teeth after eating breakfast, and others said they liked to read before going to bed. It had everyone rethinking small everyday actions for which to be grateful.

Classroom Celebrations

Holidays and other celebrations can be a great way for students to come together and make community connections. At the beginning of the year, you might have a discussion about favorite celebrations and make it a point to celebrate those as a class throughout the year. Invite families to be part of these celebrations too. Writing celebrations, social studies presentations, author studies, science projects, and math fact challenges can all be reasons to celebrate as a community. Schoolwide traditions and celebrations that everyone is invested in can bring classrooms together across the school. For example, a dragon relay for Lunar New Year can travel from classroom to classroom, bringing well wishes and good luck for the new year.

Planning for Noninstructional Time

Recess and lunchtime provide opportunities for students to make connections with each other as well as with students from other classes. It is important to use Interactive Modeling and role-play to teach students ways they can talk to each other in the lunchroom or on the playground. Some years students will need more support with this. In this case, consider giving students a prompt to talk about during lunch, or task them with a challenge before recess and then debrief them about it after quiet time. For example, you might ask them to interact with four different people from other classes during recess, and then afterward discuss what they discovered or what went well. Another idea might be "try something new," and then to celebrate the new foods, games, or experiences students tried. You could also ask three or four students what they plan to do at recess and let other students know about this activity so no one is left out during this free time. For example, you might say, "Fatima said she'll play soccer today, so if you would also like to play soccer, see her in the yard. Sky said they'll be playing with chalk today, so if you also want to play with chalk, see them on the playground. And Antonio said he'll be playing tag, so see him on the playground if you would like to play tag too. I know that you will be inclusive so everyone can play and have fun." Students will be able to take care of each other when the main classroom teacher is not present, and it's another opportunity to build connections.

Establishing Rules and Investing Students in the Rules

In the first week of school, after previewing the units of study for the year, students can spend short sessions brainstorming a list of possible hopes and dreams. This might be a chance to begin teaching the routine of using notebooks. Begin the brainstorm by having fourth graders reflect on something about which they are proud from the year before. Model your own hopes and set a goal, such as "This year, I hope that everyone will discover some new books they love to read." Spreading this brainstorming activity out over a few days gives students a chance to grow their ideas.

Throughout the week, observing students brainstorm is a powerful way to get to know them. Encourage students who have goals that are not realistic for the year to focus their goal on something more attainable within a ten-month period. Include qualifiers, such as "What do you hope to learn in our classroom this year?" or "What are some social or academic skills you hope to work on this school year?" If students don't seem enthusiastic about their goals, ask questions to better understand what motivates them. For example, you might ask, "Why is _____ important to you?"

At the end of the first week, have students choose one goal to illustrate, share with the class, and display. These goals should be placed in a space in the classroom where they can be easily seen so that you and your students can frequently return to them.

Then it's time to guide the rules-creation process:

- **Connect hopes and dreams to rules.** At the end of the first week of school, once their goals are shared and displayed, students are ready to begin the process of rules creation. This might sound like "Look again at our hopes and dreams. What are some agreements that could help us work together to achieve our goals?" By framing rules creation this way, you enable students to understand that rules are positive guidelines that allow everyone to reach their hopes and dreams. At this point, students can begin to brainstorm rules; let them know that they will return to brainstorming the following week.

- **Brainstorm the rules.** In the second week of school, spending a little time each day brainstorming a list of rules will allow students to deepen their understanding of the significance of the rules. As students brainstorm, encourage them to frame ideas positively (what we will do rather than what we won't do) and generate a wide variety of ideas. List these ideas on a chart and add any ideas that you think students have missed.

- **Categorize the rules.** After generating a list of possible rules, lead students in categorizing them. Depending on the group of students, this might involve a few more short sessions and partner chatting to discuss which rules fit together. You are aiming to combine and condense the list to three to five categories.

- **State the rules.** Once the rules have been categorized, each category is then stated as a rule or agreement. The wording each year will be different, but the final rules should have something to do with taking care of (1) yourself, (2) others, and (3) the learning environment. Here is an example of a fourth grade class's rules:

4-418's Agreements

Be respectful of people and things.

Do your best.

Be safe.

- **Publish the rules.** It's time to make the rules official by the end of the second week. Ask students if they agree that these rules will help the class work together so that everyone can reach their goals. This agreement can be arrived at by using a thumb gauge (thumbs-up, thumbs-sideways, or thumbs-down). If anyone disagrees, you can ask for possible edits or ask students to try the rules out for the day and check in on them again at closing circle. Have a few students create a poster to display the rules, leaving space for everyone (all students and teachers) to sign. (Inviting adults who come into the room on a regular basis to sign also promotes an inclusive community.) By signing the rules, students solidify their agreement. This is a document that is referred to every day through teacher language, adapting when necessary. For example, you might say, "Show how to come to the meeting area in a way that is respectful of people and things and is safe."

Some additional ways to practice bringing the rules to life include the following:

See the appendix, p. 323, for more on Interactive Modeling.

Schoolwide Rules

If your school has pre-existing schoolwide rules, rules creation can be modified. Students still begin by generating a list of hopes and dreams and then articulating rules or needs necessary to achieve those hopes and dreams. Then, students can connect their rule brainstorm and needs to the school's existing rules. For example, a student might say they need a quiet space to achieve their hope to read all the books in a series. This need can be connected to the school rule "Be respectful of people and things."

- **Modeling the rules.** Use Interactive Modeling every day, throughout the day. You will start at the beginning of the year using all seven steps, but as students get familiar with these steps, you might modify the process by asking a student to model the behavior instead of the teacher (step 2). You might omit the second time students observe and notice (steps 4 and 5). But you can help set students up for success by proactively adding Interactive Modeling before (1) a transition you know will be tricky (for example, transitioning from a lesson with math manipulatives to packing up in the afternoon); (2) a lesson for which students need materials in the meeting area (for example, reading notebook, sticky notes, and a pencil); or (3) something the class hasn't done in a while (for example, a greeting that you did a few days ago). In fact, Morning Meeting always goes better when time is spent modeling the greeting, sharing, and group activity first. By going slowly at the beginning, you can go fast later on, not needing to stop to give reminders.

- **Role-playing the rules.** Role-play is another way to practice the rules and set students up for success. Role-play can be used reactively when you notice a counterproductive behavior that you realize would be helpful for everyone in the class to have an opportunity to notice and practice correcting. For example, if you observe a book club in which not everyone shares an idea, the next day you might role-play as a class how to include everyone. However, you can also role-play proactively. Inclusion is a common theme in fourth grade, so you might role-play how to include everyone in a group of four before beginning book clubs. Other common issues to role-play in fourth grade include perseverance (or what to do when a task feels too hard or you don't understand), peer mediation or problem-solving, issues of fairness, and supporting someone who makes a mistake.

- **Embedding practice throughout the day.** As you get more comfortable with proactive strategies and practices, you will begin to see how they fit in throughout the day, all day long. Teachers often look at an academic objective and think, "What social and emotional competencies (cooperation, assertiveness, responsibility, empathy, self-control) do students need practice with in order to also practice this academic skill?" For example, if students are working to solve multistep word problems and you want them to practice on a whiteboard with you (from their desks or in the meeting area), this is also an opportunity for students to practice the social and emotional competencies of responsibility and self-control by actively listening while also taking care of their materials. This connects the academic, social, and emotional skills to the classroom rules, and when this connection is made explicit, students are set up for success and the classroom rules are brought to life throughout the day.

When children's needs for belonging, significance, and fun are met, their energy is more available for learning. Building positive relationships with students and families and between students allows children to know that they are an important part of the community. While this is a primary aspect of the beginning of the school year, we continue to use observations and conversations with students to continuously support this community growth throughout the year.

Proactive Approach to Discipline

It is important to set children up for success with direct instruction and guided practice in prosocial skills, and there are many ways to do this. At the beginning of the year, take your time and go slowly as you implement these strategies and techniques. There might be years when it takes four weeks, and there might be years when it takes a couple of months to fully set children up for success.

After completing the rules-creation process, make the rules come alive by referring to them frequently and in a positive way. Teacher language can be used to reinforce and remind students about specific actions and how they connect to the rules. We also want to rely on the rules during challenging times. These challenging times might happen regularly (recess, lunch, Friday afternoons) or occasionally (school vacations, school assemblies, field trips, guest teacher days). Preparing students for these challenging times before they happen sets students up for success and instills the sense that they follow the rules because it is part of being in a safe, caring community of learners. This is when we begin the conversation about logical consequences with students.

Fourth graders are quick to anger and quick to forgive, they are sensitive to fairness and friendship issues, they can get into arguments within small groups, and they can be critical of others. Knowing this, you can predict that there will be times throughout the year that you will need to support students with getting back on track with the rules, and logical consequences can support this. Here are some guidelines for using logical consequences with fourth graders:

- **Loss of privilege.** If students are having difficulty meeting expectations during an activity, they might lose a privilege connected to that activity. For example, a student does not meet the expectation of being careful with a tablet during a math station, so the student loses the privilege of using the tablet for that period. Instead, they practice the skill with pencil and paper.

- **Break it, fix it.** When students affect others by breaking something or hurting someone's feelings, regardless of intent, they can learn to take responsibility for their mistake. For example, you might notice a student acting out of character. When you talk to the student privately, she confides that a classmate said something that upset her. You might offer to support the students to fix the problem by using a tool such as problem-solving for two. This logical consequence can help students restore what was broken.

- **Positive time-out.** This strategy helps students, and teachers, to reset mentally and emotionally just as they are beginning to lose self-control, while allowing the rest of the class to continue with their learning. Introduce this logical consequence in a positive way: "Everyone needs a break sometimes (even adults!), and that's okay. At the beginning of the year, I will help you to notice when you need a break, but later in the year we will talk about knowing ourselves and recognizing when we need a break." Make sure all adults in the space understand that this is not a punishment, but an opportunity to recharge. Some classes have more than one space in the room where students can take a break—wherever it is, make sure students can still see and hear the lesson so that they may rejoin quickly after they reset. When first introducing positive time-out through Interactive Modeling, make sure every student has a chance to practice it and continue to use the logical consequence democratically.

Maintaining a Strong Community

Throughout the year, students will change a lot physically, cognitively, socially, and emotionally. This individual growth can foster a supportive, positive community of learners. When you build a strong foundation around relationships at the beginning of the year, students will grow in independence throughout the year, facilitating their own small groups, taking the lead on some whole-class discussions or energizers, and taking risks in their learning. Carefully notice and celebrate these changes with students through reinforcing language individually or as a whole community.

There are certain times during the year when it will be important to take additional steps to maintain a positive classroom community:

- **School vacations.** Vacations can be a challenging time for the classroom community. Some students might feel excited and look forward to the break, while other students might feel anxious to be out of their routine. Students might also dread school breaks because breakfast and lunch at school are the most reliable meals during the week. By fourth grade, students are better able to understand abstract future events in addition to having experienced school vacations before, so it is appropriate to talk about them in advance, but leave space for all feelings. This might sound like stating in a neutral tone, "Next week is our midwinter break. People might have different feelings about this." This allows any reactions to be student led. If you acknowledge that some people might have mixed feelings (you can be excited about having a break, but also feel down about missing your friends), students might be willing to take the risk to share their worries or disappointments too. It is an opportunity for students to recognize different perspectives and empathize, understanding that all feelings about school vacations are valid. Similarly, it's important for students to reconnect after the vacation. Maybe some students traveled while others stayed home. Leave space for those differences and choose carefully what you model to the class. Depending on your class, you may want to share that you traveled, but perhaps you want to model the fun you had exploring a local park or doing laundry as a family to show that all experiences are welcome to share. School vacations and long weekends are a great time to revisit classroom rules to reset and set students up for success.

- **Difficult events.** When difficult events happen, it can be challenging for students and the class community. Each class is different, and there are many resources to support conversations around difficult events. Some organizations with resources include the Zinn Education Project, Rethinking Schools, and Learning for Justice. Be prepared to have these challenging and sensitive conversations with students by practicing with colleagues, family, or friends, and have a specific goal in mind, such as understanding different perspectives. Students are still young, so you want these conversations to be developmentally appropriate, and be aware of individual student traumas. Have students lead the conversations if they want to bring something up—if no one brings up the topic, students may not even be aware of what's going on. But if students naturally bring up a challenging topic during Morning Meeting or arrival, leave space and help guide students by using a lens of curiosity and compassion, while letting students know that they are safe in school and loved. Make time for reflection about difficult events as a class or individually through journaling.

- **End of the school year.** At the end of the year, students may feel anxious about the following year. Some questions they might ask include "Where will my new classroom be?" "Where will my friends be?" "Will I be held back?" "Where will my fourth grade teacher(s) be?" "How will my routines change this summer?" "What will fifth grade be like?" "Will fifth grade be in a different building?" Students may be self-conscious and might not realize that their questions are common and shared by others. Invite students to write their questions on an index card anonymously, and collect them. Take some time to preview the questions and point out to students what you noticed: that many questions were similar. Invite students to predict the answers as part of a whole-class conversation. For example, the class might consider the question "What will we learn in fifth grade?" Students might predict, "Maybe we will learn more about fractions." "Maybe we'll read longer chapter books and write longer stories." They have enough background knowledge about school to be able to make these guesses. Fifth grade teachers and students can stop by or make a video to answer common questions in order to ease these concerns. A "moving up" Morning Meeting might be hosted by a fifth grade teacher (if students don't yet know who their teacher will be). Fourth graders can write letters to people who helped them to reach their hopes and dreams (for example, custodians, school aides, special area teachers, caregivers, siblings, peers, and so on) and say goodbye for the summer. They can write a letter to their teacher for the next year to introduce themselves.

Pause and Ponder

- What is an intention you want to set for yourself when it comes to teacher language?

- In what ways will students get to know each other at the beginning of the year? How might that shift in the middle of the year? At the end of the year?

- How might you encourage the classroom environment to be more inclusive?

- What are proactive approaches to discipline that you want to explore more?

Final Thought

"Our words and tone of voice play a critical role in establishing the nature of our relationships with students and can also influence students' relationships with each other."

—Paula Denton, *The Power of Our Words*

Grade 5

Fifth grade is an exciting time for students as many near the end of their elementary school years. Often, academics become more rigorous, with more independent exploration and group projects in fifth grade. Usually eager to work on learning tasks, fifth graders begin to develop high levels of interest for certain subjects and develop an awareness of how they learn best. It is also a year when students maintain strong friendships and establish new ones. During this time of excitement and growth, teachers may overlook the importance of building positive learning communities with and for students. Teachers may be eager to dive right in to content-based learning at the onset of the school year. However, establishing a positive community early on and maintaining positive relationships is a central tenet of teaching. After all, teachers do not teach subjects; teachers teach *children*. They teach students vital skills such as how to act, how to care, how to contribute, and ultimately how to learn. This learning happens best when time is dedicated to building relationships all throughout the school year. Positive relationships are the gateway that leads to academic, social, and emotional learning for all students.

Teachers build relationships with students in a variety of ways. Teacher language helps to create positive learning communities. Teachers who value the importance of positive community dedicate time to get to know students and to help students get to know one another. In positive learning communities, teachers and students establish rules and value their importance in guiding the community. Throughout the school year, teachers use a variety of proactive strategies to develop a community that meets students' needs. After the positive learning community is established, teachers use strategies to maintain the strong community so that it supports students' academic, social, and emotional learning. Committing time and energy throughout the entire school year to building relationships is a key ingredient in ensuring that all students are recognized and valued and, ultimately, in determining how well they learn.

Teacher Tone and Demeaner

A key way to build relationships and communicate expectations with students is through the careful use of teacher language. Teacher language is not just what the teacher says; it is also how the teacher says it. Fifth graders are keen observers and pick up on tone of voice, body language, voice inflections, and so much more in addition to the words that are said. A teacher's words can damage individual or collective relationships; on the other hand, with consistent use of positive teacher language and modeling, teachers can communicate in ways that strengthen the learning community for all members. Keeping in line with the characteristics outlined in the overview of this chapter, it is important for fifth grade teachers to pay particular attention to their teacher language and how it plays a vital role in establishing relationships and building positive learning communities. Remember to:

- **Be direct and genuine.** A teacher's words can build trusting relationships. Fifth graders appreciate and benefit from clear directives, often in the form of statements. For example, instead of saying, "Could you take out your calculators for math now?" it is better to be clear and direct when addressing fifth graders. "Take out your calculators" identifies exactly what is required at that moment. Additionally, it is important that tone of voice and body language match. If a teacher says, "Clean up your microscopes and put away your science folders" at the end of science class with a rushed and frantic tone of voice, fifth graders will notice. The moments that follow will likely match the teacher's nonverbal message. On the other hand, making that statement with a calm and matter-of-fact tone will lead to a calm and productive transition. When teachers use clear statements, it helps students understand what is expected, builds trust, and helps to sustain a positive community.

- **Convey faith in children's abilities and intentions.** A teacher's language conveys assumptions and expectations for students. As mentioned, fifth graders pick up implicit messages from a teacher. For example, if a teacher says, "I'll be watching to see that you show your work as you solve your math problems today," it sends the message that the teacher believes students will meet this expectation. The words show students that the teacher believes they are capable of high-quality work. In order for a teacher's language to convey faith in children's abilities and intentions, it is important that teachers spend time observing students. It is helpful for students to hear straightforward, reinforcing statements when they are meeting desired expectations.

- **Focus on action.** Fifth graders need to hear concrete, specific communication from the teacher, rather than abstract terms. This is true whether giving proactive reinforcements or reactive redirections. For example, instead of the teacher saying, "Great job with your poem," it is helpful for students to hear what made the poem great. A statement such as "The simile you used in your opening line really grabbed your reader's attention" focuses on the specific action the student demonstrated. At the same time, when responding to misbehavior, teachers should focus on the action. "Don't be mean at recess" is a common response teachers may use when students have a disagreement over the rules of a game at recess. This statement implies the teacher is judging the students and is not focused on what action needed to be corrected. "Take turns while playing games fairly" focuses on what the students should do instead. Statements that are judgmental are not focused on the students' actions, do not help students to change the course of action, and can undermine the teacher's relationship with the students.

- **Keep it brief.** Although they are maturing in many ways, fifth graders (just like any other age group) benefit from teacher brevity. Less is best with fifth graders. Teachers can use brief statements or questions to promote a positive community. For example, "Stay in your assigned space with your partner during writing workshop today" directs students as to exactly what to do without a long explanation. A teacher may also pose a question in this scenario by asking, "Where should you work with your partner during writing workshop today?" Asking a question keeps the teacher language brief and empowers students to think for themselves. Use caution when asking questions, however—make sure your students were previously told the expectation, and use a closed-ended question so as to avoid off-topic or unintended responses.

- **Know when to be silent.** After asking a question, be sure to provide wait time for students to think of their response. Wait time helps to build community and sends the message that we want students to be thoughtful before responding and that they don't need to respond immediately. It also builds an inclusive tone to the classroom by leveling the playing field for students who think at different rates. Teachers can also use teacher language to build inclusion in the classroom. For example, saying, "Boys and girls, it is time to take out your writer's notebooks" separates the class into two groups. More inclusive statements that promote community include "Fifth graders, it is time to take out your writer's notebooks" or "Writers, take out your notebooks." These statements identify all students as part of one class community. Additionally, instead of saying something like "You are going to set up your table area for science now," saying, "We're going to set up table areas for science now" makes the message sound more collaborative in nature. With careful attention to the need for silence and using inclusive statements, teachers can sustain trusting relationships that promote positive communities.

There are four specific types of teacher language teachers use with fifth grade students: reinforcing language, reminding language, redirecting language, and envisioning language. The chart below identifies when a fifth grade teacher can use each type and what it might sound like.

Type of Teacher Language	When to Use It	How It Might Sound	Sentence Stems
Reinforcing language	• To recognize students' positive attributes and success in meeting expectations.	• "You paid attention to the steps needed to solve this equation." • "You remembered to charge your laptop and place it in the correct storage bin."	• "You remembered to . . ." • "I see you . . ." • "I notice you . . ." • "This helps . . ."
Reminding language	• To remind students of previously taught expectations, either proactively or reactively.	• "Who remembers the steps for cleaning up our learning materials?" • "Remember to take turns with your partner so you both have a chance to share ideas."	• "Remember to . . ." • "Remind us . . ." • "Show us . . ." • "How do we . . . ?" • "How can we . . . ?"
Redirecting language	• To redirect students back to the proper trajectory of previously established expectations.	• "Sit in a different space where you can pay attention." • "Stop. It is time to clean up your work area."	• "Stop. (State desired behavior)." • "Do _____, now." • "You need to . . ."
Envisioning language	• To set a positive tone or vision for future work and to engage students in problem-solving.	• "In our classroom, everyone will feel welcomed and included." • "What do respectful listeners do? What should it look like when you are with your reading partner today?"	• "We will . . ." • "When you/ we . . . , then . . ."

In addition to these types of teacher language, many fifth grade teachers see the benefits of using open-ended questions to build positive community. As stated in *The Power of Our Words*, "Open-ended questions are those for which there is no single right or wrong answer. Any reasoned and relevant response to an open-ended question is a good answer" (Denton 2015, 47). This strategy is particularly useful in building community among fifth graders. "What are some strategies you could use to solve this math problem?" promotes the idea that there is more than one way to solve the question. Questions like this lend themselves to whole-class discussions, encourage students to view other perspectives, and support students in their learning while promoting inclusive, positive learning communities. Fifth grade teachers should use open-ended questions frequently—when getting to know students, at the beginning of new units, when reflecting on work, and all throughout academic learning. This type of teacher language is discussed further in Chapter 4.

Keep these teacher language ideas in mind when communicating with students individually or collectively. Adhering to the characteristics of teacher language allows teachers to build positive learning communities that support student learning while maintaining healthy relationships.

Getting to Know One Another

In order to build positive relationships, we have to take time to build connections with students, incorporate daily rituals that build community, design activities that help students get to know others, and structure the school day with positive interactions inside and outside the classroom. Some classroom rituals you might consider incorporating into your fifth grade classroom include the following:

- **Morning Meeting.** Some educators may think that the practice of having a daily Morning Meeting with fifth graders is childish and unnecessary. This is not true! When we carefully plan Morning Meeting, as well as frequently explain the purpose of this practice to fifth graders, it serves as a beneficial cornerstone to building a positive learning community.

- **Greetings.** This is a simple yet powerful way to build relationships with students. When students greet one another, they feel a sense of belonging in the classroom. A friendly interaction can start the day off on a positive note and prepare the student for a successful day of learning. It is especially helpful for the teacher to stand at the door and greet each and every student with an informal greeting. Teachers always have things they can work on, grade, or prepare; however, dedicating this time to interact with students benefits the teacher-student relationship. If you departmentalize in fifth grade, still remember to offer a quick, informal greeting to each student. If using a virtual format, greet each student by name with a friendly smile as they enter the virtual meeting room. During either in-person or remote learning, greeting each student by name allows all students to feel welcome, gives the teacher a chance to check in with students, and strengthens the important teacher-student relationship. In addition to greeting students informally as they arrive in the morning, you may find it helpful to use this structure as part of Morning Meeting.

Some Good Fifth Grade Greetings

- **Have students partner with a neighbor in the circle.** Determine which partner will start. Then have partners greet each other in a friendly way.

- **Greet several people nearby.** Divide the circle into small groups and have students greet each other within their group. Decide on the group size yourself, or let students decide.

- **Mix and mingle.** Give students a minute or two to move around and greet several classmates. Challenge students to greet people they don't normally hang out with at recess or lunch. Remind students to take their time and make sure their greetings are sincere and meaningful.

- **Category greeting.** Once students know each other well, challenge them to greet students who have a certain attribute. Split the class into two groups. You might begin by telling the first group to greet someone in the other group who likes art. Now give the other group a turn: "Greet someone in the other group who has a sibling in our school." Have the class brainstorm attributes, making sure that everyone will be included and that the attributes are appropriate.

- **Greet and share.** To extend a simple greeting, have students greet another person and then talk about an assigned topic for a minute or two. Again, students might brainstorm topics together, or you might choose something related to that day's curriculum. For example: "Once you and your partner have greeted each other, talk about the science work we did yesterday with batteries. What are you thinking about trying today when you work with batteries again?"

Sharing. In order to build inclusive, positive learning communities, time must be dedicated to allowing students to share with and learn from one another. This time could take place during a class Morning Meeting or during a lesson later in the school day. In order to keep sharing purposeful and fun for students, use a variety of formats and topics. Sharing is an effective way to practice or introduce new interactive learning structures. Teachers can also encourage students to share about themselves, their cultures, their backgrounds, and their lives outside of school. Here are some ideas that can be incorporated in academic learning or during a Morning Meeting:

See the appendix, p. 318, for more on interactive learning structures.

Good Fifth Grade Sharing Topics and Themes

- Family trips
- Family celebrations
- Friends
- Weekend events
- Pets
- Sports events
- Favorite music and movies
- Collections
- Favorite books and authors
- Writing pieces
- Progress on science or social studies projects
- Possible career interests
- Special talent or skill

Note: Another great way to build community early in the year is to have students brainstorm additional appropriate topics.

○ **All about me.** Provide students with a survey to identify their hobbies and interests. Use open-ended questions to ask students about their lives in school as well as things they enjoy doing outside of school, and have students share the survey results with partners, small groups, or the whole class.

○ **Class photo album.** Give each student a piece of paper on which they can print and paste pictures of themselves, their families, and things that interest them. Have the students share their individual page with classmates, and then put all of the pages together to create a class photo album to display throughout the year.

○ **Puzzle pieces on bulletin boards.** Have students create collages about themselves on huge puzzle pieces. Then have students connect the puzzle pieces together. Hold a class discussion about working together and honoring each individual's uniqueness and display the connected puzzle on a bulletin board.

○ **Personal timeline.** When learning about sequencing events in a story, or how to read a timeline in social studies, have students create a personal timeline about their own lives. Students should identify five to seven key events from their lives (learned a new hobby, moved from a different state, began a new activity, and so on) to share about themselves. Have students share their timelines with partners, in small groups, or at a class meeting and display the timelines for everyone to see.

Closing circle. Just as Morning Meeting sets fifth graders up for a great day of learning, closing circle serves as the bookend for a productive school day. Fifth graders appreciate a structured time to reflect or to celebrate the day of learning. It is helpful for teachers to guide the times of reflection with open-ended questions. "What worked well for you and your partner during writing workshop today?" lends itself to fifth graders reflecting on the processes used earlier that day. Such discussions and reflections help students feel connected to their classmates and supports the positive learning community. On the other hand, there will be times when students reflect on something that was difficult earlier in the day. A teacher might say, "I noticed some of our classmates said it was difficult to focus during science group work today. Let's set aside some time tomorrow to talk about how we can improve." A reflection like this encourages the community to take a negative and turn it into a new goal. Whether your class uses the time for a positive or constructive reflection, or to participate in a simple celebration to close out the day, spending five to ten minutes together at the end of the school day (or even a few moments at the end of a class period if your fifth graders switch classes) helps to sustain the positive learning community.

Class meetings. There are times during the school year when class meetings are necessary. Such meetings should take place during the school day, separate from Morning Meeting or closing circle. Reflection meetings take place in the whole-group meeting space. In some instances, the teacher will have students reflect on the process used during a class period or over the course of a longer project. Open-ended questions such as "What worked well for you with this assignment?" or "If you could do this project again, what would you do differently?" guide fifth graders in reflecting on the process used during an activity. At other times, the teacher will have students share an in-progress assignment or a finished product. As students share their work, classmates learn from one another and learn how to offer empathetic questions and comments. These types of meetings have a collaborative tone and support the positive learning community. Class problem-solving meetings are for addressing whole-class issues, like students excluding others at recess or talking about off-topic subjects during science group work. When these instances occur, it is important to hold these meetings when both the students and the teacher are calm, and not in the moment of transgression.

Classroom Celebrations and Holiday Events

Classroom celebrations are an effective way for fifth graders to build community and to have fun in school. These are also opportunities to promote cultural events in the curriculum. Instead of simply having a party at the end of the school day, teachers should consider ways to recognize holidays in order to learn more about different cultures, to engage in a meaningful learning activity, and to have fun. For example, exploring traditions around the world for celebrating the winter solstice is a high-interest activity that capitalizes on the excitement many students feel at this time of year. Individually or in small groups, students could study one of these cultural celebrations and give a short research presentation to the class. In math class, each group (with the help of an adult) could follow a recipe for a traditional dish or snack from the culture they studied.

Planning for Noninstructional Time

A positive learning community extends beyond the classroom walls. Recess and lunch provide opportunities for fifth graders to apply the skills learned in their classrooms in a more unstructured setting. Often, these parts of the school day combine multiple class communities with less adult supervision. Whether or not this is the case in your school, it is important that structures are put in place to ensure that this time of the day is a break for students to reenergize and interact with peers in a meaningful way. Here are some tips to ensure recess and lunch support the positive learning communities found in classrooms:

- Ensure that the adults supervising these areas provide students with clear expectations.

- Teach, model, practice, and reinforce the skills and routines students will need to be successful.

- Use a consistent signal—an auditory signal like a whistle at recess or a bell in the lunchroom, along with a visual signal, such as a hand-raise—when students' attention is needed.

If you are a teacher who does not supervise recess and lunch, offer support to the colleagues who do provide supervision:

- Review rules and expectations frequently, especially at the beginning of the school year.

- Use structured reflection with a "Sounds Like, Looks Like, Feels Like" chart for things students will encounter, such as entering the recess area, joining a game at recess, using equipment at recess, lining up at recess, entering the lunchroom, waiting in line, eating and conversing with peers, cleaning up one's space, and responding to the signal.

- Invite recess and lunch staff to join Morning Meetings from time to time so they can build relationships with students in a different context.

- Join students at recess or lunch on occasion. Although teachers always have things they can work on or set up when students are not in the classroom, it is helpful for students to see teachers join in recess games or sit in the cafeteria to have lunch. This is another way to build relationships and promote positive community while modeling appropriate social skills for students.

For our teaching to be most effective, it is important that teachers take the time to get to know their students. By using structures like class meetings and special projects and by engaging in activities such as lunch and recess, teachers can get to know their students beyond the classroom walls, and students can get to know one another better as well. When students feel connected to their teachers and peers, they are more readily available for learning.

Establishing Rules and Investing Students in the Rules

Building a positive learning community includes setting up clear and purposeful classroom expectations. At the beginning of the year, teachers should anchor all students in common expectations that apply to all students. These should be non-negotiable norms, such as how to respond to the quiet signal, how to walk down the hallway, where to store personal belongings, and anything else that teachers want students to do one way due to safety or efficiency reasons. Interactive Modeling is an effective strategy to use to teach these expectations to students.

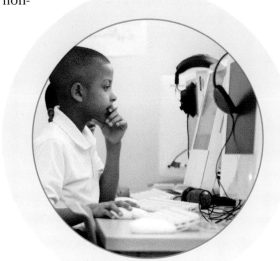

After the first few days of school, time should be dedicated to creating classroom rules. This process usually starts during the first week of school for fifth graders and follows these sequential steps:

1. **Generate excitement for fifth grade.** Preview units of study with your students. Use textbooks, websites, and other learning materials to highlight projects and other activities students will complete during the year.

2. **Brainstorm hopes and dreams.** Share your hopes and dreams for the school year with students. For example, you might say, "This year, I hope all fifth graders enjoy reading new books and making new friends." You might also share a personal goal you have for the year, too, such as "I hope to use lots of new energizers to keep our learning fun this year." Then ask students, "What do you hope to learn in fifth grade this year?" Have students select at least one academic and one personal hope and dream. Fifth graders enjoy journaling these in a writer's notebook, and this may take a few days for some fifth graders to complete. Consider having students work on this as a homework assignment if additional time is needed. Here are some sample hopes and dreams:

Academic Hopes and Dreams	Personal Hopes and Dreams
• Read bigger chapter books	• Make new friends
• Write a five-paragraph essay	• Stay organized
• Learn how to create a slideshow/movie	• Develop study skills
• Understand how to complete long division	• Join a new club at school

Have students write, draw, or make a collage to display their hopes and dreams for the class. Use a format that is developmentally appropriate for fifth graders, such as writing the goals in a paragraph on fancy paper, writing goals on a cloud image, using a sports theme such as softballs and baseballs, or having students display their hopes and dreams around photos of themselves.

Have students share their hopes and dreams, and then display the hopes and dreams on a bulletin board or somewhere in the classroom. Dedicate this space to hopes and dreams for the entire school year.

3. **Cocreate rules with students.** Ask students guiding questions such as "If Jacob wants to read larger chapter books, what rules will we need to help him reach his goal?" or "What rules will we need to help Amelia make more friends in fifth grade?" These questions help students see the classroom rules as a guide for helping everyone to achieve their hopes and dreams. Have students brainstorm a list individually or with small groups. An effective strategy is to have students write the rules on sticky notes.

4. **Consolidate the list.** Have students share the list of rules they generated. Next, make the point that there are too many rules to remember. Ask students, "Which of these rules seem to go together? For example, 'Raise your hand to speak' and 'Take turns with partners' both deal with respecting others. What other rules help to respect others?" Have students discuss and share all the rules they come up with. If students wrote the rules on sticky notes, sort them into separate

piles. Guide students in developing three to five rules, ensuring that general categories include respecting yourself, respecting others, and respecting the classroom and materials. The rules should be stated positively; for example, "Be kind and respect others" as opposed to "Don't be mean." Stating rules in the positive describes what action students *should* follow. Make sure that the final list of rules is few in number (three to five is ideal) and identify global, positive statements for students to follow.

5. **Display the rules.** Post the rules in a visible area in the room that is easy to refer to. If possible, have the rules close to the hopes and dreams display to remind students of the connection between these two practices. It is also helpful for students to share their hopes and dreams with their families. Include this information in a parent newsletter or on your classroom website, along with a narrative that provides parents with an overview of the students' hopes and dreams and of the rules-creation process. More information about soliciting parents' hopes and dreams is discussed in Chapter 5. If you use a learning management system, be sure to post the rules in this space, too, so students can reference them throughout the school year.

Existing Rules

If you are in a school setting where classroom rules are already in place, have students generate hopes and dreams followed by group brainstorming of rules needed. Then, instead of consolidating rules from a large list into three to five global rules, have students take the large list and make connections with the preexisting rules.

FIFTH GRADE RULES

Respect your own learning.

Be kind and support others.

Take care of our learning materials and classroom.

When teachers and students invest the time to create rules together, that investment is returned as the year goes on. Students will see the purpose of the rules and will work to follow them, providing the time needed to focus on learning academics and other skills. The rules-creation process outlined above is the central tenet in building a positive learning community.

Proactive Approach to Discipline

Much of the groundwork for establishing a positive learning community takes place at the beginning of the school year. Careful use of teacher language, helping students get to know one another and their teachers, and modeling and discussing the rules are paramount proactive strategies. Taking time to revisit rules, recognizing how well you know students, and holding realistic expectations help to ensure the positive learning community remains strong all school year long. However, there will be circumstances throughout the school year that challenge the strength of the positive learning community. Proactive discipline is a core component to setting a positive learning community up for success.

When misbehavior occurs, it is important that teachers realize misbehavior is a message that needs to be decoded and responded to. Teachers need to have predictable and ready-to-use responses to misbehavior—a tool kit of sorts. When misbehavior occurs, teachers need to remember that one size does not fit all. By taking the time to know the students we teach individually, collectively, and developmentally, teachers are best equipped to respond to misbehavior with a developmentally appropriate response. Here are some helpful strategies fifth grade teachers can add to their tool kit:

- **Proximity and visual/verbal cues.** Move closer to anyone who is misbehaving or off task, or use a visual or verbal cue to redirect them. For example, if two students are having a side conversation while a classmate shares at Morning Meeting, move closer to that pair of students, use a hand-raise, or point to an anchor chart posted in the room that identifies what respectful listening looks like, sounds like, and feels like.

- **Reminding and redirecting language.** Use a sentence starter that reminds students of previously taught expectations. For example, if students are supposed to be using laptops for research, but you notice some using it to play a game, ask, "Who can remind us what you are using your laptop for?" You could also state, "You need to use your laptop to complete research," or "Stop. You need to complete your research now."

- **Logical Consequences.** Consequences that are respectful, related, and realistic are the most effective tools in your discipline tool kit. Consider these three options:

  ○ **Break it, fix it.** If something is broken, a mess is made, or someone has been hurt in some way, students take responsibility to fix it or clean it up. For example, if a student spills milk in the cafeteria, they should get paper towels to wipe it up.

  ○ **Loss of privilege.** If a privilege is misused, it is removed for a short period of time. For example, if two students are talking about last weekend's soccer game when they should be completing a study guide together, they lose the privilege of working together. They can try again another time.

  ○ **Positive time-out.** If a student has lost self-control, the student goes to a designated area for a minute or two to calm down. For fifth graders, this can be teacher directed or student initiated, depending on the circumstance.

All of the responses to misbehavior, particularly logical consequences, need to be taught before they are implemented by the teacher. Some fifth graders struggle with the application of logical consequences, particularly time-out.

- **Calming stations.** Another helpful strategy is using Interactive Modeling to teach students how to reset. In one fifth grade classroom, a teacher uses a "calming station" in the back corner of the room. It includes two chairs, a traditional chair and a wobble chair. There is a one-minute sand timer as well as a basket with some fidgets (spinner, stress ball, bendy pencils, and so on). The teacher directs a student to go to the calming station. The student chooses which chair to sit in and completes one of the following activities for one rotation of the sand timer: sit quietly, choose a fidget item from the basket, complete chair push-ups, perform some yoga stretches, practice deep breathing, or practice mindfulness. After one minute, the student may choose to repeat the process one more time or return to the learning task. All of these strategies and procedures are taught ahead of time so students know the purpose of them. By discussing and practicing the strategies, fifth graders realize how to develop internal control of their actions and how to regain self-control using a structure similar to time-out. After they have practice with using a structure like this, consider allowing students to decide for themselves when taking a break to regain self-control is needed.

Whatever strategy you choose to implement with students, it is important to remember that the goals are to stop the rule-breaking behavior, to help students regain self-control, and to reestablish the positive learning community. With a positive teacher-student relationship already in place, and careful use of teacher language, students will see that the teacher is supporting the student with empathy and care. When situations arise that challenge the strength of the learning community, it is important that the teacher maintain the authoritative leadership style described in Chapter 2. It is the action, not the character, that is the mistake that needs to be fixed. Students must see that the rules apply to everyone in the class and that the teacher will hold students to following the rules. Using strategies like the ones mentioned allows the teacher to preserve the dignity of individual students and the group. The positive learning community is reestablished, and the focus on learning and being part of a positive community resumes.

Maintaining a Strong Community

Positive communities thrive when certain foundations for learning are in place in the classroom. These foundations serve as proactive ways to set students up to be successful and to keep the momentum of the beginning of the school year alive all year long. With careful attention to proactive discipline, fifth grade teachers can sustain the positive learning community by using some of the following strategies:

- **Reflect on and revisit rules.** After rules are established, refer to the rules often with class discussion and Interactive Modeling. For example, before introducing a new learning material to your students, such as a tablet, use open-ended questions to bring the rules to life. "How can we follow our rule for respecting class materials when you begin to use the tablet today?" is a question that helps the rules go from something posted on the classroom wall to something that guides thoughtful behavior in the classroom. Open-ended questions that guide discussions around the application of the classroom rules should take place multiple times in a given school day.

Consider quizzing your students on the rules, too. If you ask your students, "What are our classroom rules?" how many rules do you think they will recall? It's a simple question, but one that is challenging for students in classrooms where the rules are not discussed, modeled, and reflected on frequently.

Schedule opportunities to revisit the rules throughout the school year. After an extended school vacation, at the beginning of a new month or grading period, or even at the beginning of a new unit are perfect times to revisit the rules. Some teachers also have students revisit their hopes and dreams during this time and consider creating new ones if needed.

A significant amount of time is dedicated to discussing, modeling, and practicing the rules early on in the school year. In many circumstances, the time dedicated to applying classroom rules drops dramatically as the year goes on and the teacher's focus shifts from building community to following curriculum pacing guidelines. In order to sustain positive learning communities, rules should be connected to everything happening in the classroom.

- **Know your students.** Another foundation for good learning is to ensure you know your students well. This requires frequent individual and whole-group check-ins and observing students in both structured and unstructured settings. Donald Graves, an educational theorist, describes an exercise in which you create three columns and list the following:

  - Column 1: Who is in your class? Write a list of all of your students you can remember, not alphabetically or by student number, but as they come to mind.

○ Column 2: What interests each student? Next to each student's name, write down something unique you know about that child—a hobby, a talent, and so on.

○ Column 3: Does the student know you know this? Put a check next to any item you are sure the student knows you are aware of.

You may be surprised by the outcomes of this exercise. It is helpful to complete this activity often throughout the school year. As a tip, for the students that this exercise indicates you do not know as well as others, make a conscious effort to ask an extra question when you greet the student at the door in the morning. Or position that student's desk near the teacher desk the next time you switch the seating arrangements in your classroom. Taking the time to know, notice, and acknowledge students is a powerful tool in building relationships that lay the foundation for learning.

● **Set and maintain realistic expectations (physical, social, and emotional).** Throughout the school year, reflect on the expectations you have for the learning community and adjust as needed. Consider the following:

○ **Physical.** Does the layout of the classroom need to be rethought to better support student movement? Are students having enough movement during the day? Should more hands-on learning, energizers, or interactive learning structures be incorporated throughout the day?

○ **Social.** Are there enough opportunities for students to interact with a variety of classmates throughout the day? If off-task conversations or blurting out occur, do I need to include more time for sharing? Would more interactive learning structures around academic and social topics throughout the day benefit the students?

○ **Emotional.** Do students have the necessary skills to complete a task? Would they benefit from lessons or discussions around necessary skills like cooperation, assertiveness, responsibility, empathy, or self-control?

Taking time to reflect is a vital step in the learning process. Teachers should engage in reflective practices often to ensure that the foundations for learning are in place for all students and the positive learning community remains consistent.

Just as teachers need to carefully arrange the physical layout of the classroom with the ideas discussed in Chapter 2, it is important that teachers dedicate time throughout the school year to organize the emotional structure of the learning community. Relationships are the crux of what teachers do with students each and every day. When we pay careful attention to teacher language, incorporate classroom activities that promote positive community, and focus attention on maintaining the positive learning community all year long, students will see how much we, as their teachers, care for them and they will be set up to do their best learning.

Pause and Ponder

- What is an area of teacher language that you can improve on to support building a positive community with your fifth graders?

- What strategies will you use to get to know your students at the beginning of the school year? Later in the school year?

- How will you structure the rules-creation process so students view rules as positive guidelines to support the learning community?

- What are some times during the school year that you can revisit the rules so that students can focus on them all year long?

- Which strategies from the tool kit will you use to respond to misbehavior and maintain the positive learning community?

Final Thought

"Students don't care how much you know, until they know how much you care."

—Anonymous

Chapter 4
Engaging Academics

● ●

Overview

Consider the last time you learned something for the first time—a new skill, a hobby, or a new teaching practice. What made the learning engaging? Was it because it was something you had been interested in and had made it a goal of yours? Was it because you had time to practice and problem-solve the new skill? As a result of learning, did you reflect on your experience and set new goals?

The most engaging learning is a result of a three-part natural learning cycle that begins with meaningful goals—meaningful for the learner and connected with their interests and needs. The second phase involves providing time and opportunities for learners to actively explore, experiment, and problem-solve to meet their goals. The final phase is reflecting on the explorations and setting new goals, which fuels the natural learning cycle again.

As educators, keeping the natural learning cycle in mind when planning leads to continuous learning. In this chapter, we will explore key practices in creating a learning environment that makes academics engaging for all students, characterized by learning that is pedagogically sound and lesson design that is based on the natural learning cycle.

Lesson Design
A three-part lesson structure, consisting of an opening, body, and closing, reflects the natural learning cycle and is used to effectively design lessons

around learning objectives so that the learning is purposeful and meaningful.

Opening

The first part is to create a purposeful opening that gets students hooked and excited about what they are about to learn and why it matters. Lessons designed with a clear purpose increase student motivation, provide context for how the lesson fits with what they already know, and lead students to set their own learning goals. The skillful use of envisioning language and open-ended questions serves as a springboard for students' learning. For example, you might introduce a lesson by stating, "When you write your letters to the principal and school board, you'll be letting them know the importance of having playground equipment that meets your needs. Your words will paint a picture of your dream for equipment that can be used by all." As a result, students can make a personal connection with the learning and have a clear understanding of how to complete the tasks.

Body

The body of the lesson is characterized by *action and interaction*. This is an opportunity for students to try out and practice a new skill, explore new content, construct their own knowledge, and apply their learning. In the example above, during the body of the lesson, students would engage in research, craft a letter using the RAFT (role, audience, format, and topic) writing strategy, and share their progress with their peers. Learning is student focused—built on encouraging student strengths and interests, providing autonomy, and giving high-quality feedback. Evidence of an effective lesson body includes students engaged in their work—on track and focused on their goal with the teacher spending time observing, facilitating, coaching, and supporting students based on their needs.

Closing

A well-planned closing provides the fuel for continued learning with *purposeful reflection*. This allows time for students to think about the *what* (the content) and the *how* (the process) of the learning experience and provides opportunities for students to share and make connections to other learning. There are a variety of ways to structure the closing. The reflection might be individual, with students using a journal or exit ticket, or the reflection can involve sharing with a partner, a small group, or the whole class. Open-ended questions begin the closing of the lesson. Examples include questions such as "What's one big idea you have learned?" "What has stuck with you?" "What might you do differently the next time?" Reinforcing the positives you noticed during the lesson is a way to continue to nurture the positive community and acknowledge academic growth.

Effective Questioning Techniques

For students to be successful, they need to learn how to engage in their academic work. Effective questioning is a practice that sparks curiosity, wonder, and interest and promotes intrinsic motivation. *Create purposeful questions* that directly connect the lesson goals to the work that the students will be doing. Purposeful questions invite students to become fully engaged in their learning and are open ended. Open-ended questions are questions for which there is not a single right or wrong answer. For example, here's a purposeful question that could be used in math class: "When learning about two-digit multiplication, what prior knowledge might you need to access?" Consider how you might have students share their responses—through a journal response, in a partner share, or by using an interactive learning structure—and how student responses will inform your teaching.

For optimal engagement throughout the lesson design process, vary the type of questions asked, whether you posed them during the opening to stimulate student interest, during the body to deepen students' under-standing, or in the closing to help students reflect on the learning. Effec-tive questions invite students to become fully engaged in their learning. When questions are student centered, you show your students that their curiosity matters. As you listen for understanding, utilize wait time and formulate follow-up questions as needed. You are modeling how to be an effective listener and showing them that their thinking is important. The use of diagnostic and open-ended questions provides opportunities to extend the lesson and deepen understanding. When using diagnostic questions to assess students' knowledge, ask for supporting evidence of correct responses and utilize follow-up questions to clarify vague responses; with incorrect responses, be cognizant of how to address misconceptions in a way that preserves the student's dignity. As you ask effective questions, listen and respond. Use the tool that is carried with us—teacher language—to nurture our positive community.

By directly teaching students the skill of asking effective questions, we are giving our students the tools to become lifelong learners and to take ownership of their learning. Knowing the difference between a statement and a question is the first step. Using Interactive Modeling to teach and practice how to ask effective and meaningful questions, and displaying charts with examples, continues to build students' understanding of effective questions. Incorporate role-play in your lessons to teach students how body language, coupled with the words we use, conveys genuine interest in the speaker and subject matter. Morning Meeting, closing circle, interactive learning structures, and role-play provide opportunities for students to practice asking and responding to respectful questions.

Setting High Expectations

An essential part of engaging academics is setting high expectations for all students. When we know our students and know our pedagogy, we can create lessons that provide an appropriate level of challenge in order for students to spend most of their time working in their "zone of proximal development," a concept introduced by the twentieth-century psychologist Lev Vygotsky (1978). The zone of proximal development is the range of tasks that a student can perform with the help and guidance of others—peers or teacher—but cannot yet perform independently. Lessons are designed to push students beyond what they already know how to do so that they develop academic competencies such as perseverance, an academic mindset, and a tool box of different learning strategies. The benefits of time spent developing a positive community come to fruition as students learn that the classroom is a safe place to ask questions, make mistakes, and deepen and extend their learning. Our teacher language sets the tone for engaging academics as it conveys our faith in students'

Academic Choice

Academic Choice is a practice that follows the natural learning cycle. During Academic Choice, students have choices to make about the content (what they learn) and/or process (how they learn), which builds metacognition through the purposeful use of open-ended questions. Academic Choice is a way to structure a lesson or activity that creates a sense of purpose for students' learning. When students have choices in their learning, they become highly engaged. There are three distinct phases in Academic Choice:

- Planning

- Working

- Reflecting

During the *planning phase*, students engage in decision-making as they consider why they might choose one option over another. Start with an open-ended question such as "Why would you choose one over another?" Students then respond and share their thought process with a peer or small group, or with the whole group, and commit to a choice.

Students follow through on their plan during the *working phase*. The teacher coaches and supports students as they are engaged in the process of working by asking open-ended questions, such as "How could you challenge yourself further?"

During the *reflecting phase*, students reflect on the work that they did and the learning that occurred. Options for reflections include students presenting their work to the group and discussing an aspect of their product or process, writing a journal entry, or using a rubric to conduct a self-evaluation of their work. Open-ended questions for this phase include "How did your choice work for you?" and "What are you proud of?"

abilities to meet the expectations and engage in higher-level thinking. Academic Choice and interactive learning structures are ways to structure and engage students in higher-level thinking while developing their speaking, listening, and thinking skills.

Observation Strengthens Instruction

An essential part of teaching is spending time observing students. Observation is instrumental in getting to know our students individually, culturally, and developmentally, and it informs our expectations, reactions, and attitudes about our students. Through observation, teachers are provided with immediate feedback and are able to identify and clear up student misconceptions and differentiate instruction in the moment, as well as inform future lessons, so that the instruction is engaging and appropriately challenging and provides an optimal learning experience for all students. During observation, in addition to receiving information, teachers provide in-the-moment feedback to students. The feedback that we give shows students that we know them, support their vision of themselves as learners, want to learn more about their thinking, and want to help them better understand their own learning. For example, during the working phase, I notice a student who writes for a few minutes and then tears the page from the writer's notebook and crumples it up. I share my noticing with the student and discover that the student wants his paper to be perfect. When he realizes he has made a spelling mistake, he crumples the paper. Together we are able to identify a few strategies for him to use so that he can focus on capturing his ideas and learning, and to persevere through challenges. Responding with genuine, positive teacher language that includes reinforcing language and open-ended questions enhances the effectiveness of the learning process.

Culturally Responsive Teaching and Engaging Academics

Creating engaging academics is a result of knowing our students—individually, culturally, and developmentally. Culturally responsive teaching builds upon our students' individual and cultural experiences in addition to utilizing their prior knowledge to draw them into the content and support their growth. The importance of including students' cultural references in all aspects of learning is at the heart of culturally responsive teaching (Ladson-Billings 2009). Culturally responsive teaching celebrates learning within the cultural contexts of students and empowers students to take ownership of learning and the learning environment. Engaging academics and culturally responsive teaching recognize the importance of building strong relationships with our students and showing faith in students' abilities by communicating high expectations in the lesson design. In addition to communicating high expectations, teachers are called to design culturally relevant lessons that are purposeful, active, interactive, appropriately challenging, and connected to students' interests and strengths, and that give students some autonomy through choice. Our instruction is planned to create and promote the positive perspectives of all students and to nurture a positive community that is safe and academically challenging. As we plan our instruction, we need to acknowledge that our experiences growing up may be different from those of our students, be aware of the biases that we carry, and actively research and include cultural references in our lessons.

As you turn to the grade-level specific sections in this chapter, you will find strategies and approaches listed for engaging academics that are developmentally appropriate and culturally responsive. You will be shown how to use your understanding of your students, effective management, and positive community to design and implement lessons that are engaging for your students.

Grade ❸

"For today's Morning Meeting sharing," the teacher explains, "we are going to do Inside-Outside Circles." The teacher points to a student to begin counting off by 2s, asking students to hold up the number of fingers that corresponds to the number they have counted off. When everyone has their number displayed, the teacher directs the 1s to stand and form a circle. The students have used this structure before and immediately turn their bodies to face out. The teacher holds up two fingers, prompting the rest of the students to stand in front of a partner. The teacher instructs, "We just started our weather unit yesterday. With your partner, share a fact about the weather that you already know." There is high energy as students share everything they know about weather, halted only by the ringing of the chime. The teacher directs students in the outer circle to take a step to their right to chat with a new partner, this time asking them to share an "I wonder" question about weather. With the sound of the chime, the teacher prompts a student to share their partner's weather wondering. After a few students enlighten the group about their partners' curiosity about the topic, the teacher has the class move to a new partner for the final time. She prompts them by asking, "If you could become an expert in hurricanes, tornadoes, or blizzards, which would you choose, and why?" Once students have shared, the teacher rings the chime and instructs students to return to the edge of the carpet for their activity. Before moving on, she says, "Raise your hand if you would want to become a hurricane expert." Several hands are quick to go up. After asking about tornadoes and blizzards, she plants a seed of enthusiasm: "I am so excited for us to get to science later because you are going to get to become a hurricane, tornado, or blizzard expert!"

In the above scene, the teacher took advantage of the academic content that can be incorporated into Morning Meeting, allowing students to practice their social interactions with others while also reviewing content that will support their work throughout the day. By providing a hook into the day's science lesson, she also ensured that students would have time to think about a choice that would be presented to them. We know that third graders need to practice decision-making and need time to reflect

on how to make a decision that is in their best interest. This way of pre-teaching what would become an Academic Choice lesson for students gave them time to think and generate an excitement for learning. Later in the day, when the teacher formally introduces the Academic Choice lesson, in which students are able to select what they are learning, the time spent during Morning Meeting will have facilitated the setting of expectations and will mean that students will have more time during the lesson to get started and have their eyes and minds engaged in the weather resources. As we focus on engaging academics throughout this section, consider how time can be maximized and a culture for learning can be embedded throughout every moment of the day, even when students think they are just having fun!

Designing Lessons

In addition to developmentally responsive teaching, positive community, and effective management, we come to engaging academics. Like a puzzle, the classroom experience would not be complete without each of these four elements happening in unison. A common theme throughout is the importance of knowing the students you teach. It is about understanding who they are, their goals, their strengths, their weaknesses, and their learning styles. We know there are common trends and themes for students at each age; however, we teach individuals. As previously mentioned, from year to year, each group of students may reflect similarities to the class before them, but they will also require lesson modifications and personalizations that reflect their class composition. When starting the school year, keep in mind that your students are still like second graders in their knowledge and skills. Over the summer, some may have spent time with relatives outside of the country for extended weeks, and some may have looked after younger siblings while parents worked; when they return, they may demonstrate a "summer slide" on reading or other assessments. It is important to be mindful of the possibility of learning loss across portions of the school year, such as during long breaks and when pivoting to school closures for various reasons. We must remember to revisit the routines and expectations after those periods and build student confidence and skills in order to set students up to resume academic learning.

We strive for students to feel engaged, motivated, and enthusiastic about their learning. We know that all learners, regardless of grade level, benefit from hands-on and experiential learning. We also know that it is unrealistic to be able to provide that for every lesson across the curriculum. The use of games, special projects, Academic Choice, field trips, and more can help breathe life into the curriculum. These should not be considered enrichment or something to use when the lessons are finished. Instead, they are for us to embed within the lessons, becoming a foundation for us when planning units. It is also important to remember that our third graders can become overzealous at times, so maintaining their enthusiasm, while helping them break down projects and ideas into bite-size chunks, will create a more successful experience; for their social and emotional development, this strategy models for them a key life and academic mindset skill. As you progress through various practices to support engagement, put yourself in the learner's seat to think about how you would benefit, even as an adult, from these structures. Sometimes as educators, we are so focused on leading the show that we forget what it is like to be in the audience.

Teaching Practices for Third Graders

The six main characteristics of engaging academics are:

1. Learning is active.

2. Learning is interactive.

3. Learning is appropriately challenging.

4. Learning is purposeful.

5. Learning is connected to students' interests and strengths.

6. Learning is designed to give students some autonomy and control.

These characteristics form the basis for teaching practices that support students' needs and maximize student engagement.

Interactive Learning Structures

Third graders want to have opportunities to socialize with their peers. If that need is not being met, they will fulfill it themselves. While this is one possibility, the use of more interactive learning structures is the more proactive and academically minded option! These provide students with the essential speaking, listening, and thinking opportunities they need, promoting social interactions with their classmates and fostering peer relationships. Students are learning cooperation, assertiveness, responsibility, empathy, and self-control through their frequent practice.

See the appendix, p. 318, for sample interactive learning structures.

Morning Meeting is the optimal time to introduce and teach each interactive learning structure, so students can use them during academic lessons throughout the day. Many teachers will display a list in the classroom of interactive learning structures that have been taught. On days when you notice students need more opportunities to talk or you spontaneously decide that you want them to have time to talk with a partner, the list will make it easy for you to determine the best structure at that moment.

Interactive Modeling is just one of the many practices that are your key to success. There are a few elements you should think through in preparation for setting students up for a positive experience:

- **Establish a quiet signal.** You will use the quiet signal often; however, you will want to ensure that it is firmly established before using interactive learning structures. During these activities, there will be a lot of conversation throughout the room. Make sure to model with students that finishing a thought within five to ten seconds before giving you their full attention only builds respect for listening and allows the speaker to feel valued.

- **Plan how you will teach the structure.** Is Morning Meeting the best time? If not, when is the best time? How do you want it to look in your classroom? Knowing your students, what are some aspects of the structure you want to proactively address with them? Using the structure during Morning Meeting will give students the opportunity to practice it and to incorporate more personalized information, allowing them to make connections to the material and setting them up for when you use the structure later in the day for academic content. Consider the Inside-Outside Circles structure from the opening scenario. This was focused on science content, but the first time the teacher introduced it, she could have asked students to share their favorite food, what they did over the weekend, or which superpower they would like to have, and why.

- **Provide time limits.** Students need to know how much time they will have to complete the structure. Knowing that third graders are still learning how to gauge their time, consider a visual timer or countdowns. For example, you might tell them, "You will have five minutes for the Museum Walk. I will let you know when you have one minute left." This teaches time management, as students learn how to prioritize and gauge their time—a life skill.

- **Develop a system for how students will take turns.** Sometimes students at this age have trouble navigating who will go first. You may tell them the person with the first name beginning with the letter closest to "A" can go first. You may have students quickly decide if they are "peanut butter" or "jelly," to which you can share, "The jelly partner goes first." Ultimately you want students to develop the turn-taking naturally and model how to determine who goes first; however, at the beginning of the year especially, maximizing time for discussion is more important than having students spend a lot of time navigating who goes first. Another tip to consider: In a group of two, determine who will go first and have that partner talk for the entire time. Encourage the other partner to ask questions to facilitate the speaker. At the end of the time frame, have the students switch roles. This ensures that both partners get to talk. It also builds conversational and questioning skills. Of course, you will want to use Interactive Modeling and even a Fishbowl structure to support social and emotional skills.

Academic Choice

"You have a choice to make for your science work today" is what the teacher says. What the students hear is "You have a choice, and I trust you to be in control of your own learning." Academic Choice allows students to feel a purpose, offers an innate sense of challenge, and lets students use their strengths and interests. In the overview, you read about the practice of Academic Choice. Now you need to start considering how you will utilize it for your students, not as an "if you are finished" option, but rather as a way of structuring the lesson objectives. Whether you are giving students the option of what they will learn, how they will demonstrate this knowledge, or both, there are a few considerations you will need to factor in to your planning.

Some Academic Choice lessons lend themselves to individual work, while others can be incorporated in a partnership or small-group setting. Consider the developmental implications, along with the specific needs of your students. Teacher-assigned groups that change frequently can meet the needs of students. Proactively role-playing and teaching students to anticipate and deal with possible challenges will set students up for success. Notice students who always want to work by themselves and those who always want a partner—they need to develop skills for both settings, and careful observations will ensure students are varying their level of interaction.

Be aware of the process versus the product. Academic Choice is engaging for students, but some will require your support in decision-making.

You are trusting them to be creative, make choices, and navigate with the broad objectives you provided. Some third graders will relish this and others will be worried if they are doing the right thing and desire checking in with you every step of the way. Sharing their final product is important; however, the process of planning, working, and reflecting is just as important.

Some students may make a choice only to want to change their mind. This is where knowing your students is important. If you have planned a weeklong Academic Choice lesson and after the first day students are not gathering as much information about their topic as they need to (perhaps because there is not a lot of information), letting them make a change would provide opportunity for reflection and be a better choice. If you have planned a one-day Academic Choice lesson and a student changes their mind halfway through, it would only interrupt their level of success for the day, so if you have students who may not be prepared to stay with their choices, you may wish to proactively share in your directions that the decision they make is the decision they stick with for that day. A student could be upset by not being able to change their choice; for them, that will be the biggest learning experience of this process. Yes, we want our students to be happy and successful; however, we also want to support their social and emotional needs by helping them understand that there are times we can make a change and other times when we need to stick with our choice until the end, but either way, we still learn from the decisions we make. Being consistent and clear and planning for your students in advance will set them up for success.

Energizers

We have all been there, sitting at a meeting for over an hour and anxious to get up and stretch our legs. As adults, we know what we can do if we start to feel restless; however, our third graders are still developing this understanding. When they have been sitting for a while, there will suddenly be enthusiasm for visiting the bathroom or the nurse, sharpening a pencil, or getting a tissue. This is where energizers are the secret to sustaining engagement during lengthy blocks of learning.

Energizers can be calm or lively, and they always involve movement, whether standing up or sitting down. They promote a sense of community, as everyone participates together; they can also facilitate academic skills and learning. While the students will see them as just fun, take time to point out how they are practicing their content skills, in addition to cooperation, self-control, and other social and emotional competencies. Here are a few helpful tips for utilizing energizers with your students:

- **Model, model, model!** You know your students, developmentally and individually. You will need to model each energizer for them, taking into consideration the need to maintain personal space, appropriate physical contact, volume, and self-control. Some energizers get students laughing and highly energized. Your students *can* be successful; they will just need your proactive support and clear expectations.

- **Take it slow.** You want every student to feel comfortable, so selecting low-risk energizers, mirroring the low-risk Morning Meeting components, will ensure that all students participate and build their level of trust and success together. Just as some energizers are your favorites, each year's class will develop their top preferences too.

- **Keep a list.** Similar to how you chart the interactive learning structures and Morning Meeting components you have introduced, charting the energizers you use is a powerful tool to support you and the students. A chart will allow you to quickly select an energizer, give an idea to a colleague who stops in to watch your class for a few minutes, and even allow students to develop independence. As the year goes on, when you know the most successful energizers, you might even select a student to be the leader.

- **Think of energizers as time-savers.** You may be wondering how you can fit introducing an energizer into your already full schedule. Just as Morning Meeting can be used for introducing interactive learning structures, you will find that energizers and the Morning Meeting activity go hand in hand. If you teach Human Protractor to begin the day, you can use it again later during math. Think about the energizers that can provide echoes across content areas too! Double This, Double That can be used in the regular form, along with math, language arts, science, social studies, art, music, and more!

See the appendix, p. 313, for these and other energizers.

See the appendix, p. 317, for more on Guided Discovery.

Guided Discovery

"What do you know about stamps?" The teacher posed this question to the class. Hands rose immediately, as third graders have had many experiences with stamps and ink pads over the years. "How have you used them in the past?" The teacher selected several students, who gave responses about how to care for stamps and experiences with how hard to press on stamps. "What new ideas can you think of for how stamps could help us with new learning?" Some students commented on how shape stamps could help them with fractions, while another suggested they could use them for patterns. One student raised his hand and shared, "If you use a few triangles, a square, and a rhombus, you could make your own tangram." "How might you do that?" the teacher posed, inviting the student to demonstrate this idea. The class was eager to view and begin exploring their own ideas.

> ## Materials to Introduce Using Guided Discovery
>
> Guided Discovery can be used to introduce drawing supplies (colored pencils, markers), math manipulatives (pattern blocks, base ten blocks), and student textbooks. It's also helpful to use Guided Discovery for materials students have used in earlier grades, such as crayons and rulers. Their familiarity will boost students' confidence and creativity in coming up with new ways to use those materials.

Through the use of the Guided Discovery strategy, students will be able to think creatively and critically about different ways to use materials. The use of open-ended questions allows students to draw on their personal experiences, while exploring, interacting with others, and practicing the cleanup and care of these materials. Remember, this strategy is most effective with materials that will be available to students over time, compared to a one-day experience. The reinforcing and reminding language used during this time will set students up for success. Consider how much time you will save over the course of the year, when students have modeled and practiced the care for materials too.

Morning Meeting

In the scenario shared at the beginning of this section, the teacher used Morning Meeting with a science focus. This practice is more than a tool to build a positive sense of community and support the social and emotional needs of students to set them up for a productive day ahead; it is also a powerful academic time. One teacher noticed her students needed to support their math facts, so she incorporated math practice into the activity. Another teacher noticed that students needed support with punctuation and capitalization, so he incorporated physical motions and sounds into the reading of the morning message to facilitate additional practice for students.

One third grade teacher shared that as she began to learn more about the practices included in this book she saw how Morning Meeting, as well as other learning structures, could support students' development. She noted, "I used to think that this approach was about the students planning Morning Meeting, but now I know it is about me carefully designing it to support their social, emotional, and academic skills."

Setting High Expectations

Noticing everything a student or a class can't do is an easy trap for educators to fall into. Of course, there are skills students do not yet have because of their age and developmental stage. Instead, we need to shift our perspective to focus on asking, "What does each student do well?" "What is each child's strength?" Students require high expectations, modeling, and support to continue to grow and develop across all aspects of their lives, from math and reading skills to problem-solving strategies and peer relations. When we start from a place of strength and use reinforcing language to support what students are doing well, we develop a deep level of trust that will allow us to support their areas for growth. Within the authoritative leadership style is nested the role of coach, supporting and encouraging our students, enabling them to develop the self-confidence and breadth of positive experiences that will facilitate their success not only for the year they are with us, but also in the future.

Assessing Third Graders

Suggested Assessments

- **Checklists.** Students can simply check off project requirements as they complete them.

- **Rubrics.** Students can help create their own rubrics for what qualities or elements should be in their final projects.

- **Self-assessments.** Teach students how to honestly appraise their own work (focusing on positives without ignoring challenges).

- **Lists.** Bulleted lists of "things done well," coupled with one or two "suggestions for next time" can help encourage thoughtful reflection.

- **Narratives.** Writing a simple note or letter that highlights what a student did well and gives one or two ideas for improvement personalizes your feedback.

Assessments to Avoid

- **Peer assessments.** Third graders shouldn't be placed in a situation where they have to assess one another. Let assessment remain the teacher's job.

- **Letter grades.** Impersonal and often subjective, letter grades used in isolation give little information that students can use to improve their work.

- **One-word feedback.** Words such as "Great!" or "Sloppy" give children little to go on. Instead, offer specific assessments that reinforce the positives and offer suggestions for growth.

- $\checkmark+, \checkmark, \checkmark-.$ Like letter grades, check marks tend to be too general to offer valuable feedback.

- **Public assessments.** Students should not be assessed in front of others. Once they've done a presentation or shared their work, a private conference or paper-based assessment is more appropriate.

Goal Setting

"I did it!" Morgan whispered to her teacher during a reading conference. "Today is Thursday and I just finished chapter six, which I wanted to do by the end of the week." "I wish you could see your face right now, Morgan," the teacher smiled. "You look so proud of yourself. You have really worked hard to make it happen. I'm excited to see what your next goal will be." The teacher's use of reinforcing language allowed the student to take ownership of this accomplishment. Morgan was achieving this goal for herself and not for her teacher. Establishing a culture for goal setting, as Morgan was relishing having done in the moment of success, the teacher was already prompting her to think of her next goal to encourage her to be self-reflective and to remember that when one goal is done, the next has just begun.

In previous chapters, we talked about the importance of establishing hopes and dreams at the beginning of the school year. These help us to ground our rules and expectations, investing students in becoming a community so everyone can succeed. While third graders are beginning to understand more abstract concepts, they benefit from concrete visuals and expectations. Goal setting allows students to celebrate little successes on their way to their end-of-the-year dreams. There are many ways to establish goals for students, whether they are set weekly or developed at the beginning of each unit. It is important to model your own goals with students, so they learn how to make them specific and manageable. When students have a focus, it keeps them engaged and makes learning purposeful. Consider having students share their goals during Morning Meeting or with a content area partner. Having students write their goals down and displaying them in a designated space reinforces commitment to follow through. With goals individualized, *all* students in the classroom can be successful. A student who is struggling with a concept will have a manageable target, and a higher-performing student will see that even if they "already know this," they can continue to challenge themselves.

Equality Versus Equity

It is amazing how students will rise to meet our expectations, especially when we establish a high bar for excellence and implement expectations continuously and consistently. We also need to remember that each student is different and that we need to meet their specific needs. Consider how prompts for directions will allow all students to be successful. For example, you might tell students, "By the end of science today, you should have at least two facts to share about the type of weather you chose." This gives a student who may be a slower reader a manageable number to achieve, while encouraging another student that they can keep going, even if they already have two facts. The more you know your students, the more you know how much you can help them to accelerate their progress and how you can plan for modifications so they are successful. This approach helps to maintain a positive community, keeps learners engaged, and ensures effective management to maximize learning for all.

Open-Ended Questions

Third graders are curious, creative, and eager to share their experiences. The use of open-ended questions will meet their need to exercise those qualities, in addition to helping them to develop their reasoning ability, knowledge, independence, and self-reflection. Refer back to the opening scenario, when the teacher used the Inside-Outside Circles interactive learning structure to facilitate sharing during Morning Meeting. The scenario prompted students to reflect on the type of weather they were interested in and encouraged them to make a personal connection, putting the students themselves at the center of their learning. By encouraging students to share "why," you are helping them to develop deeper thinking skills and draw on their own experiences. The next prompt was for students to share their questions about weather. Asking students what they want to answer invites their enthusiasm and engagement, while creating a culture of wonder within the classroom. This approach encourages students' higher-level thinking skills and gives them an investment in their learning. Finally, asking students to determine which type of weather they would want to become an expert in, and why, gave them a sense of autonomy and competence and instilled a greater investment in their learning.

The use of open-ended questions within lessons is imperative for students; encouraging them to share their questions outside of a specific lesson led one teacher to create a "wonder wall." This wall, full of sticky notes of every color with contributions from every student, allowed these third graders to share what they were curious about and generated a community-building experience. Students frequently added questions and read their classmates' questions. Sometimes the teacher provided an answer or brainstormed possible responses as a transition activity, and at other times students responded to each other. "I found the answer to Michael's question about why cats sleep so much!" a student responded when asked about something that stood out to them during their independent reading time. This ties into the initial idea that our classrooms can be learning environments—even when students think they are only having fun!

The following open-ended question stems are not only for you to model for students; they also make powerful anchor charts for your wonder wall:

What are some ways that _____?

What are some things you _____?

What surprised you about _____?

How might you _____?

How did you support your group today? Describe one way.

How could you say that using your own words?

When would be a good time to _____?

When might you try using _____?

Where else do you see _____?

Why might you choose _____ instead of _____?

The Power of Observation

In an article referencing her work in *The Power of Our Words* (2015) and *The First Six Weeks of School* (2000), Paula Denton refers to the importance of taking time to observe students: "Teachers who occasionally stand still and watch their students will learn things they'd never learn otherwise" (2008). While it is important to always pause and observe, at the beginning of the year it is especially imperative, so you can learn about each individual and how you can create a community together. We may be tempted to make predictions about students based on instinct and on experiences we've had with other students in the past. It is important to consider the power our observations hold. During an Interactive Modeling lesson, we want students to be attuned to noticing what we are doing. This is our opportunity to pay it forward and show them that we are noticing what they are doing so we can set them up for success. Consider the following times to observe and questions you may ask to guide your observations. Consider as well how these observations can inform your decision-making and planning:

Observation Opportunities		
Arrival	• Who unpacks quickly? • Who takes longer to unpack? • Which students greet each other? • Who is very happy? • Who looks like they are upset?	I may need to: • Use reinforcing language for what is going well. • Use reminding prompts. • Use Interactive Modeling to show students the routines. • Post a visual list for what students should do when they arrive. • Give an individual student a checklist to facilitate independence. • Check in with a student to make sure they are doing well.
Morning Meeting	• Which students always greet one another? • Who is greeted last? • Who always shares, and who wants to pass? • Who is more reluctant to participate in certain activities?	I may need to: • Use reinforcing language for what is going well. • Vary the greetings so students are encouraged to interact with more peers. • Ask for a volunteer to be greeted last. • Model engaging someone who is not my closest friend. • Meet with a student to prepare them for the sharing topic. • Have a conversation with a reluctant participant to learn more.
Transitions	• Which students transition quickly? • What is the reason some students take longer to transition? • Who needs more support in organization to get materials ready?	I may need to: • Use reinforcing language for what is going well. • Use Interactive Modeling. • Use a visual timer or song to improve transitions. • Use a visual checklist so students know what materials they need to get out.

Observation Opportunities

Starting independent work	• Why is a student not starting right away? • Are they distracted? • Are they asking someone for the directions again?	I may need to: • Use reinforcing language for what is going well. • Ask students to restate the directions before getting started. • Use reminding language to ensure a collective understanding. • Provide individual check-in with a student.
Small-group activities	• Which students take a leadership role? • Which students need encouragement and support to participate? • How are students resolving a conflict? • What is causing them to get off task? • How are students using materials?	I may need to: • Use reinforcing language for what is going well. • Use role-play to support social and emotional topics that arise during group work to facilitate problem-solving strategies. • Revisit Guided Discovery for materials usage and care.
Lunch and recess	• Who plays together outside? • Are groupings the same as/ different from those in the classroom? • How are students talking and interacting with one another? • Who prefers to be in a large group and who prefers to be on their own?	I may need to: • Use reinforcing language for what is going well. • Be mindful of seating arrangements when we return to the classroom. • Use interactive learning structures to support relationship building.

As with all of the tools and strategies in this book, you need to make them your own. Consider using an observation clipboard, where you can jot down what you hear students saying and note what they are doing.

Recording your observations on paper will allow you to look for trends to support students and their successes. You may also notice how these trends vary over the course of the year, as students grow, develop a sense of community with one another, and internalize what it means to be a third grader. Sometimes students say and do things differently when we are in their immediate presence than when we are across the room or at the other end of the playground. Observations will give you a clearer picture and different perspective for understanding each child.

Becoming a Reflective Practitioner

As has often been observed, we do not learn from experience; we learn from reflecting on experience.

The power of observation does not stop at our students; it also includes us in our pivotal role within the classroom. When was the last time you saw yourself teach? If you are unable to remember when, then it is time to set up your recording device on a stand or ask a colleague to do the recording honors. Within college programs, watching ourselves teach is always a requirement, along with a reflective essay. Whether you are a novice or veteran, watching yourself can be uncomfortable and enlightening. There might be moments when you wonder why you said or did something and other moments that you impress yourself. An unbiased observation will allow you to reflect on what you are proud of and which areas you would like to focus on for improvement. Consider some of the following questions you might ask yourself after watching your initial recording:

- "Which characteristic of teacher language is a strength, and which would be good to focus on improving?"

- "How often am I using reinforcing language to proactively support students?"

- "How often am I using reminding and redirecting language?"

- "Which teacher language stems do I repeat, and which should I incorporate?"

- "How often am I using open-ended questions?"

- "Am I supporting students equally?"

- "Do I call on some students more than others? (If so, why might I be doing that?)"

- "Do I implement the expectations and rules consistently?"

As you review your video and begin to ask yourself some of these questions, along with many more that will come to mind, remember to be empathetic and kind to yourself. This will give you the opportunity to look at your own internal biases and allow you to become more self-aware, so you can create the learning environment that you desire for your students.

After this, consider what goals you are setting for yourself and how you can build support from a trusted colleague. You may have the benefit of working with another adult in the room, with whom you can share your goals and from whom you can seek observations of you. Teaching can be isolating and you may be in the room by yourself, in which case having these conversations with your grade-level team or a colleague can give you an accountability partner for support. Often, administrators during a preobservation conference will ask if there is anything in particular you would like them to observe for feedback. This can be a powerful opportunity to share that you are working on, for example, including more reinforcing language and to ask them to share their observations of how you are doing with this goal.

Pause and Ponder

- Which strategies will you start with to support student engagement?

- Which interactive learning structures and energizers will support your students?

- How can Morning Meeting be maximized for student success?

- How can you set high expectations and structure goal setting?

- Which open-ended prompts will you focus on using?

- How will you plan to reflect on student observations?

- How will you plan to become a reflective practitioner of your teaching craft?

Final Thought

"Sometimes, in the midst of our busy days and our need to meet curriculum goals, we lose sight of a fundamental fact: To create academically engaging classrooms, we need to know our students—as a group and as individuals. Although not every child will love every lesson we plan, we want to make sure that something in each lesson speaks to each child."

—*The Joyful Classroom*

Grade **4**

"Today our goal is to identify the main idea using reciprocal reading," the teacher explains to the fourth grade class. "You have three articles about activism from which to choose. The first article is about climate change, the second article is about gender, and the third article is about animals. Why might someone choose to read the article about climate change?" "Maybe because they're passionate about the environment," one student responds. "Maybe because our read-aloud story connects to climate change," another student says. "Maybe because they are curious about that topic," a third student shares.

After students share the reasons for choosing all the article options, students hold up one, two, or three fingers to indicate their choice as the teacher writes down their choices on a premade chart. Students transition into their practiced reciprocal reading routine: they move to their groups, each with their own copy of the text. Students talk about the text, mark up the text, and ultimately work together to identify the main idea of the text.

When the work time is finished, the class gathers in the meeting area to share the main ideas of the articles. Students return to their desks to write a journal entry in response to the following questions: How did your choice help you understand social justice issues? What was one problem you had as you were working? How did you solve it?

This scene shows an engaging academic lesson that integrates developmentally responsive teaching, effective management, and positive community. It demonstrates the characteristics of engaging academics: it was active, interactive, appropriately challenging, purposeful, and connected to students' interests; and it encouraged student autonomy. This section will review teaching practices for fourth graders and will break down ways to design engaging lessons like this, set high expectations for students, and observe students to guide instruction.

Designing Lessons

When designing lessons for fourth graders, it is important to plan with students' physical, social and emotional, and cognitive development in mind. Chip Wood's *Yardsticks* is a resource with many specific ideas for fourth grade academic areas, including those set out in the following table.

Developmentally Appropriate Lessons for Fourth Graders	
Subject Area	**Provide Opportunities for Students to . . .**
Reading	• Work in reading groups, focusing on comprehension and interpretation. • Begin to research and use related reading material. • Explore poetry year-round. • Read more, and do fewer book projects. • Read graphic novels, comic books, and trade books.
Writing	• Demonstrate the revision process with first and final drafts. • Write descriptively. • Strategize what to do when they have "writer's block." • Explore themes around world issues, divorce, moving away, death, disease, other worries, friends, time travel, letters to request information, and reports. • Write longer stories and poems.
Math	• Solve word problems. • Practice and master multiplication tables. • Explore math concepts with concrete objects and pictorial representations. • Practice division. • Use maps to measure and compute. • Work with fractions and decimals.

Subject Area	Provide Opportunities for Students to . . .
Across the curriculum	• Use and practice fine motor skills. • Use drama to play with language. • Work with choice partner. • Exercise. • Take part in group activities. • Assist community organizations or younger grades.

These developmental guidelines can be a place to start when designing lessons.

With development in mind, consider your goals and objectives. Depending on what you teach, there may be more than one. For example, students may be working on the fourth grade standard of determining the main idea of an informational text and explaining key details, as in the anecdote at the beginning of this section. Knowing that fourth graders work well together in reading groups, you might consider a standard from the Fly Five social and emotional learning curriculum (see Chapter 6), such as "cooperates as a group leader or member of a group." As an English as a New Language (ENL) teacher, you might also include a speaking and listening objective such as the New York State Next Generation standard "[E]ngage effectively in a range of collaborative discussions with diverse partners . . ." (New York State Education Department 2017, 60). With these standards in mind, three lesson objectives for the opening anecdote might be:

- **Academic objective:** Students will analyze an informational text and summarize the main idea of each section.

- **Social and emotional objective:** Students will effectively communicate with all members of the group.

- **Language objective:** Students will explain to group members the main idea from the informational text using the sentence frames "I think _____" or "I see _____."

At first it takes time to find ways to be purposeful in integrating multiple objectives, but with practice, embedding them together throughout the day makes for incredibly powerful and effective lessons. Integrating objectives also exemplifies the guiding principle that teaching social and emotional skills is as important as teaching academic content.

As was discussed in the overview, lesson design follows a three-part structure: opening, body, and closing. It can be tempting to cut the opening and closing in order to give students more time to practice the content. However, this structure is very purposeful in the way that it follows the natural learning cycle. Students are more invested and will go deeper with the content when the purpose of the content is clearly explained at the beginning of the lesson and when they have time to reflect and consolidate their learning.

The Importance of an Effective Closing

During fully remote learning, many teachers were only able to meet live, or synchronously, with their students in ten- to twenty-minute increments in order to limit screen time. Some teachers creatively introduced a schedule that highlights the importance of the closing part of the lesson: students independently watched a short video or read slides asynchronously for the opening of the lesson. Students then worked independently and sometimes in small groups, and teachers could post feedback and coach student work. The live instruction was devoted to the closing, where students shared their learning and reflected on their process with the class. Having experienced the power and significance of this structure, these teachers have returned to the building with a renewed sense of the importance of the third part of this three-part structure. They set a timer in order to ensure that the class gets to this key part of the lesson, which connects the learning and purpose for students.

Open-ended questions can support students' learning in all three parts of this lesson structure, but they can be particularly powerful during the closing. This question might relate to the content objective ("What helped you to determine the main idea in the article?"), it might support students in thinking about how their actions affected the outcomes of the work

("What worked well in your reading groups? What might you do differently the next time you work with a group to summarize an article?"), or it might encourage students to learn from each other ("How did working together in a small group help you to determine the main idea of the article?").

Teaching Practices for Fourth Graders

There are many teaching practices that you can use to increase engagement. Engaging academics has six main characteristics:

1. Learning is active.

2. Learning is interactive.

3. Learning is appropriately challenging.

4. Learning is purposeful.

5. Learning is connected to students' interests and strengths.

6. Learning is designed to give students some autonomy and control.

Incorporating these characteristics into your lessons is essential to making learning productive and fun. Engaging academics is also the domain where we see the big connections with the domains discussed in the previous three chapters: developmentally responsive teaching, effective management, and positive community. It has been demonstrated that when students know they belong, it increases their academic motivation and achievement (Goodenow 1993). In the practices discussed below, you will see the ways in which these four domains relate and connect to one another.

Academic Choice

Academic Choice is a teacher-guided approach for students to have control over what they learn and how they learn it. Academic Choice is a powerhouse of lesson design because it includes all six characteristics of engaging academics. The anecdote at the beginning of this chapter exemplified an Academic Choice lesson and this three-part structure: planning (opening), working (body), and reflecting (closing). In that example, all students

were working to summarize the main idea. They did not have choice in the content (what they learn), but they did have choice in the process (how they learn) by being able to select an article topic that interested them. With fourth graders, it's also a great option to allow students to sometimes choose their own partner, knowing that they need social interaction and that they like to work with a partner of their choice.

An Academic Choice lesson contributes to students' sense of autonomy and control. At the beginning of the year, when many students are exhibiting the characteristics of nine-year-olds, it's common for them to say things like "I hate this" or "This is boring" when tasks are not appropriately challenging. Having a sense of control will help to mitigate these typical behaviors. By the middle and the end of the year, this structure is a great way to support eager and curious ten-year-olds.

We also know that, with all of their growing energy, fourth graders benefit from exercise. Academic Choice can meet fourth graders' needs for being active by getting them moving around the room during the working phase of the lesson. Students often excitedly stand while building something or passionately hunch over a task.

Academic Choice also helps to differentiate instruction. With our guidance, students can make a choice that feels just right—we can encourage students to stretch themselves yet still help them to feel successful by allowing them to make choices that are connected to their strengths and interests. This is another way we can support a range of ages in the class.

Guided Discovery

See the appendix, p. 317, for more on Guided Discovery.

Guided Discovery is a strategy used to introduce materials in the classroom. It builds anticipation and interest and, through open-ended questions, helps students to explore the many ways they might use a tool. In fourth grade, Guided Discovery can be a way to assess students' prior knowledge of a tool (such as crayons or rulers) and support students exploring familiar tools in new ways. It's important for students to explore materials well before they need them for a specific task or assignment.

Guided Discovery can also be a proactive discipline strategy, since students are more likely to stay focused on and engaged with an academic task when they have had a chance to explore.

Interactive Modeling

This strategy is used to show students one particular way to do something. In Interactive Modeling, students actively participate in a seven-step process with the teacher. It might be used to teach students how to use the standard algorithm or their writing notebook. Fourth graders have a lot of prior knowledge when it comes to school, but showing them how to be successful in the particular setting of the fourth grade classroom, and with the specific academic skills they will need to learn, will help them to reduce their anxieties.

Interactive Learning Structures

This is a strategy that provides opportunities for deep learning because children can move and talk to one another. Fourth graders need to move, and interactive learning structures can prevent that fourth grade energy from spilling over into acting out. Fourth graders enjoy talking and explaining and can appreciate others' perspectives. Engaged learning should create a buzz of energy in the classroom. Use Interactive Modeling to teach an auditory and silent quiet signal in order to get students' attention to move on.

The Language of Learning

Speaking and listening are skills we must teach even though developmentally, fourth graders do like to talk and are good at listening. Often, people assume that by fourth grade students know what it means to "listen" or "work together," but there are actually a lot of underlying skills implied that need to be explicitly taught in order to support whole-class, small-group, and partner discussions. The table below shows when to introduce various speaking and listening skills throughout the school year for third and fourth graders.

Speaking and Listening Skills		
Weeks 1–4	**Early to Middle of Year**	**Middle to End of Year**
• Focusing attention	• Developing listening comprehension skills	• Presenting evidence
• Sustaining attention	• Staying on topic	• Persuading others
• Showing interest	• Speaking with clarity	• Agreeing
• Taking turns	• Asking purposeful questions	• Disagreeing
• Speaking confidently	• Answering questions	• Partially agreeing
• Core question skills	• Organizing thoughts	• Responding to disagreements
	• Distinguishing facts from opinions	

Adapted from *The Language of Learning,* by Margaret Berry Wilson (Center for Responsive Schools 2015)

Small-Group Learning

Building in opportunities for small-group work is a strategy that allows students to be active and interactive. The teacher plays the essential role of keeping collaborative work productive. Fourth graders are generally flexible and work well in groups, but it is important to proactively teach students how these groups can be productive and successful. You can use Interactive Modeling or role-play to support this. When creating small groups, you might consider using the following:

See the appendix, p. 318, for this and other interactive learning structures.

- **Random groupings.** Counting off by 6s, for instance, or randomly passing out pieces of academically related pictures and asking students to find their partners or groups helps to mix up groups frequently so students have the opportunity to work with different classmates.

- **Student-selected groups.** We know fourth graders like to choose partners, but it's important to have a good foundation in place first by establishing a positive and inclusive community. Build up to academic student-selected groups by first having students self-select partners during greetings. Then guide them in choosing work partners with interactive learning structures like Mix and Mingle to Music. When that is successful, have students choose partners for longer tasks, and then two pairs can join together to create a small group.

- **Assign small groups.** You may want students to work on specific tasks in small groups, such as a guided reading group for language arts or a mixed-language-acquisition small group for a science project. In these cases, you might find it useful to also assign jobs or roles like leader, recorder, timekeeper, and materials manager. You might ask a small group to model working together for the rest of the class before starting a work period.

Morning Meeting

Morning Meeting is an opportunity to begin integrating academic and social and emotional learning at the beginning of the day. Many teachers plan Morning Meeting last, after they have designed lessons for the rest of the day, so that they can include a review or a preview of academic objectives in at least one or two of the four Morning Meeting components (greeting, sharing, group activity, morning message).

For example, you might begin with a greeting that previews the day's vocabulary. Then you might transition into a special news dialogue share. This is an opportunity for students to practice stating the main idea that they are working on in reading.Listening students have the opportunity to practice asking purposeful questions, an essential listening/speaking and academic skill. In the group activity Just Like Me, the teacher makes statements like "I like cacti," "I like to write in a journal," "I like face painting," and "I have younger siblings," and students indicate if they agree. At the end, the teacher connects these statements to the class's recent read-aloud, *My Diary From Here to There* by Amada Irma Pérez, in which the main character immigrates to the United States from Mexico. The teacher helps students to make text-to-self connections. Finally, the morning message helps to transition the class into the next period by reviewing the previous day's science content with some vocabulary and previews what scientists will be doing today.

During Morning Meeting, students should be spending more time being active and interactive and practicing skills, and less time being passive. When designing a lesson, keep in mind that the greatest amount of students' time should be spent speaking and doing and only a small amount passively watching. Be sure to consider this ratio when designing your lessons.

These practices demonstrate ways that we can engage students and contribute to their sense of belonging, significance, and fun. Learning will go deeper when it is purposeful and all four domains are connected. It's like a four-legged chair or table: when one of the legs is shorter or longer than the others, it is not the most effective equipment. But when all four legs are the same height, the furniture is stable and strong. The next section will discuss ways to raise the table up through high expectations.

Setting High Expectations

It is important to have expectations for fourth graders that are both high and realistic. Below are some guidelines to consider to keep those expectations high:

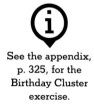

See the appendix, p. 325, for the Birthday Cluster exercise.

- **Consider what is developmentally appropriate.** As was suggested in Chapter 1, review *Yardsticks* at the beginning of the year and use the Birthday Cluster exercise as a starting point. Throughout the year, if students exhibit behaviors that are not within the range of expected characteristics for nine- and ten-year-olds, see if you notice behaviors characteristic of other ages. Students who are exhibiting some behaviors that are typical of children two years younger or two years older are within a normal developmental range. It's likely that it's our expectations as teachers that need to shift to meet students where they are.

- **Get to know your students.** In Chapter 3, we discussed ways of building a positive community, and part of that is knowing our students. Two characteristics of engaging academics are that learning should be appropriately challenging and should connect to students' strengths and interests. When we talk about whether or not a task or assignment is appropriately challenging, we might think of a rubber band: we want it to stretch, but we don't want it to break. When tasks are too hard, students can get frustrated and give up. When tasks are too easy, students can get bored and their energy might be spent in other, less productive ways. We therefore need to know our students. This means talking with students and their families or caregivers about their likes and dislikes and their hopes and dreams. It also means observing students; this will be discussed further in the next section.

- **Assess progress.** Preassessments, postassessments, mid-unit assessments, and self-assessments are all ways to get to know students in order to set high and realistic expectations. You might involve students in creating rubrics, which can increase student understanding of objectives and expectations as well as cause students to be more invested and perform at a high standard. All of these can show you what students are doing well or already know and what they need to work on to stretch their thinking. These assessments can also be a tool that you and a student discuss in a one-on-one conference: fourth graders take pride in their school-work, and talking with a teacher about their strengths and stretches based on assessments will continue to encourage autonomy and give them control of their learning.

- **Be mindful of teacher language.** When students are able to visualize their accomplishments, they are more likely to succeed. Envisioning language allows students to develop a growth mindset and shows them that they can do challenging things. Fourth graders appreciate being noticed for their efforts, and reinforcing language allows students to know that you see their efforts. When it comes to engaging academics, this might sound like "You added figurative language to your poem. This metaphor about light is going to help your readers visualize this part." As mentioned earlier, open-ended questions can invite students to meet a challenge in the opening part of a lesson or to reflect on their learning during the closing part of a lesson. They can also be used to coach individual students while they are working. For example, you might ask, "How is this strategy helping you?" or "What more would you like to learn about this?"

When we know our students personally, developmentally, culturally, and cognitively, we can design lessons that engage and challenge them appropriately. When our expectations are high, we can design and deliver high-quality, rigorous, and engaging instruction for all students.

Observing Students

We can get to know students in so many ways through our observations. This is such an important tool for teachers. Teachers observe all throughout the day and are constantly gathering data: student body language and facial expressions during a lesson; student discussion during Morning Meeting, in reading groups, and with science partners; interactions while playing soccer at recess; behavior during the transition from the meeting area to writing independently; and the list could go on and on. When we actively observe students, we learn more about them as a group and

as individuals, and this information can be used in designing effective and engaging lessons. Here are some things to look for when actively observing:

- **Peer relationships.** Who sits together? Who plays together at recess? Fourth graders are highly sensitive to fairness issues and are quick to anger and quick to forgive. They may also have a sense of who is in and out, and problematic cliques may form. Looking for who is included and excluded informs your social and emotional teaching as well as your approach to designing opportunities for interactions in lessons.

- **Physical activity.** Who eagerly participates in energizers? Who needs encouragement? Who often sits and reads or chats with a friend at recess? Who seems to have an endless amount of energy at recess? Fourth graders can be restless and need lots of outdoor time with physical activity. These observations and developmental characteristics may be considerations when planning your daily schedule or designing lessons that are active.

- **Mental energy.** Who takes time to get started working? Who rushes through a task quickly? Which students keep trying through a challenge? Which students get easily frustrated or give up? Some of our older students take pride in their schoolwork and pay close attention to directions and organization, while our younger fourth graders may be impatient, become easily frustrated, and feel worried or anxious. These developmental considerations can help inform your observations, and in turn can help you design lessons that are appropriately challenging or plan for teacher language that will encourage student success.

- **Learning styles.** Do some students participate more with visuals? Do some students like to use pictures or graphic organizers to understand concepts? Do some students prefer to be tactile with manipulatives? Do some students prefer written directions? These observations can help you to support and design lessons that engage your students with choices and scaffolds to support their learning.

- **Language and cognitive skills.** How do students express themselves with words? Do students understand others' perspectives? Do students understand abstract or figurative language? How quickly do students process or synthesize information? These types of observations can support lesson designs that are appropriately challenging and with student strengths in mind.

When observing these areas, take notes of students' words and actions. Low-inference notes and checklists can help you to make decisions based on facts rather than on assumptions. For example, a teacher observing a student during a math assessment might note, "Isabella looked out window—8:48–8:53." Later, the teacher might check in with Isabella and ask, "How did the test feel to you?" By asking this question with a curious and compassionate tone, the teacher might gain insight into Isabella's thoughts from that short observation. Insights such as this one will further inform decisions about lesson design.

As humans, we all have internal biases. These unconscious and unintentional attitudes influence our expectations, observations, assessments, lesson designs, and relationships with students' families. These biases can affect student investment and achievement. As educators, our constant observations and the need for making split-second decisions cause us to enact our internal biases throughout the day. It's important to be aware of these biases. Educator and author Zaretta Hammond (2019) advises teachers to work from the "inside out" to do their own work around implicit bias and cultural proficiency. As was suggested in Chapter 3, invite a trusted colleague to observe you or record a lesson and think critically about these biases. What patterns or tendencies do you notice? Just as we do with our students, do this work with curiosity and compassion. More of this self-care will be discussed in Chapter 6.

Pause and Ponder

- What strategies or techniques do you want to begin to use to design purposeful, engaging lessons?

- How can you embed social and emotional and academic objectives throughout the day?

- How will you set high and realistic expectations with students?

- How might you use observations to inform your engaging lessons?

- How will you balance your own growth mindset with curiosity and compassion when addressing internal biases?

Final Thought

"Students enter our school doors with a vision of themselves as learners, filled with hopes and dreams for learning. . . . With them, they bring an innate curiosity and a thirst to discover words, numbers, music, and art; to hear, tell, and make meaning of stories from the past and stories that are yet unfolding; to explore the wonders of faraway planets and uncover the marvels of the one named Earth—and most importantly, to learn all the nitty-gritty details of whatever captures their own interests and helps to manifest their hidden gifts and talents."

—Dr. Lora Hodges, foreword to *The Language of Learning*

Grade ⑤

"Today, you will work on an activity that will demonstrate the research you completed about a European explorer recently," the teacher says at the opening of a social studies period. "I will share three options you will choose from to show what you learned," the teacher continues. "Then you will have time today and tomorrow to work through your choice. On the final day of this project, you will have the chance to share your learning with others and reflect on your work." Next, the teacher explains the three choices: preparing an electronic slide show, writing a historical fiction story, or recording a talking statue presentation. The teacher takes time to model each choice and to answer students' questions. The teacher also uses Interactive Modeling to show students the materials available to complete the work. As the class finishes planning for this social studies activity, the teacher instructs students as to where they can work on this assignment; holds a brief discussion about following the classroom rules to care for oneself, classmates, and the learning materials while completing this assignment; and signals to the class that they are ready to begin. The teacher concludes, "Consider which choice will best help you to show what you learned about your explorer. You can indicate your choice by writing your name under the choice board on the dry-erase board and then begin your work . . ."

The scenario described above is an example of the beginning of a lesson that incorporates Academic Choice, a teaching practice that allows students to be actively focused with appropriately challenging tasks. In incorporating choice, teachers create conditions for students to take ownership of their learning by having the opportunity to make a choice and use their strengths. Students also have opportunities to interact with peers around academic content. Academic Choice is one way that teachers can meet fifth graders' developmental needs—such as the needs for physical movement, social interaction, and consistent reinforcement, as discussed in Chapter 1. There are six characteristics that lay the foundation for creating engaging academics:

1. Learning is active.

2. Learning is interactive.

3. Learning is appropriately challenging.

4. Learning is purposeful.

5. Learning is connected to students' interests and strengths.

6. Learning is designed to give students some autonomy and control.

In order to create optimal learning environments with these six character-istics in mind, teachers must design lessons and use teaching practices, such as Academic Choice, to support students' needs. Teachers must hold students to high expectations for maximum learning gains to occur. Lastly, teachers need to observe students and reflect on teaching practices to best support student learning. Designing lessons, using teaching practices that call for active student involvement, setting high expectations, and observing students are practices that are critical to creating the founda-tions for engaging academics for fifth graders.

Designing Lessons

Knowledge of child development is crucial to designing meaningful lessons for fifth graders. Fifth graders' needs, including the needs for movement, interaction, and reinforcement, can be met with careful planning by the teacher. There are many teaching practices—such as Academic Choice, Morning Meeting, and Interactive Modeling—that teachers can use to meet these needs. Additionally, teachers must be deliberate in creating an environment that supports engaged learners. It is also important to remember that fifth graders need explicit instruction and practice with the skills needed to be engaged in their work.

Effective lessons begin with an objective. Use pacing guides, state or local standards, and your knowledge of child development to identify a meaning-ful lesson objective(s). To help fifth graders see a purpose for the lesson, explicitly state the objective. "Why do we have to know this?" is a common question heard in fifth grade classrooms. To make learning purposeful, connect the learning to real-world examples. For instance, you might say, "Today, we are going to learn how to find elapsed time. This is a skill you will use as you get older and have to plan your schedule." In some instances, it may be challenging to find a real-world example. In such cases, connect the lesson objective with previous and future objectives. For example, you might begin a geometry lesson by explaining, "In fourth grade, you learned how to find the area of parallelograms. Today, we are going to practice finding the area of trapezoids so that later on you can find the area of any quadrilateral." Statements like these allow students to see their current learning as a bridge that connects past and future learning experiences. Clear learning objectives serve as the foundation for an effective lesson.

Tips to Keep in Mind for Engaging Academics

- **Before beginning any interactive learning structure, use Interactive Modeling to teach students how to use and care for learning materials.**

- **Teach and use signals for quiet attention.** Be consistent with using these during all times of the school day.

- **Teach new interactive learning structures during Morning Meeting to maximize time on task during academic subjects.** For example, if you plan on having students engage in a partner chat, have them practice this during Morning Meeting. Doing so allows students to gain familiarity with the structure before using it in an academic lesson.

- **Provide time limits for students.** State the time limits when giving directions, and use a visual timer to support students' independence and responsibility.

- **Give clear directions.** Keep in mind the characteristics of teacher language, particularly brevity. Be brief with directions, and consider scaffolding them, providing just the necessary directions for each step of the lesson. Posting visual directions using a projector or marker board helps fifth graders revisit the directions and can easily be referred to as a visual reminder if needed.

- **Discuss and use a visual noise chart.** It may also be helpful to hold up the noise level on your fingers at times as a visual cue for students.

A well-designed lesson utilizes a three-part structure—opening, body, and closing. During the opening, the teacher identifies a purpose for the lesson. It is the time when the teacher explicitly states the lesson's learning objective. Using envisioning language and open-ended questions, as well as interactive learning structures, the teacher creates excitement for the lesson. Next is the body of the lesson, which may include some brief direct teaching. During this phase, students work individually, with partners, in small groups, or all together to work toward achieving the learning objective. It is an opportunity for students to actively explore the new content. Finally, a well-designed lesson wraps up with a closing. This is a time for students to reflect on their learning. It is also a time when the teacher can use a formative assessment to gauge students' grasp of the lesson objective and to direct future instruction.

Throughout all three phases of a well-designed lesson, teachers should use open-ended questions to support student engagement. Teachers may feel crunched for time and be tempted to focus on only the body of the lesson, in which students work with new content. Avoid this temptation by planning all three parts of a lesson, and dedicate time for planning, working, and reflecting to best support students' learning.

Well-designed lessons with clear objectives and a three-part structure serve as a form of proactive classroom management. Well-designed lessons reduce misbehavior and allow students to see a purpose for their learning. Lessons designed in this manner provide an appropriate pace for learning and offer students opportunities to reflect and solidify learning gains. In some instances of misbehavior, after addressing the misbehavior with a reactive response as discussed in Chapter 3, the teacher should consider redesigning the lesson to better support student learning. For example, if your students engage in side conversations during a lesson, you could incorporate an interactive learning structure. Making this adjustment will support students with staying on task with their learning.

Teaching Practices for Fifth Graders

Designing lessons with an opening, body, and closing creates the foundation for engaging academics. During each of these three phases, there are many teaching practices educators can use to enhance student engagement. Some teaching practices can be used at other times in the day as well. Below are some options that teachers can use during an academic lesson or at other times in the school day.

Academic Choice

Academic Choice is a strategy that can highlight any of the six characteristics of engaging academics. In this three-part structure, students plan, work, and reflect on their learning. During an Academic Choice lesson, students make a choice about the content (what) they will learn or the process (how) they will use to learn it. For example, the scenario described in the opening of this chapter is a lesson in which students made a process choice in that they chose which way to demonstrate their research. The lesson may have included a content choice, too, if students chose the explorer to research prior to the start of this Academic Choice experience.

How to Give Clear Directions

1. State the task.

2. Identify the roles and responsibilities for partner and group work.

3. Inform students about the amount of time for the task.

4. Answer any student questions.

5. Signal for students to begin.

Noise Chart

0 = Silent; independent work

1 = Whisper level; best with partners

2 = Quiet voice; best with small groups

3 = Presentation voice; best when speaking with the whole class

At the beginning of an Academic Choice lesson, students hear the learning goal for the lesson. During the planning phase, teachers tell students what options are available to choose from. Teachers model and discuss the available choices and answer students' questions at this time. Then students are encouraged to consider which option will work best for them, and make a choice. Next is the working phase. During this time, students follow through with their plan. As students work, teachers circulate and monitor their activity, offering reinforcing and reminding statements when applicable and providing students with open-ended questions to stretch their thinking. The working phase is also a time when teachers reteach skills individually or in small groups as necessary. At the end of an Academic Choice lesson, students reflect. During the reflecting phase, teachers ask open-ended questions about the content or process used and students share their work. This is a time when students solidify their learning gains.

It is important to keep in mind that Academic Choice lessons can be as short as ten minutes, while others may take place over the course of a few days. As you plan an Academic Choice lesson, keep in mind the importance of making the work engaging for students while considering the amount of time the lesson will take.

Although not part of a traditional Academic Choice lesson, teachers should also consider providing other types of choices to students. For example, allow students to make a *who* choice: "Would you like to work on this activity independently, with a partner, or in a small group?" At other times, teachers may provide students with a *where* choice: "You can work on this activity at your desk or in the whole-group carpet space." When students have choice in their learning, their motivation increases, allowing them to be truly engaged in their work. Also, consider some of the choices listed in the chart on this page for additional ideas.

Ideas for Academic Choice Activities

Constructions
- Game
- Puzzle
- Book
- Maze
- Museum display
- Brochure
- Newspaper
- Magazine
- Model
- Mobile
- Diorama
- Puppet
- Set of cards
- Collage

Drama
- Pantomime
- Play or skit
- Student-made video
- Chant or cheer
- Demonstration of skill or process
- Movement piece
- Living "freeze frame" or tableau

Drawing/Painting
- Illustration (comic strip, picture book, brochure, etc.)
- Mural
- Still life
- Scene
- Card (thank you, holiday, friendship, etc.)
- Decorative border
- Calligraphy

Looking, Studying, Observing
- Study a map or globe
- Study a picture (painting, photo, illustration, etc.)
- Observe an object closely and record observations (with naked eyes, microscope, telescope, magnifying lens, etc.)

Manipulating
- Experiment with different ways to use materials
- Conduct a formal experiment
- Play a game
- Work a puzzle

Music
- Write and sing a song or jingle
- Create and perform a rhythm to express ideas and information
- Create and perform a tune to express ideas and information

Oral Presentation
- Speech
- Monologue
- Debate
- Reader's theater
- Script for radio show or podcast
- Poem or passage of text
- Story

Reading
- Library book
- Textbook
- Website, blog post
- Magazine or newspaper article
- Encyclopedia, dictionary, thesaurus, online source
- Brochure
- Handout
- Graph, chart, diagram, or poster
- Document

Representing Graphically
- Map
- Flowchart
- Timeline
- Graph
- Venn diagram
- Poster
- Chart or table
- Web
- PowerPoint presentation

Speaking and Listening
- Plan and conduct an interview with a knowledgeable person
- Listen to an audio file
- Listen to a speech or lecture
- Participate in a discussion
- Listen to and watch a video clip or DVD
- Learn a song, rap, chant, or poem

Writing
- Story
- Poetry
- Scripts/dialogue
- Instructions
- News article
- Blog post
- Persuasive essay or paragraph
- Journal or diary entry
- Memoir
- Riddles
- Comic strip
- Research report
- Worksheet
- Quiz
- Letter
- New version of a well-known story or fairy tale

Interactive Learning Structures

See the appendix, p. 318, for sample interactive learning structures.

Interactive learning structures can be used during the opening, body, or closing of a lesson. These structures can be simple or complex. They offer a safe way for students to interact around new learning. Interactive learning structures also provide students with opportunities to practice listening, speaking, and thinking skills. Fifth graders' needs for social interaction and movement can often be met using interactive learning structures. Using these structures results in high levels of engagement for students.

Small-Group Learning

Working with peers provides students with a safe space to try something new and learn from mistakes. Some fifth graders may be reluctant to participate in whole-group settings; however, they may find working in partnerships or small groups to be beneficial. Small groups help teachers to differentiate and better address various learning styles, needs, and aptitudes while meeting students' need for interaction. Many times in fifth grade classrooms, teachers create groups of mixed ability or similar ability depending on learners' needs. For example, in reading workshop, students may be grouped homogeneously based on reading levels so that students are reading appropriately leveled books. At other times, students may be grouped randomly or heterogeneously, such when they are grouped with other students for a science project, allowing them to work with different peers and to practice important skills such as cooperation, assertiveness, responsibility, empathy, and self-control.

There also may be times when groups are student created. For example, in the scenario described at the beginning of this section, students who made a similar process choice for how to demonstrate their explorer research might work together. To help students work effectively together in small groups, consider creating groups of three or four students. When groups are larger, students may struggle with staying engaged with their work. Additionally, assigning roles to students during group work helps to support the group dynamics. Here are some roles to consider:

- Recorder
- Starter/timekeeper

- Presenter

- Materials manager

In order for small-group learning to be effective, take time at the beginning of the school year to create a positive learning community, using some strategies like the ones outlined in Chapter 3. Doing so will create a strong, trusting foundation that supports students working well with others while staying engaged with their learning.

Interactive Modeling

When teaching academic skills, there are many times when teachers want students to complete an academic task using only one method, often for efficiency purposes. In instances like these, Interactive Modeling is an effective teaching strategy. Using the seven-step process of Interactive Modeling to teach academic skills is an engaging approach for fifth graders. It empowers students to notice how to complete the new skill and provides opportunities to practice it, the chance to be retaught it, and reinforcement for completing it successfully. The teacher models the skill with minimal dialogue, thereby allowing the students to focus specifically on how to carry out the skill and giving them a clear mental image of what it should look like. How to plot a point on an ordered pair in math is an example of a fifth grade academic skill that Interactive Modeling can be used to teach. In language arts, fifth grade teachers might use Interactive Modeling to teach how to complete a works consulted page for research writing.

See the appendix, p. 323, for more on Interactive Modeling.

Morning Meeting

A goal of Morning Meeting is to merge academic and social and emotional learning. As such, using Morning Meeting to preview, teach, or review academic content is an engaging practice for fifth graders. All four components of Morning Meeting—greeting, sharing, group activity, and morning message—can incorporate academic content. For example, if you recently taught students how to convert fractions, decimals, and percents, consider using this skill for a partner greeting. Create different sets of three equal values—such as ½, 0.5, and 50%—on index cards. Then distribute the sets of cards to students and have them find their match and greet one another. If your students recently completed a novel study, consider having them share in partnerships about the character they connected with the most, and why.

The group activity component is an effective way to incorporate academics into Morning Meeting too. After you finish a unit learning about European explorers in social studies, play group memory with your fifth graders. This activity will help students review each explorer's country of origin. Create a set of matching cards: write "Hernando de Soto" on one card and "Spanish explorer" on another; "Amerigo Vespucci" on one card and "Italian explorer" on another; and so on. Then put all of the cards face down on the floor, and have students take turns, one by one, by flipping two cards at a time and deciding if the cards are a match. An activity such as this could serve as an energizer later in the day, too.

Lastly, the morning message also serves as a way to engage students with their learning. For example, if you plan to graph data later in the day during math, consider collecting data on the morning message about a topic that interests fifth graders.

As you consider ways to incorporate academics into Morning Meeting, keep in mind that building community and practicing social skills are goals for this practice as well. Use caution in preparing a Morning Meeting that solely reviews or previews academic content.

Culturally Responsive Teaching

Just as it is important to know the students we teach individually and developmentally, as discussed in Chapter 1, and it is equally important to create a positive learning community, as discussed in Chapter 3, it is paramount that culturally responsive strategies are in place. Whether you are new to teaching or have years of experience, remember that each class community, as well as each individual in the class, is unique, and brings their own cultures and backgrounds to the learning community. Fifth grade teachers can demonstrate this mindset by conveying empathy during all interactions with students. It is important to create a nurturing and caring environment, one that sends the message to students that each of them is an important and valued member of the community and that we all want to learn about one another. Honoring all students' backgrounds is a helpful way to develop a culturally responsive pedagogy. Here are some helpful tips to cultivate a culturally responsive academic learning community for and with your fifth graders:

- **Include "get to know you" activities.** Be intentional about planning activities that allow students to share about their cultures and learn from one another. (See Chapter 3 for more on these activities.)

- **Involve all students during class discussions.** Consider using craft sticks or a name randomizer app to create equity for student participation.

- **Provide choices for books to read.** For example, if the current unit of study is biography, allow students to choose a person to read about whom they are interested in or who represents their culture.

- **Use writing workshop time to build in cultural awareness.** When working on narrative writing, have students write about a custom they enjoy celebrating.

- **Encourage student input on projects.** When using Academic Choice, provide an option for "create your own," in which students can choose a process to meet the learning goal. Or if using a rubric to assess students, allow students to cocreate a rubric with you.

Skills Students Need

In order for students to take part in an engaging academic lesson, certain skills need to be modeled, practiced, and reinforced for students. As mentioned previously, students need speaking, listening, and thinking skills to engage in tasks like interactive learning structures or small-group learning. Using Interactive Modeling, you can teach the skills that fifth graders need to be successful. (See the table in the fourth grade section, page 193, for examples of speaking and listening skills to teach.) Consider teaching these skills during Morning Meeting, and then reinforcing students' success with these skills as they are used later in the school day.

Setting High Expectations

Holding fifth graders to high expectations is an important tool in creating engaging academics. When fifth grade teachers hold students to high standards, and support students throughout the learning process, students develop perseverance, an academic mindset, and new learning strategies. These skills are necessary for students not only during their fifth grade year, but all throughout their schooling experience. The life lessons students learn by overcoming obstacles and achieving new successes will last well beyond their fifth grade year. With careful planning, teachers can create the conditions necessary for high expectations to be in place.

There are many ways that teachers can set high expectations that are appropriate for fifth grade. Here are some strategies that work best.

Preassessments

Using a preassessment at the beginning of a new unit or topic is helpful for both the student and the teacher. For students, it previews material that they will soon learn. It also gives students the chance to demonstrate skills or knowledge they already have in place. It allows teachers to gather baseline assessments and tailor instruction to meet the needs of the class. Since each group of students is unique, the time needed to teach certain skills will vary from one group to the next. Preassessments also help teachers to support any learning loss a group of students may be experiencing, such as the gaps in learning that some students experienced during the COVID-19 pandemic, or learning loss experienced during extended breaks from school. If a preassessment identifies significant learning loss for a group of students for a given topic, consider reaching out to the previous year's teachers or a specialist to support planning a supplemental lesson.

When designing a preassessment for a unit on fractions, for example, consider using an online form, since online forms can be set to grade immediately when students are finished. This allows teachers to focus their time and energy on how to interpret and use the results of a preassessment, instead of needing time to grade the assessment.

A preassessment should be used as a formative assessment only; it should not count toward a report card grade like a summative assessment might. Although fifth graders may have had experience with preassessments in past years, it is important to remind students of the purpose in order to minimize their frustrations or nervous feelings.

Teachers should use the results of a preassessment to determine the pacing of lessons and the amount of time needed on a topic. The results can also be used to differentiate instruction based on a student's zone of proximal development (Vygotsky 1978). The zone of proximal development is the just-right fit for a student to engage with a task; it is not so easy that boredom may emerge, and it is not so difficult that frustration could occur. A student's zone of proximal development is the area where a student can learn new content with support from the teacher and classmates. Teachers should strive to have students operate in an area of their zone of proximal development often, as it supports on-task behavior, creates engaging academics, and allows students to make meaningful learning gains.

Cocreated Rubrics

Another helpful way to set high expectations with students is to work together with them to create rubrics. A cocreated rubric allows students to take ownership of their learning and develop metacognitive skills. It encourages students and teachers to define standards for good work together and helps to create a positive learning community. For cocreated rubrics to be successful, it is helpful for the teacher to clearly explain the goals of the activity. If possible, it is also helpful to show students samples of previous students' work, to help your current students see what a completed product should look like.

Single-Point Rubrics

There are similarities between single-point rubrics and traditional rubrics. Both identify criteria for proficient work and identify the expectations for students. However, a single-point rubric emphasizes the process students have demonstrated by using open-ended sections to identify areas of growth and areas where students have exceeded expectations. Including this information on the rubric allows the teacher to set meaningful goals and provide reinforcing language for areas of exceeding expectations for each individual student. Below is an example of a single-point rubric.

Colonial History Presentation—Single-Point Rubric		
Areas for Growth	**Criteria for Proficient Work**	**Areas of Exceeding Expectations**
	Research and Note-Taking Skills • Include accurate information. • Use at least two websites. • Include *all* "must-haves." • Include five options.	
	Slideshow • Make sure mechanics are correct. • Include most of your note-taking. • Pictures relate to facts.	
	Presentation Skills • Speak for two to six minutes. • Maintain eye contact with audience (or camera). • Speak clearly.	

Portfolio Collection

Have students collect their work throughout the school year. This may include the results of summative assessments, such as tests or quizzes, as well as other projects. Toward the end of the school year, have a portfolio sharing day when students can share their artifacts with classmates and family members, if they are invited to attend. A portfolio helps students to reflect on what new learning they achieved during the school year. It also helps students to reflect on the processes they used to gain new learning and develops their sense of the importance of using different learning strategies. As the use of technology has become more prevalent in recent years, many classrooms are shifting toward using a digital portfolio collection as well. Consider using this option if it works well in your setting.

Reinforcing Language

Keep in mind the importance of teacher language, particularly reinforcing language, as discussed in Chapter 3. In addition to supporting the creation of a positive learning community, reinforcing language also helps establish engaging academics. Think of reinforcing language like a scaffold to a building—it is used to uphold and support students' academic abilities. Without that scaffold in place, students might continue to use their skills effectively. However, by providing students with specific reinforcing language in response to their positive abilities, students become aware that they are meeting high expectations and are more likely to continue to use and develop that skill in the future. Teachers should use reinforcing language often during academic lessons.

Open-Ended Questions

Open-ended questions are an effective tool for building a positive community, as discussed in Chapter 3. They also are vital to creating engaging academics that invite students to reflect and challenge students to grow. When we as teachers ask open-ended questions, with a sincere curiosity and a willingness to accept any reasoned response, we send the message to students that their learning is important.

Open-ended questions can be used during all three phases of a well-designed lesson. By using them throughout a lesson, teachers empower students to think critically and stay engaged in their learning. Open-ended questions are also an effective tool to use during the three phases of Academic Choice, during a closing circle, or at any other time when students are being encouraged to reflect. The following offers examples of how open-ended questions can be used during an opening, body, or closing of a lesson.

Open-Ended Questions in a Well-Designed Lesson		
Opening	Body	Closing
• What do you notice about this learning material? What kind of things might you learn from it? • How does this learning goal connect with other learning? • Why might learning about _____ be important?	• What thinking is helping you _____? • What do you think will happen next? • How else might you think about _____? • In what ways have you thought about _____?	• What was hard about that? • What would you do differently if you did this again? • What are you most proud of? Why?

Observation and Reflection

Two additional teacher practices that support engaging academics are observing students while they work and reflecting on instructional practices. When teachers take time to observe students while they work and continuously reflect on their own teaching as well as on their students' development, valuable information is obtained. Teachers can use the information gathered to inform future educational decisions to best support students' learning.

The Importance of Observing Students

An integral part of developing engaging academics for learning communities is to actively observe students. When teachers observe students, they are able to make decisions based on facts instead of on assumptions. It is also a time when teachers can clear up misconceptions. For example, if students demonstrate confusion about a task, the teacher can respond with reminding language to get students back on track. If the teacher observes that students misunderstand the content, the teacher can reteach the skills individually or to a small group. When teachers actively observe students as they work, teachers are able to differentiate in the moment. Teachers are able to stretch students' learning with open-ended questions and can provide reinforcing language to recognize students' efforts and successes. Reminding and redirecting language can be used in conjunction with observing students too. Student observations can provide useful information in planning the opening for the next lesson as well.

Observing students also serves as a method of formative assessment. In addition to using preassessments, observing students at work helps teachers to support them in their learning. If a teacher has students reflect on their progress throughout the lesson, the teacher will then have a good idea if progress is being made, based on what is observed during the body of the lesson. When teachers use preassessments, observe students at work, have students reflect on their progress, and use formative assessments during the closing of a lesson, students are held to high standards and are more likely to achieve greater learning gains.

Depending on the number of students you work with, observing students can be challenging, particularly if you are hoping to look at and reinforce individual students' use of specific skills. To support your observations, consider making a spreadsheet checklist. Creating a checklist allows you to keep track of which students you have observed completing various tasks. For example, if you have students completing a multistep research report, prepare a checklist that lists the students and identifies all of the required tasks for the assignment. For a research report, you might have the steps in this sequential order: select a topic, collect research, outline report, write rough draft, peer edit, publish good copy. Having these tasks on a checklist enables you to keep track of which students you have noticed completing the steps. It also may be helpful to include some space on the checklist for reinforcing language comments that recognize students' individual efforts as well as space for anecdotal notes from your observations. These comments could be shared with students in the moment or at a later time, such as on a grading rubric or a report card comment. Lastly, if you have access to a tablet, consider creating the checklist using an electronic form, which can help you to more easily organize your observations and collaborate in real time with coteachers. If using an electronic spreadsheet, including premade sentence starters for anecdotal notes is another strategy that makes recording observations of students more manageable. See the sentence starters in the following table for some ideas.

Sentence Starters When Observing Students Research

[Student's name], you used a variety of sources (electronic, print, etc.) to find your information.

[Student's name], you organized your notes by subtopic. This will help you organize your report into clear body paragraphs.

[Student's name], your notes are neat and demonstrate pride in your work.

[Student's name], you collected a lot of meaningful images that you will be able to use to enhance your slideshow presentation.

Lastly, when observing students with the purpose of giving them feedback, strive to do this in a timely manner. Doing so allows students to apply constructive feedback right away. Timely feedback also honors students' efforts by sending the message that there is value in their work and effort with the learning process.

Reflecting on Teaching Practices

Becoming a reflective practitioner is important for teachers and impacts their work with students. Just as teachers deliberately plan time for students to reflect, perhaps at the end of an Academic Choice experience or during the closing of a lesson, teachers must take time to reflect in order to make informed decisions that benefit students. Reflecting on teaching practices helps teachers become their best self. Here are some ways to collect examples of teaching in action that can be used for further reflection:

- **Video/audio recorder.** Capture authentic clips of your teaching in action.

- **Focused observation.** Ask an administrator or colleague to observe you, looking to see that a particular practice is in place. For example, if you are working at using more reinforcing language during a lesson, ask the observer to make note of those instances while observing.

- **Peer collaboration.** Work with a colleague to support one another. For example, if you hope to include more social interaction during a lesson, plan the lesson with a colleague while keeping this goal in mind.

After you have collected these artifacts, reflect on the items carefully. Make note of how students are experiencing your instruction by considering some of the following:

- **Use of teacher language.** Are the characteristics of teacher language in place during your interactions with students? Are there more reinforcing language examples than reminding or redirecting? Consider posting sentence starters around your classroom or in a prominent place at your desk so you can focus on using more reinforcing language.

- **Process used.** Do lessons have a clear opening, body, and closing? Is there a balance between individual, partner, small-group, and whole-group activities? Consider the flow of the lesson, and make adjustments as needed.

- **Language, cognitive, and social skills.** Are there skills missing that need to be retaught? For example, do students have difficulty with listening to a partner and remembering details? Consider reteaching these skills with Interactive Modeling and give students the chance to practice during an upcoming Morning Meeting.

- **Physical and mental energy.** Are students' energy levels too low or too high? Incorporating more energizers and interactive learning structures can help to maintain student engagement.

As you pay attention to these items in your reflection, consider the impact they have on students. The things you notice while observing students and reflecting on your teaching practices work hand in hand with the realistic physical, social, and emotional expectations discussed in Chapter 3. Be reflective and willing to adjust your teaching methods in order to support your students' needs.

Additionally, use the practice of reflection to become aware of your own implicit biases. Biases can directly impact a teacher's work with students. As a result, it is important to become aware of biases and to take action in response to them. For example, some teachers may favor one group of students over another. Here are some things to pay attention to as you reflect on your craft: Is there a balance between calling on boys and girls during a discussion? Is there a balance between calling on students from different ethnic groups or cultures? Biases are a delicate and personal matter, and no two teachers have the same biases. However, becoming aware of biases, such as simple ones involving whom you call on during class, is important when reflecting on our teaching practices. Being honest about our biases, recognizing them in our practice, and making a plan to address them to build culturally responsive classrooms is of paramount importance for us as teachers as we work to support all students with their academic and social and emotional learning.

Pause and Ponder

- What improvements can you make in using a three-part lesson design (opening, body, closing) to create engaging academics for fifth graders?

- Think about an upcoming unit of study. What teaching practices described in this chapter can you use to make the content more engaging for your students?

- Which speaking and listening skills do your fifth graders need explicit instruction and practice with?

- What are some open-ended questions you can use to deepen students' engagement during the opening, body, or closing of an upcoming lesson?

- How can you use student observations to make informed decisions for an upcoming unit of study?

- What reflective strategies can you use in your practice to support your work with students?

Final Thought

"When teachers build the six characteristics of engaging academics into lessons, they help students meet rigorous learning standards in a dynamic way."

—*The Joyful Classroom*

Chapter 5
Connecting With Parents

● ●

Overview

When you hear the word "connection," what comes to mind? Being on the same page? Finding a common purpose or common ground? Feeling seen, heard, and valued? Connection is that moment when you see another, they see you, and you feel known. Our students seek it from their peers and teachers, we seek it from our colleagues and students, and the parents of our students seek it in the school community. Connecting with care lays the path toward partnering with families and building respectful relationships that lead to fruitful collaboration. When teachers actively seek and build positive connections with their students' families, students do better both academically and socially. Research conducted by the Global Family Research Project (Weiss, Lopez, and Caspe 2018) shows that one of the strongest predictors of children's learning, overall development, and well-being is family and community engagement. Parental involvement is a leading component of a child's success in school.

Connecting and Engaging With Parents

Where to begin? Connecting and engaging with parents takes an investment of time. Reflecting on your experiences as a student provides insight into your own understanding of and feelings about school-to-home connections. Think about the partnerships your parents had with your teachers. Which teacher(s) made school an inviting place for your family? What did the teacher(s) do to make school welcoming for your family? Which teacher(s) did your parents trust and speak highly of? What did the teacher(s) say and do to build and grow the relationship throughout the school year? How did the partnership between your parents and teacher(s) support your success? If you have children who are currently in school or who have finished school, which teacher(s) have you connected with? How did the teacher(s) make you feel welcomed and valued as a partner in your child's education? How did they maintain the connection throughout the school year?

Now reflect on your role as an educator. To teach our children well, we have to know them—individually, culturally, and developmentally. This extends to knowing and partnering with their families and valuing their families' contributions. Consider the perspective of your students' parents. Parents are the first and primary teachers of their children and want what is best for them. A parent's perspective on school is influenced by their own school experiences, their familiarity with the school, their beliefs about education, and the experiences their child has had during previous school years. These factors can positively or negatively influence a parent's feelings and ideas about school. It is important to keep this in mind so that you can seek and build connections with families from a place of empathy.

Parents are experts on their children and on their family's environment. They know how their child processes and responds to directions, what energizes them, what their interests are, what they delight in, and how they deal with disappointment. Parents are able to give us a fuller picture of their child. As teachers, we know about child development, the curriculum, and strategies and practices to help children learn. We are called to

"Parents"

Students come from homes with a variety of family structures. Students might be raised by grandparents, siblings, aunts and uncles, foster families, and other caregivers. All of these individuals are to be honored for devoting their time, attention, and love to raising children, and we include all of them in our thinking in this chapter.

It's difficult to find one word that encompasses all these caregivers. In this book, for ease of reading, we use the term "parent" to represent all the caregivers involved in a child's life.

orient, inform, and welcome families to the classroom and school community. Each of us—parents and teachers—has expertise to contribute as we work together toward a common interest: setting the student up for success. A strong foundation built on trust is paramount to a successful collaboration that values the input of all involved in raising the student. Parents are much more likely to work collaboratively to support the child's education when they trust that the teacher knows and appreciates their child.

Strategies for a Strong Connection

In approaching the school year, proactively set the table for families to join as partners in the yearlong journey, and envision ways to strengthen the connection daily, weekly, monthly, and in the spontaneous moments when you cross paths with the family. Devoting time and energy to building relationships with students and their families in the first six weeks of the school year sets a positive tone that allows parents to feel welcomed and valued. The strategies for connecting with families are similar to the strategies that apply to our partnerships with our colleagues and administration. In all of our communications with families, our goal is to create a collaborative school-home relationship.

Reach Out Early

Set a positive tone for the school year by reaching out, inviting, welcoming, and connecting with parents early with positive information about your classroom. Consider using both the time prior to the start of school and the first six weeks of school to introduce yourself, invite parents in to see your classroom, give a sneak peek at what the coming year holds, and provide information about ways to connect, including how they can contact you. Strategies for connection prior to the start of the school year include inviting families to visit and tour the classroom; sending an introductory letter, postcard, video, or email; and conducting listening conferences. Each of the grade-level-specific sections in this chapter offers additional suggestions about how to connect with your students' families.

Listen and Empathize

Invite parents to share their thoughts and insights about their child, and actively listen to show genuine interest. The information parents provide will help you teach their child. All parents want to do whatever they can to help their child to succeed in school. Reassure parents that they are welcome and that you value their input. Listen with openness, respond with understanding, and provide realistic and genuine feedback. Communicate positive intentions to parents by utilizing any of the following sentences or conversation starters:

- "I can tell this is really important to you."

- "Can you share more about that?"

- "What is something that has worked for your child that you are willing to share with me?"

- "I appreciate your bringing this to my attention."

- "It sounds like you are really thinking about what might best support your child. Here are some ways I can help."

Keep in mind that when parents are concerned about how their child is doing in school, they might be fearful and anxious and come across as defensive or adversarial. Our goal is to ease the parent's fear as we listen, gather information, and empathize, recognizing that parents are a valuable resource in solving any problems and misunderstandings.

Communicate Regularly and Consistently

By regularly informing parents about the goings-on of the classroom, you are investing in the partnership. Maintain regular positive communication with parents throughout the year. Keep the information brief, focused, and positive. Topics to share include classroom activities, the class's and their child's accomplishments, upcoming special projects or events, and developmental changes you might see in their child. Ensure that parents are informed of classroom and school happenings and that they understand the rationale behind the activities.

Try to follow a consistent schedule and format in communicating with families. If parents know what to expect and when to expect it, they are more likely to review and respond to your communication. Consider technology tools to aid in communication, keeping in mind the family's preferred way of receiving information, which you can gather through beginning-of-the-year surveys and conferences.

Let Parents Know How They Can Help

All parents want their children to succeed. Parental involvement is a leading component of a child's success in school. Invite parents to take an active role in their child's education. Let them know what they can do to help their child. Survey parents about their interests and skills and invite them to share their hobbies, expertise, and family traditions as part of special classroom projects and activities. Show that you value the contributions that parents bring to the community. When families are connected, teachers feel more supported.

In forging connections with families, it is important to remember that parents and teachers share similar hopes and goals for students. In deciding the mode of communication to use with your students' parents, use your knowledge of the individual families and consider their preferences (email, newsletter, text, phone). Also keep in mind any need they might have for translation. You will also want to make sure that the systems you develop for communicating will be ones you can manage over the course of the school year.

The grade-level sections in this chapter suggest and offer practical, specific, and realistic ways to actively build and strengthen connections between school and home, to address particular grade-level concerns, to communicate with parents, to hold productive parent-teacher meetings, and to involve parents in events and activities. When we make parents valued partners in the education of their children, all involved become more connected with school, resulting in our students becoming more fully engaged and enthusiastic.

Grade ❸

At the end of the school year, a third grade teacher received this letter from a parent:

> *I want to take a minute to thank you for everything you have done for Isabella this year. I have seen her excited to go to school. She is reading every night without any reminders and she does her homework independently. This has been a rough year for our family, especially with the divorce and illnesses. I always knew she was safe with you and had someone to talk to, even if she kept things inside at home. I appreciate your frequent communication and open door. We are grateful for you.*

This letter from the last day of school was a result of a year of developing connections, maintaining collaboration, and building a school-home partnership to support the social, emotional, and academic success of the students in the class. As you read this section, keep this end-of-year note tucked in the back of your mind, or maybe recall a similar one that you have received from a student's family member. There will certainly be some challenging experiences with parents over the course of any school year; however, we want to remember these lasting, positive messages, which guide and reinforce why we do what we do.

Building and Strengthening Connections

Throughout the third grade year, relationships with families will go through three distinct phases: bold beginnings, mindful middles, and effective endings. As you read about these three phases in the following pages, and begin to digest and reflect on them, consider how you might adapt the ideas presented to meet your particular communication style. The success of our students is grounded in the strength of the relationships we can build to bridge the school-home connection.

Bold Beginnings

Moving into third grade is a distinctive jump for students in elementary school. Third graders' stamina is increasing, and they are more independent in reading and writing. Math concepts are building upon one another. In social studies, students are applying their reading and writing skills while learning about more abstract concepts, including civic standards, the nature of relationships, and their own position in the world. In science, students are increasing their understanding of the scientific process and applying critical thinking skills as they learn more about engineering and technology, and how to incorporate mathematics into these areas. Third graders are growing their academic competencies and learning how to study and take notes. Depending upon your district, third grade often marks the beginning of state assessments too.

Our job is to support both the students and their families. We can get them off to a positive start by connecting with them before the school year starts. Here are some ways to facilitate a bold beginning:

- **Before-school visits.** Consider inviting families to visit and tour the classroom prior to the start of the year, if this is not currently a practice in your school. This informal event can allow students, and their families, to see how the room is arranged and view where supplies are kept, and it gives you the chance to make face-to-face contact with both students and parents. Students appreciate being able to find their desk before school starts as well. You may decide to be available for a full day for families to visit at their leisure, or you may have a few windows of availability for a few days, such as Monday, Wednesday, and Friday afternoon from one o'clock to three o'clock, to allow flexibility for this initial meeting. This positive experience will allow families to feel known, and you can answer any questions they may have so you, the students, and their families can begin a successful school year together.

- **Letter or video.** Some teachers send a welcome letter prior to the start of the school year. You can introduce yourself, sharing an overview of your professional experience and a few facts about yourself. Another option is to create a video recording that can be shared, so students and families get to see you and hear your voice, and you can welcome them with an inviting and personal tone. Whether you send a letter or share a video, you can let students and their families know about what they will learn over the course of the year and the materials they will need, and share the daily schedule.

- **Questionnaire or survey.** It's also helpful to provide a survey for parents to complete, either electronically in advance of the first day of school or on paper to be returned on the first day of school. A well-designed survey can give you insight into the children in your class and their parents' hopes and goals for them. You can also find out parents' preferred method of communication and the best time of day for contact, in addition to their child's interests, strengths, allergies, and any other pertinent information that will help you support the child throughout the year.

See the appendix, p. 329, for a beginning-of-the-year survey.

- **First-week-of-school communication.** Starting from a place of positivity and utilizing your reinforcing language, set a schedule for yourself to make a connection with each family during the first week or two of school to share information, insights, and observations about their child's transition and what you are learning about them. If you have a class of twenty children, select four families each day to connect with, using the preferred method of communication they have noted in their initial survey. In the first days of school you will have already learned about each student's hopes and dreams, pets at home, hobbies, and interests. Sharing what you have learned will allow the parents to feel their child is known. They will feel that your interest in their child is genuine, which is an important component in building trust. This will be helpful in case you need to communicate about more difficult or challenging situations in the future.

- **Formal Back to School Night.** Each school and grade-level team will organize this event in their own way. Some schools will have the whole third grade team share with all third grade parents about the curriculum and expectations for the year, prior to individual classroom visits. Some teachers and schools have the students attend with the parents, empowering them to give the classroom tour. This is not a time for individual conferences about student progress, and it is important to set that expectation from the beginning. Some teachers will organize a back to school night so that it includes a Morning Meeting so parents can see how students begin each day feeling that they belong, are significant, and can have fun learning together.

- **Digital media.** With so much of our lives being digital, the use of a website, social media, or other platform can provide a view of what students are doing in class—starting with the first week of school. Maintaining a student-centered philosophy, you may invite students to share and write postings as they reflect on their learning from the week. Remember that if you plan to post students' photos to a class or school social media platform, it is important to ensure that families have first completed media consent forms.

Mindful Middles

Throughout the course of the year, your use of digital communication and weekly or monthly newsletters will let families know what students are working on. Keeping current and consistent with the information you are sharing is important, so while it can be tempting to want to use multiple methods of communication, consider the sustainability of maintaining these methods throughout the year. Here are some ways to communicate with families:

- **Friday letter.** In some classrooms, students write a letter to a family member on Fridays, talking about what they learned during the week, their current goals, and what they consider to be a source of pride. Family members may write a letter back too. As a teacher, you can use this as an opportunity to share a comment about the student's success and even suggest an area of growth to focus on in the week ahead.

- **Individual updates.** While report cards and comments provide parents with quarterly updates on their child's progress, communication should be more regular than these district benchmarks. It is far better to give parents regular updates than for them to feel surprised about a situation with their child that you have seen unfolding over a few weeks. Although there will be times when you will need to communicate about areas of concern, you should usually keep these individual updates brief and positive. While it can be easy to notice what is not going well, sharing a positive note about a success will be even more powerful.

Effective Endings

Even when the school year is drawing to a close, communication and collaboration should remain strong. You have worked hard to establish familial relationships all year, and the classroom community has grown and developed.

- **Celebration of learning.** Consider having an end-of-year celebration of learning, in which children get to share student-selected pieces from their portfolios. This can be a special, memorable event, and it can also empower students to reflect and to grow their skills and confidence. As students will have created projects and authentic learning experiences through Academic Choice, they can help to make this special occasion their own. For example, after doing a reader's theater unit, students in one class were inspired to create their own scripts and in small groups reenact some of their favorite activities and projects from throughout the year. This cross-curricular experience highlighted the importance of building a class community.

- **Meaningful reflections.** As you have students reflect on their hopes and dreams and growth throughout the year, including parents in this process can further solidify the school-home connection that you have fostered all year. Some teachers send an email to parents asking them to share positive experiences and growth they have seen in their child over the course of the year. Others will invite families to write a letter to the child, to share pleasant memories from throughout the year and acknowledge the growth the child has experienced. It is important to keep these reflections positive; the end of one school year launches excitement and enthusiasm for the next. The purpose of these steps is to ensure students feel supported, successful, and ready to work to their potential in the year to come.

Communicating With Families

As you are planning communication with families, keep the follow three ideas in mind:

1. **Power of positivity.** It can be easy to reach out only when there is a concern or incident to discuss; however, building rapport with parents comes from knowing their child well and sharing positive updates. Consider scheduling a reminder in your email or writing on your calendar which child's parents you will contact each day. Making a point of connecting with each family monthly will allow them to see the successes in their child's day, while keeping the lines of communication open. Yes, you are juggling a lot, but this proactive practice can help you when challenging concerns arise.

2. **Challenging situations.** It is important to plan how you will tackle the challenging situations that arise. Parents should hear from you about events that arise before they hear it from their child. While some parents may find email to be their preferred means of communication, depending on the nature of the incident or concern, a quick phone conversation can help you avoid the challenges email can present. In writing, it can be hard to discern exactly what is being said, the tone can be misinterpreted, and it may raise more questions and concerns on the part of the reader. If you have academic or behavior concerns that do not reflect one particular incident but are ongoing, and you'd like to just have a conversation about it, using email to set up a time to talk is appropriate. Make sure you give parents an idea of what you want to discuss. Having an idea of the nature of the conversation to come will ease parental worries.

3. **Document communication.** In the moment, we may feel confident we will remember the specifics, but days are busy and parent communications are many. Keeping a phone call log with the date and time, the person you spoke to, and a few key takeaways from the conversation will help you to maintain accurate records for future reference. This can also be helpful information to share with administration and colleagues if the need arises. In your email, consider keeping a "Parent Communication" folder with a subfolder inside for each student. This is easy to set up quickly, and it will keep you organized and your inbox emptier.

Special Concerns of Third Grade Parents

Certain developmental characteristics are hallmarks of third grade, and parents are often concerned about them. At the beginning of the year, proactively plan for how you can share information on these topics, so parents can recognize that their concerns are shared. It is important to always be clear, honest, and positive with parents. Taking time to hear and acknowledge parents' concerns, and listening to their input, will make them feel valued as an expert on their child.

Between the open house and the initial parent-teacher conference, provide parents with the developmental information for third graders. Make sure that parents are aware that developmental growth occurs at different rates for each child and that children's physical, cognitive, and social growth rates may differ. As parents are working with their child on homework and observing them at home, sometimes they may have concerns about academic skills or behaviors that they notice, and it's helpful for them to learn that these academic skills or behaviors are developmentally appropriate.

Reading and Writing

Parents listen to their children read, and they watch their children as they write. They may be concerned about messy handwriting, and they may see that the reading is more developed than the writing. This is to be expected of third graders, who are so eager to get their ideas down and who strive to fill up as many pages as they can that neatness is compromised along the way.

You can reassure parents by sharing with them that the goal in third grade is to encourage children's ability to develop ideas and compose complex thoughts. In third grade, it is common for students to read fluently but to struggle more with comprehension, as they are learning about character feelings and traits, and synthesizing, analyzing, and consolidating their understanding of texts and structures.

Grading and Progress

Parents of third graders are often increasingly concerned about grades and standardized tests. At schools with gifted and talented programs, parents may be concerned about how to get their child into these programs and whether they should hire a tutor so their child can get into the advanced math class. For many parents, the jargon of education and assessments can also be difficult to understand. From DRA to BAS and IEPs, schools use many abbreviations. We can support parents during this time by helping them to get a clear picture of where their child is and what the benchmark expectations are to measure progress.

Prepare yourself for the discrepancies that data can show, as test scores may be different from results of classroom evaluations. One parent emailed a teacher to question this discrepancy: "I am concerned about my child in math. The standardized tests showed my child was partially effective, however every test this year has been above 90 percent and she never needs help with homework."

Helping parents navigate the analysis of assessments is important. In the case above, the teacher took time to explain that the testing was a snapshot of two days in the third grader's year. Students are just learning how to take these assessments, which often require a level of stamina they have not needed in the past and test-taking strategies they are just learning. The teacher's acknowledgment of the child's daily performance, along with positive comments based on classroom observations and assessments, helped to ease the parent's concerns.

Homework

Homework is a highly debated topic, with varying philosophies. Do you work in a school that does not give homework? If that's the case, remember to instill the habit of being a daily reader in your students, so they can enjoy books when they leave your classroom. Many studies point to the benefits of nightly reading as a precursor to future success. If you do give homework, remember that this can be difficult for families to manage, especially for those with children who require assistance to complete the tasks.

Here are some strategies to consider when assigning homework:

- **Make homework manageable.** Large packets and long-term projects can be overwhelming, especially since developmentally, third graders do not have sufficiently advanced time management skills to handle this work independently. Instead of asking students to complete a page of twenty math problems, consider having them choose any eight they want. The element of choice is important, and if they have learned the skills and know the material, they will not learn more from completing twenty than they will from completing eight.

- **Create purposeful and interesting assignments.** We know third graders love to share their personal experiences and make connections with others. Think about how homework can lay the foundation for the next day. If you're going to work on graphing the next day, ask students to create a survey question and then get responses from five people. Students will be eager for math the next day so they can share their ideas and data. If you are starting a personal narrative unit, ask students to make a list of three events that happened in their life that they think someone would be interested to learn more about. The next day, use an interactive learning structure to let students share these ideas, a prewriting experience that will prepare them to put pen to paper.

- **Teach and practice homework skills and expectations.** Just as you model how students should complete their in-class daily work, you should do the same for homework. Even if you are giving only bite-size amounts, you want high-quality results. Setting aside time in class at the beginning of the year for one or more practice homework sessions will allow you to observe students and support them in developing the skills that will help them to work successfully and independently at home. This is important, as allowing expectations to slide on homework can have a negative impact on the work students complete in class. However, there will also be times when you will need to demonstrate empathy and flexibility, giving students a break from homework if they are dealing with challenging circumstances. Remember, knowing each of your students will be important for your expectations. For example, students who are traveling between two or more homes each week have a lot to manage, and at times, this means leaving a book at mom's house or forgetting their folder at grandma's.

- **Provide clear written directions.** It can be tempting to ask children to copy down homework directions. This can be challenging for many third graders, and the expectations can get lost in translation. Provide students with clear written directions. When possible, provide an example. This will help students to be successful, and it will also help family members who are checking and supporting students with homework.

- **Offer clear expectations for parents.** You make sure students know homework expectations; the same should be true for parents. Some students are in situations where they must do all homework on their own, without someone to guide them. Other students have overly eager parents who may take on the assignment and project themselves, and need to be reminded that this is their *child's* work. Let parents know where assignments can be found. Do the parents need to check an assignment book and initial that the child read it and completed the work? Does the child need to go online for homework? About how long should homework take on a daily basis? Some educators feel it should take students about twenty to thirty minutes, in addition to time for independent reading, while other districts will have different guidelines and expectations. What should parents do if their child is consistently struggling with homework and taking a long time to complete it, going far beyond the district expectations? Only you can provide these guidelines to parents. Including a frequently asked questions section on your website or in the beginning-of-the-year letter can help parents. It can also save time for you by addressing all of these matters at once, instead of fielding many questions about homework during the year. This will allow you to focus your time and energy to support those students and families who have the greatest concerns about homework and helping them develop a plan for success.

Holding Productive Parent-Teacher Meetings

Parents are experts on their own children. They require our active listening to learn more about their child outside of school as well as about any concerns they may have. We must empathize and remember the unique nature of each student in our classroom. You may find in-person parent-teacher meetings to be more stressful than other forms of communication; you are not alone. Many parents feel the same way, concerned about what you will say about their child's progress or perhaps reliving memories of their own school experiences, which can make them uncomfortable.

Parent-teacher conferences should occur within the first marking period so you can proactively discuss the child's progress and ensure a successful start for the year. As the year unfolds, and once you have established a home-school partnership, you may meet to discuss a particular concern. Here are a few tips for your initial meeting:

- **Prepare in advance.** When you reach out to let parents know the date and time of the conference, offer them the opportunity to share in advance any questions or concerns they have, telling them that the time together will go quickly and you want to make sure you address their questions and concerns. This will also give you time to gather additional data or observations about the child to support your discussion of these topics.

- **Ease the anxiety.** You may wish to start the parent meeting with a personal note, such as: "I was thinking about Greyson when I was at the bookstore the other day and saw a new book series about outer space adventures. He was telling me that the best part of his day is reading books about space with you at bedtime." An anecdote, personal story, or connection will allow the parent to see that you know their child. It will make them smile and laugh; as we know, laughter helps to ease tension and will start the conference on a positive note. Consider ahead of time questions you might ask, such as:

  ○ "What is your child enjoying about school?"

  ○ "What are some of your child's interests at home?"

- **Provide note-taking materials.** In addition to having student work samples to show parents, keep sticky notes or paper and writing implements on the table. While some parents will come with a tablet or notebook, others may need something on which to jot down notes as you are sharing. As parents raise concerns or ask questions, you can write them down too. They will feel that you are hearing them, even if they have asked a question that you will need to look into and get back to them on. Yes, it is honest and professional to tell parents that you are going to look into something and get back to them. For example, at one meeting, a parent asked, "Do you see my child being stressed and twirling his hair when he reads? We have noticed a bald spot at home and want to make sure he is okay emotionally." The teacher replied, "I'm going to make a note to observe him carefully when he reads. I'll get back to you at the end of the week to let you know."

Formula for Success

You have prepared for the conference by seeking parental input, and you began with a fun and uplifting story about the child to show you know them well. You have created a positive start to the meeting; now it is important to keep the following in mind:

1. **Remember to listen.** Your body language will let parents know you are sincere and genuinely interested in what they have to say.

2. **Ensure conversations are two-sided.** It can be easy to talk at parents; however, talking with them will make them feel valued and comfortable sharing insights and asking questions.

3. **Highlight the positive.** Parents will be eager to hear how their child is doing, and you can reassure them by telling them about their child's strengths. While you may also need to point out areas for improvement, it is important for parents to hear, especially in your first meeting, that you see the good in their child.

Involving Parents in Events and Activities

The classroom community consists of the teacher, students, and their families. Inviting parents into the classroom expands the richness of individual experiences and offers you additional sets of hands. Remember the initial survey you sent at the beginning of the year? If you included a checklist for parents to note how they would like to volunteer in the classroom, you can plan ahead for ways to include families in your classroom.

See the appendix, p. 329, for a sample volunteer checklist.

While some parents have schedules that are flexible enough for them to spend time helping out in the classroom, others may not have that flexibility but will still want to be part of and contribute to the community. Offering a variety of ways to get involved will enable everyone to feel that they are making a difference. Here are a few ways parents can help:

- **Have families share aspects of their cultures, jobs, or personal experiences with the class.** Whether bringing food in from their culture, sharing how they use math in their job at a bakery, or talking about what it was like to build homes for Habitat for Humanity, everyone has something to offer!

- **Invite parents to support classroom activities by preparing materials in advance at home.** Are you doing an experiment that requires each student to have preassembled materials? Did you laminate flashcards for a math fact game that will need to be cut out? Parents can help out by doing these projects at home. For parents who are unable to get into school for one reason or another, their gift of time makes them feel they are contributing, and it helps you too.

- **Include parents in classroom celebrations.** You may have home-room parents who coordinate these events for the whole class. While a whole-group activity can be fun, you may also wish to encourage parents to take charge of small-group centers to support classroom management during classroom celebrations. One teacher shared, "After trying four centers during a classroom party—snack, game, craft, and story—I would never go back. Each child got the attention they needed, and it was easy for parents at each center. I was able to circulate, and the celebration was well structured, with each rotation providing the perfect amount of time for students to stay on task and have fun!" This teacher then used this format throughout the year, including for winter and spring parties and for celebrations around cultural studies.

It is important that all volunteers understand your guidelines and expectations. Within our classrooms there is a certain amount of confidentiality required to protect the students. Each child is growing and developing, requiring empathy and understanding. Consider holding a meeting for parent volunteers to discuss your expectations. In addition, be aware that sometimes the child of a volunteer acts entirely differently when their parent comes to visit. For instance, the child may be very excited or seek attention by asking the parent for help when you know they can be independent. It can be uncomfortable to redirect a child in front of their parent; relying on your reminding and redirecting language can help. (See Chapter 3.) The class is always watching you and how you are keeping them safe by ensuring consistent enforcement of the expectations.

Sample Guidelines for Parent Volunteers

Providing parent volunteers with clear, consistent classroom information and guidelines sets everyone up for success. You might offer something like this:

Class Routines
- Hand signal/chime. When I raise my hand or ring the chime, that's our class signal to stop working and look at me. Adults can help by doing the same.

- Bathroom sign-out. Students may sign out to use the bathroom on their own. They can help explain our process if you have questions.

Volunteer Guidelines
- Adult voice. Adult voices can sometimes carry farther than we think. When working with a student (or a small group), make sure to use a quiet voice so others can stay focused on their work.

- Discipline. If a student is refusing to do work or being at all disruptive, let me know and I will handle the situation.

- Privacy. As a volunteer in our classroom, you may see a student struggling. Please respect the privacy of all students by not discussing student-related issues outside of our classroom.

- Anything else. If you have any questions at all, please let me know.

Advice for Tricky Situations

Whether you are in your first or twentieth year in education, tricky situations will occur, and some uncomfortable questions and concerns can arise. There is also bound to be a situation you have never experienced. It is always important to listen to and empathize with parents, maintaining the professionalism and empathetic approach that you have been utilizing with them from the beginning. Frequent proactive communication with parents can establish a rapport that will help overcome this challenging situation. It is important to always remember that everyone wants the best for the child, even if each person's vision is different.

"I thought about retaining my child in first grade, but now I have decided it should happen this year," a parent confided to a third grade teacher. Unsure how to handle this situation, the teacher shared it with her administrator and received the collegial support of specialists in the building. Together, they generated goals and an action plan and documented the child's progress. Research and developmental expectations were shared to help the parent understand why this was not a decision in the best interest of the child. In this situation, the administrator's involvement and the team approach allowed the teacher to feel supported; it also showed the parent how many staff members wanted to support the child's growth and well-being.

"I'm feeling uneasy about this meeting," a novice teacher shared with her mentor about an upcoming parent conference. "I feel like sometimes the parent asks questions that I'm not prepared to answer." The mentor sat in on the meeting and was able to draw on their years of experience to answer some of the unexpected questions. When in doubt, lean on your colleagues. It can be helpful to know you have support in the room, and someone who can also document the events. Consider asking your literacy or math interventionist, mentor, guidance counselor, or administrator to join you during these tricky situations. Whether you are meeting in person or on a conference call, feeling supported will make you more comfortable. Yes, these encounters are challenging in the moment, but they will give you a bank of experience and insight to draw upon when facing the next tricky situation.

Remember, documenting parent communication and student progress and observations is important! You have a classroom of individuals with unique needs and circumstances. Maintaining communication logs and notes will provide an invaluable record. As much as you may remember the conversation specifics in the moment, as time goes by and the school year progresses, those details will inevitably blur and you will be grateful for your notes.

Pause and Ponder

- What bold beginnings will be your focus?

- How will you ensure a mindful middle for communication during the year?

- How will you plan for effective endings to the school year?

- What concerns do you want to proactively address with families?

- How will you welcome all families into the classroom community?

- To whom can you go for help with tricky situations?

Final Thought

"When families and teachers collaborate on behalf of children, they create windows of light for generations to follow."

—Unknown

Grade ④

The teacher's phone buzzed in the late morning on a Saturday with an unread message from a parent. The teacher opened it, anxious about what she would need to clarify on Monday and hesitant as to whether or not she should wait until Monday to open the message at all. But upon opening, she saw that the message read, "Angel told me I had to send you this picture of him right away. This is the soccer trophy his team won today. We hope you're having a great weekend!" The fourth grader beamed proudly out of the attached picture, holding up his trophy. The teacher excitedly asked the student about it on Monday morning, highlighting a clear connection between school and home.

Your students will have had years of school experiences before entering fourth grade, and so will their parents. Parents are also bringing with them their own educational experiences and perhaps those of their older children, as well as their expertise about their own child. You are coming into the space with your expertise in curriculum, child development, and methods that help students learn. Working together, teachers and parents can support student growth and learning. This section will offer suggestions and considerations about connecting with parents throughout the year as you work together to support their fourth grader.

Building and Strengthening Connections

As you look at your class list before the year begins, you may wish to use Chip Wood's *Yardsticks* (2017) as a reference when considering where students are developmentally as they enter fourth grade. You may even have a letter from the student or work samples from the previous year. You may also use this time to begin to envision how you will build positive relationships with parents and cultivate these connections throughout the year.

Build connections with parents before and at the beginning of the school year. Consider the following ways to communicate:

- **Mail or email letters to your students and families before the first day of school.** In the letter, introduce yourself and say a little about the main academic and social and emotional concepts they can expect to encounter in fourth grade. Include your contact information as well as the date and time of back to school night or other times when you are available to meet with parents.

- **Send parents a questionnaire.** Some things you might consider asking about include preferred language(s) for notes home and for meetings, preferred method of communication, and information about skills, hobbies, and jobs. As teachers, we can approach all parents' knowledge and skills as resources and strengths, or funds of knowledge (González, Moll, and Amanti 2005). This knowledge can be used to engage families in the classroom and to support your students' concept and skill development. Consider ways that parent skill sets might connect to the curriculum, or even consider working with parents to set up partnerships with local organizations, as fourth graders really like to help people and places in the community.

- **Ask parents about their hopes and dreams for their child's fourth grade year.** Talk with parents about two to three of their own hopes and dreams for their child in fourth grade by asking, "What's your biggest hope for your child this year?" or "What do you think is most important for your child to learn this year?" Offer parents some examples of social-emotional and academic hopes and dreams, such as the following:

  - "I wish he had more friends."

  - "I want her to like school more."

  - "I hope he reads more and enjoys it."

  - "I want her to learn her math facts."

Discussing hopes and dreams can be a way to get to know parents and students, and also to get an idea of their past experiences in school. After the first weeks of school, you may share the child's hopes and dreams with their parent. (See Chapter 3 for a discussion of students' hopes and dreams.) You can use these student- and parent-created hopes and dreams to guide parent-teacher conferences throughout the year, especially if you have only ten or fifteen minutes to meet each time.

- **When meeting with parents, ask open-ended questions and spend most of the time listening.** Parents are the experts on their children. Parents have their own experiences and perspectives related to their child's education. Giving families the time and space to meet at the beginning of the year to teach you about their child can help to start the school year in a positive way. Resist the temptation to have your first impressions of students or parents clouded by your colleagues' past interactions and perspectives. Stay curious and empathetic in order to listen more deeply. Some questions you might ask include:

  - "What is your child good at?"

  - "What and how do they like to play?"

  - "What is hard for your child?"

- **Get to know parents by asking how they would like you to address them.** Practice pronouncing their name correctly, and use their names throughout conversations to build rapport and establish a foundation of respect.

- **Use Morning Meeting as a way to get to know students and their families.** The sharing component of Morning Meeting is a great way to incorporate students' cultures into the curriculum, including teaching the class about language, clothes, art, music, history, or traditions. It might also be an opportunity to incorporate lessons about primary sources by asking students to complete short, low-risk interviews with a family member or caregiver and share what they learned with the class, such as a favorite childhood memory or an important food served at celebrations or get-togethers.

- **Consider short, monthly check-ins with parents.** Call or email parents once each month or every six weeks. Talk about something positive you notice their child doing, such as helping other students to think deeply about the read-aloud by asking purposeful questions, growth in reading stamina, or improvement related to something you have previously spoken about; try to avoid adding in advice. By fourth grade, many parents have gotten used to having little communication with teachers or to being contacted only when there is a problem. These short, positive conversations can go a long way in building connections throughout the year.

- **Invite parents to be part of unit celebrations.** For example, during an immigration unit students might interview a family member about their family's immigration story. Parents can come to school as part of the celebration as students share their stories.

- **Invite parents in for monthly get-togethers.** Many schools have a monthly period when parents are invited to join their child's class for an activity. Consider starting with a short Morning Meeting structure and encourage parents to participate. Then move into an activity related to a topic that the class is studying or ask a parent in advance to lead an activity. Parents can lead a how-to on such topics as calligraphy or origami, or can show students how to prepare a simple recipe. Encourage families to lead in their first language while modeling the steps, or invite their child to help with explaining the steps.

Special Concerns of Fourth Grade Parents

The developmental characteristics of fourth graders are important to keep in mind in order to support parents with common questions and concerns related to this age. Explain to parents that each individual child is unique, but knowing common patterns can help support their child in their growth. Parents appreciate that they're not alone when it comes to common behaviors of their fourth graders.

At the beginning of the year, parents may be confused, worried, or even frustrated with the moodiness and anxiety of their nine-year-old child. Parents are often relieved to hear that this is normal and that nine-year-olds need a lot of encouragement, listening, and understanding to support these expected behavioral characteristics.

Parents of fourth graders may begin to have questions and concerns about their child's hormones and changing bodies. For example, some parents may ask for support in reassuring their daughters about bathroom accommodations during menstruation or information on who they can go to, such as the nurse's office staff, if they need feminine products.

Parents may also have questions or concerns about extracurricular activities, especially if they are offered by the school. Students at this age are solidifying their likes and dislikes and this is a great time for them to dive into after-school or weekend programs. Parents may ask about opportunities that the school provides, and they might ask about activities offered by community groups. Be ready to share where parents can find organized sports teams, dance classes, instrument rentals, and so on.

Depending on your school and state, a frequent concern for fourth grade parents is testing. They might be interested in their child opting out of testing, or they might have concerns about the pressures and stress of high-stakes testing. As educators, we also have our own beliefs about testing. Your school may have a way that they would like you to handle these conversations, but in general, you can use envisioning language and reinforcing language to keep these conversations positive and matter-of-fact. (See Chapter 3 for more on teacher language.)

Connecting with parents is about two-way communication: you are asking parents for advice and ideas, and they are also coming to you with questions and concerns. Being proactive about what some of these common questions might be can support you in cultivating those relationships with parents.

Communicating With Parents

Here are some ways to support your communication with parents:

- **Choose a method of communication.** Find one method that you can use throughout the year—preferably one used by the entire school, so parents can use the same method for all of their children in the school. Certain apps include ways of translating messages that also replicate text messages.

- **Set a day of the week to send out brief, positive comments to parents.** Sending a short message, perhaps even including a picture of only their child performing a task, will let parents know what their child has been working on in class, and it will also let them know that communication lines are open and you are available if they have questions or ideas. It will also give them an idea of what to talk to their child about: so often at dismissal, we hear parents ask, "How was your day?" and the fourth grader may answer with a generic "Fine" or go into a description of a game that was played at recess. Your brief, personalized check-in can give parents an idea of current academic content or happenings that are more specific than daily homework assignments or monthly newsletters.

- **Consider working with the grade-level team on rotating a monthly fourth grade newsletter.** Better yet, consider ways to have students write or take photographs for the monthly newsletter. When students bring the newsletter home, they will have more to say about it if they feel ownership over the writing and photos.

- **Empathize with parents.** Parents bring with them their own educational experiences, sometimes from a different country with different norms and ways of doing things. There are parents who are uncertain about or even skeptical of the educational establishment and keep their distance due to their own past experiences. Some parents may come from cultures where there isn't a two-way school-home partnership, but rather it is expected that those two worlds are separate. Some cultures revere educators, and it is expected that the teacher will tell the child to behave at home. Understand that sometimes both you and the parents are doing the best you can to negotiate meaning with one another in an effort to support their child's success in school.

- **Consider parents as a resource in problem-solving.** Approaching parents with curiosity about what they have to say about their child can be illuminating for teachers. You will likely learn a lot about your own tendencies when parents give you tips on what works for their child at home. By going to parents to ask for advice, you are sending

Practical Strategies for Different Communication Styles

There are many benefits to learning about the cultures of our families. As was discussed in Chapter 4, embedding reflections and representations of our students' cultures throughout our curriculum and everyday classroom activities is a culturally responsive practice that allows our students to deepen their learning and sets them up for academic and social-emotional success.

Learning about the cultures of our families can support our advocacy of students and families as well. For example, an English as a New Language (ENL) teacher learned that one of her students was being evaluated for an individualized education plan based on a referral from the classroom teacher. Part of the evaluation was going to be performed with a psychologist speaking Mandarin, the language that official school records had indicated was the child's primary language at home. Upon further research, the ENL teacher learned that the student had spent his first four years with his grandparents in the Fujian province of China, so his first language was actually Fujianese, a different dialect than Mandarin. The ENL teacher made many phone calls and was eventually able to find a Fujianese translator to support the psychologist's interview. This child and his parents were able to use English, Mandarin, and Fujianese to get a more thorough and accurate evaluation because of this teacher's research.

Learning about the cultures of our families will ultimately support our partnerships with them. Some areas to be aware of:

- Nonverbal communication behavior
  - Appropriate physical distance and positioning between speakers
  - Meaning of eye contact
  - Appropriateness of touching
  - Respectful body postures

- Conversation norms
  - Who begins conversations
  - How silences may be used in conversation
  - Ways of bringing up sensitive topics

- Values related to children's learning
  - Ways adults teach children discipline, exercise authority, and reinforce rules and values
  - Attitudes toward cooperative or independent learning
  - Ways adults support children in gaining independence

- Cultural history
  - History of education, science, the arts, and so on
  - Politics
  - Folk heroes and legends

While it's important to learn about the cultures of our families, it is also important to remember that not all characteristics or values will be the same for all individuals within a particular cultural group. While you should do your research and look for information from different sources, you should also use what you know about the individual families. Remember that just as you will be adapting your communication style to accommodate theirs, they will also be adapting their communication style to their perception of yours. You both will be negotiating.

the message that they are the experts on their kids, and that their expertise is valuable in this relationship.

● **Keep in mind the different backgrounds of parents.** In some cultures it is considered insulting to teachers for parents to offer suggestions or advice about teaching their child. Some parents may feel uncomfortable because of their own negative experiences with school or because they fear that their English is not proficient enough to have a meaningful conversation about their child's education. Assume that all parents care about their child's education. We must find their most comfortable ways of communicating in order to build a partnership. There may be family engagement counselors who can offer suggestions and support in your school, district, or community.

Holding Productive Parent-Teacher Meetings

Parent-teacher conferences hold a lot of weight each year. They are often scheduled to correlate with report cards and tend to be a time when the teacher tells the parents how their child is doing in school. If we are truly following the guiding principle around teachers and parents working together, we want meetings to happen throughout the year, in different ways, and really emphasize two-way communication. You might consider thinking about parent-teacher conferences in two categories: adult-led conferences and student-led conferences.

Adult-Led Conferences

For an adult-led conference, prepare notes that you can share with the parent(s), including current goals for the child, areas of strength, areas for improvement, upcoming goals, and additional notes. These notes may also include questions to ask parents that will help you make a plan together—action steps for what the teacher can do at school and what the parents can do at home to support the child reaching their goals.

Students can also put together a portfolio of work they want to highlight for the teacher to show parents. This may include work that they are proud of for any number of reasons: maybe it was really challenging for the child and the work highlights their persistence, or maybe they directly included reflections about how they could improve their work. You can set aside a little time each Friday for students to collect these items in a portfolio and write down why they chose each item to represent their learning from the week, giving you and students time to self-assess weekly. After reviewing the portfolio, parents could also be given the option of writing a note to add to it for their child to see or even a video that they could record and send to you later to add to a digital portfolio. You may want to offer sentence stem prompts to a family (in various languages, if applicable) in order to give them some ideas of what they might say. Here are some sentence stems you might use:

- "I noticed that . . . "
- "I'm proud of . . . "
- "I know you sometimes have difficulty with . . . "
- "I'm glad to see you're working hard on . . . "
- "I can help by . . ."

It is important to remember that while this meeting may connect directly to report cards, you should also hold meetings leading up to this one in which parents can have many opportunities to see their child's classwork and how students are graded. In addition, you might send assessments or work home or post feedback to an online platform. Perhaps you have regular reflection sheets that students complete that can be sent home to be shared with parents. You might make copies of these reflection sheets and call parents in order to talk with them about them and respond to any questions they might have. (Keeping copies of the reflection sheets can also be useful in case the originals get lost in a backpack!) If a family speaks a language other than English at home and the reflection sheets are completed in English, consider calling each month with a translator in order to support the child's communication with their family.

Student-Led Conferences

Another option for a formal parent-teacher conference would be to host student-led conferences. These meetings tend to take longer (twenty to thirty minutes), but they challenge students to take responsibility for their learning and keep the meeting focused on the child. For families that include English language learners, students can also lead the conference in the language spoken at home. Alternatively, you might consider having the first formal conference be adult-led and the second formal conference be student-led, with plenty of check-ins in between. As fourth graders get older, they tend to demonstrate the characteristics of ten-year-olds—taking pride in their schoolwork and appreciating being noticed for their efforts—so a student-led conference would also be developmentally appropriate. There are several elements to consider with student-led conferences:

> ## Virtual and Phone Meetings
>
> Ask parents about their preferred method of communication for a meeting. Sometimes parents will say they are comfortable with a virtual meeting, in which case you can share digital copies of the child's portfolio. However, if a parent prefers to talk on the phone, which could be for any number of reasons, try to get creative: send a picture of student work in advance via text, email, or app so that parents have a point of reference in your meeting.

- **Inform students and parents early on, as this may be a new concept.** Bring it up early and often, so students get used to the idea. Providing weekly opportunities for students to reflect and collect work samples in their portfolio will support them in getting ready for the conference.

- **Invite students to select work samples for their portfolio each week and add a short reflection about the work chosen.** They could also include a longer reflection about the work overall. Additionally, the portfolio can include goals the student plans to focus on for the next marking period.

- **To prepare for the conference, role-play with students.** In this case, students could get in groups of two or three, where one or two students play the role of the parent, while the third plays the role of the student, leading the conference. Then students switch roles.

- **After the conference, give families the opportunity to bring the portfolio home to really look through it together.** Eventually students bring the portfolio back in order to continue adding to it for the next marking period.

- **Invite students and parents to write a reflection about the conference.** Offer sentence stems for both to support the process. Here are some sentence stems for parent reflections:

  - "I'm proud of . . ."
  - "I noticed that . . ."
  - "Keep up the good work on . . ."
  - "I see you're working hard at . . ."
  - "We can make a plan together to . . ."

Whichever formal conference option you choose, student learning, reflecting, and autonomy are really at the center of these meetings. If you or parents would like to talk in private, you can schedule another meeting. Parent meetings and check-ins should happen frequently, with student work and progress at the forefront of these conversations.

Involving Parents in Events and Activities

There are many ways you can include parents in the classroom. You might consider inviting parents in as observers, participants, sharers, or helpers. Most parents feel most comfortable as observers, so keep this in mind, especially at the beginning of the year. Conducting a survey at the beginning of the year to gauge parent availability, interest, hobbies, skills, and jobs can be a way to individually invite parents into the space.

Inviting all parents into the classroom often ensures that they feel welcome and are part of their child's learning. Many schools have monthly activity nights, such as a literacy night or math game night, to encourage families to attend after school. Some schools host a monthly Family Friday, inviting families to join for Morning Meeting and a short academic activity. Keep in mind that parents may not be able to take time off from work, so if a parent cannot attend these monthly gatherings, that's okay too. You might reach out to those parents individually and find other ways that they can participate, such as through a video call, or coordinate with them to plan for a specific day or time when they can request time off from work.

Advice for Tricky Situations

Tricky situations will happen! Difficult conversations can be due to any number of reasons, including a misunderstanding, a mistake, a behavior issue, grades, or a difference of opinion or experiences. In order to be open, honest, and empathetic even in complicated and difficult situations with parents, consider the following:

- **Try to talk when both you and the parent(s) are calm and unrushed.** If you think that a conversation might be tricky, try to get an idea of what the conversation will be about beforehand, and then schedule a meeting at a time when you can be free of distractions. Dismissal can be a great time to connect with parents as they pick up their child, but often this is not the best moment to have an actual conversation about a sensitive issue.

- **Try to understand the parent's point of view.** You can invite a trusted colleague, counselor, social worker, or administrator to offer advice, or perhaps even be present at the meeting. If the child has been at the school in previous years, an administrator or counselor has likely already interacted with the parent and child. If the child is new to the school, it can be an opportunity to have an administrator or counselor be present to introduce themselves and offer some third-party perspectives to de-escalate a challenging conversation.

- **Plan out what you will say.** Perhaps even practice a role-play with a trusted colleague, counselor, social worker, or administrator. This can help you to be empathetic and direct. You'll also have the right words ready since you'll have practiced saying them.

- **Have humility.** We are human and we can get defensive when people offer advice or tell us we should have done something differently, especially when we haven't already established a relationship of trust. Try to be mindful when this happens: Lindsay Lynch (2019) suggests a silent mantra can help you to be calm and to be open to what someone else is saying. You may also consider pausing for a few seconds after someone has said something before responding. Our ego can escalate situations, but ultimately we need to let go of it.

- **Consider the mode of communication for tricky conversations.** When you know a conversation may be challenging, it is best to meet in person or via videoconference; this allows all parties to communicate with body language and facial expressions in order to convey empathy and active listening. If a parent is unable to meet, the next best mode is a phone call, which will enable you to read tone and speak freely. Keep emails, text messages, and app messages for brief comments or summaries. Emails or online platforms can make it difficult to understand someone's tone, which can lead to misunderstandings of that person's intentions. If you do receive a written message from a parent that makes your body tense up or your heart beat faster, notice these as signs to ask a trusted colleague or administrator for advice before responding. Consider responding with a phone call when you are more calm to give the parent space to clarify their meaning, even if you need to wait until the next day. If you do reply to the email, also wait until you are calmer and have had ample time to let go of your ego.

- **Keep the child's hopes and dreams at the forefront.** If a conversation gets off track, keep bringing it back to the child's goals. You and the parent are on the same team, working together to support their child in learning and growing.

Pause and Ponder

- How can you build and strengthen parent connections throughout the year?

- How can you ensure all parents feel welcome?

- How might you keep teacher-parent meetings productive?

- How might you involve parents in classroom activities?

- What is one strategy you want to try when it comes to tricky situations with parents?

Final Thought

"Look to parents as resources in getting to know their children. As the experts on their child and their home environment, parents can help you understand how family values, child-raising practices, and expectations might translate into the student's behavior and needs at school."

—Chip Wood, *Yardsticks*

Grade 5

"Before we begin tonight's back to school night session and I share information about this school year, I want to begin with two simple words: *thank you.* Thank you for your presence tonight. Thank you for your support in getting this school year off to a great start. And thank you for the opportunity to be an important part of your child's school year. I am excited to be your child's teacher and to support your child's academic, social, and emotional growth. I know this will be a challenging and rewarding school year, and I look forward to partnering with you and your family to make it a wonderful school year for you and your child."

A mentor teacher shared this message with me before my first back to school night session. I have used this opening at the beginning of every back to school night since. A message like this lays the foundation for a trusting, working relationship that values parents' partnership. This statement shows parents that they are partners in their child's education, and that as such, their input will be solicited and valued throughout the school year.

Just as teachers take time to create a welcoming, positive classroom environment that includes all students, teachers must dedicate time to building and strengthening connections with students' families. Connecting with parents early on during the school year is paramount to supporting a child's learning and growth. Parents of fifth graders have special concerns as their children near the end of their elementary school years and face the unknowns of middle school. As a result, frequent communication between the teacher and parents is beneficial for all. Parents know their child best, and when positive connections between students' families and their teachers are established and maintained, students are set up for a successful, productive year of learning.

Building and Strengthening Connections

Connecting with parents can be intimidating for teachers. Whether you are a seasoned veteran or new to the profession, communicating with families can be challenging based on a number of factors: What is the family's preferred mode of communication? How much or how little communication does the family desire? What is the most effective way to share positive news or constructive feedback? And how can a teacher effectively balance connecting with all students' families on top of a list of countless other professional responsibilities?

Just as groups of students from one year to the next are unique, so are our relationships with parents. Dedicating time to building connections with parents at the beginning of the school year, and strengthening those connections over the course of the year, provides teachers with the confidence needed to work as collaborative partners with parents to support a student's learning. Developing strong, positive connections ensures that all parents feel valued and welcomed in the community and enables both parents and the teacher to positively impact a student's learning.

Building Connections at the Start of the School Year

Well before they greet students on the first day of school, teachers have an endless list of responsibilities and tasks to consider in order to start the school year with positive momentum. Connecting with parents is something that could easily be overlooked. In the midst of reviewing student lists, preparing supplies, laying out the classroom, attending meetings, along with so many other responsibilities to get ready for the school year, it is vital that teachers dedicate time to make connections with students and their families. When positive connections are established, communicating—whether sharing good news or providing constructive feedback—becomes easier for both the teacher and parents. The following are some options for building connections at the start of the school year. Choose one or some of the approaches that match your style, are realistic for you in balancing the demands for the beginning of the school year, and fit your school culture.

- **Teacher introduction: letter, email, phone call, or video.** Connect with your students and their families before the first day of school. Many teachers use a combination of a welcome letter and an email. Others make individual phone calls or video calls to students and their families. Use a method that works well for you and that meets the goals of this initial connection: to introduce yourself, to share your excitement for the upcoming school year, and to begin to get to know your students and their families.

- **Informal "listening conference."** At the beginning of the 2020–2021 school year, during the COVID-19 pandemic, my school started the year with a 100 percent virtual format. I feared that not being in the classroom would result in the initial connections that I make with students and their families not being as strong as I would like. To overcome this, during the first two weeks of school I scheduled virtual "listening conferences" with each family—three ten-minute conferences at the end of my lunch break. Since I had already introduced myself to students and parents with newsletters and a video message, I used these conferences as an opportunity to ask parents individualized questions such as:

  - "What does your child like to play?"
  - "How does your child learn best?"
  - "What's a subject your child enjoys?"
  - "What does your child find challenging?"
  - "Does your child have access to independent reading books?"
  - "What is your biggest hope for your child this school year?"
  - "What else would you like me to know about your child?"

The answers to these questions were very insightful. I kept notes during the conferences and added them to my communication log. Having one-on-one, informal meetings early on in the school year helped me form quicker and stronger connections with my students' families than in previous years even while facing the challenges of

COVID-19. The benefits of these conferences were so significant that I plan to continue this practice regardless of the schooling format.

- **Hopes and dreams and learning preferences survey.** As previously mentioned, you should plan to send families an introductory letter. As part of that communication, you may also wish to ask your students' families what their hopes and dreams are for their child's upcoming school year. Your students' families know them best and can share valuable information about goals that can be worked on during the year ahead. It is helpful to provide parents with some examples of hopes and dreams. In addition to asking parents to share hopes and dreams for the school year, you can also include a survey (paper or electronic) about their child's learning preferences. Be patient and realistic when asking parents for this information— some families will respond immediately, others will wait a few weeks into the school year to respond, while others may not respond at all. Some families will provide a lot of information; others will share just a few thoughts. Remember that any amount of information will be helpful for you in getting to know each child's strengths and goals. Include reminders about these surveys in your initial parent communications, and thank parents for their time and the information provided.

Using Electronic Forms for Surveys

Consider collecting survey information electronically. Electronic forms help you to easily organize the data collected. In addition, some parents are more likely to complete an electronic form than they are to fill out a paper survey.

- **Meet and greet.** It is also helpful to have an informal meet and greet prior to the first day of school. This is an opportunity for students to meet the teacher in person. It also allows students the chance to see the classroom and become familiar with their new setting. If appropriate, allow students to bring in school supplies to lighten their load for the first day of school. A helpful tip is to schedule a few different sessions, perhaps with staggered start times over a few hours, to make the meet and greet more informal and to allow for more personalized interactions. You can also provide students with a brief scavenger hunt to complete that asks students some simple questions—"Where is the pencil sharpener?" "Where are the laptops stored?" "How many student desks are in the room?"—to familiarize them with their new classroom. Consider setting up a virtual meet and greet to accommodate students and families who are unable to attend in person.

- **Back to School Night.** Many schools schedule schoolwide back to school night sessions during the first few weeks of school. Back to school nights are a great opportunity for parents to meet the teacher as well as one another. Use this opportunity to introduce yourself, present curriculum information, and preview special events for the school year. It is also helpful to share child development information with parents so they can know the typical development patterns for ten- and eleven-year-olds. If using a slideshow to present information, post the slideshow or a recording of the session on your class website for parents who are unable to attend the session.

Strengthening Connections Throughout the School Year

Using strategies like those mentioned in the previous section helps to establish positive relationships that are focused on creating a productive school year experience. These initial interactions build trust among all members of the class community—students, educators, and families. After establishing these positive connections, use the following strategies to strengthen parents' connections to their child's learning throughout the school year:

- **Class newsletter.** A weekly, biweekly, or monthly newsletter is an effective way to communicate updates to families. Include a quick recap of what was learned in each academic area as well as information about special events. Use the newsletter to announce upcoming assessments, project due dates, or any other pertinent information for parents. It is also helpful to include an "Ask Me About" section in the newsletter to support parents' and students' discussions about school at home and to keep families connected to current class topics. Include open-ended questions like the examples below to facilitate students' discussions with family members.

○ Which strategy for double-digit multiplication works best for you and why?

○ How has the character Bud changed from the beginning to the end of *Bud, Not Buddy* by Christopher Paul Curtis?

○ Why did European explorers travel to North America?

○ What is something you are proud of from this past week?

○ What are some examples of how you honored the classroom rule of supporting others this week?

Class Newsletters

A class newsletter helps you stay connected with students' families. Here are some tips for creating and distributing them:

- Use the same format each week to help parents navigate the newsletter more easily. For example, put announcements and information about upcoming tests in the same place each week.

- Use bullet points and boldfaced words to highlight important messages and to keep information brief.

- Create an email distribution list. Collect parents' preferred email addresses from student files and during initial parent meetings.

- Email or distribute the newsletter on the same day each week to provide consistency for parents.

- Provide paper copies for students whose families have limited or no email access.

If you work on a team, consider creating a shared newsletter for your grade level and divide up the sections of the newsletter to lighten the load.

- **Classroom website.** Many schools provide teachers with a classroom web page located on the school's website. If your district does not, there are many online platforms that teachers can use to create a website. Use your classroom website to share your contact information as well as links to any learning management systems or any social media platforms that will be used to connect with families throughout the year. It is also helpful to provide an overview of each academic area on your website. Additionally, include pictures and video clips on your website to give families a snapshot of events in your classroom. (Check your school policy on posting students' images online.) Consider posting a copy of the weekly newsletter on your website, too, offering families another method for receiving information. Use your website as an extension of your physical classroom by updating it frequently with news about the class's activities and about topics students are exploring; this will keep families informed and help them feel connected.

- **Learning management systems.** Invite parents to join the online learning management system your class is using. Many learning management systems have notification options that will autogenerate email reminders for students and parents about upcoming assignment due dates and keep parents informed of what students are working on in class.

Providing All Parents With a Voice

The school-home connection is strengthened when parents and families know that their input and engagement is welcome. Here are a few ways to make sure that parents know that their voices are heard and that their insights about their child are valuable and welcome.

- **End-of-marking-period parent surveys.** Throughout the school year, plan on using surveys for parents to share feedback. A good time for this type of parent survey is at the end of each marking period. Just as we have students reflect on what they have learned and accomplished during their marking period, and possibly set new goals, it is helpful to have parents do the same. In the survey, have parents share what they are proud of their child achieving during this grade period, how they have seen their child grow from the previous grade period, and what they would like to have their child work on during the upcoming grade period, as well as any other information they would like to provide. Also, if assigning homework or long-term projects, consider asking parents about the amount of time students are spending on these assignments at home to see if adjustments need to be made. It is also helpful to include an open-ended question at the end of the survey, such as "What other information would you like to share with me?" to let parents know you are open to receiving their input. Using these types of surveys encourages parents to stay connected, to communicate concerns, and to have their voice heard throughout the school year.

- **Using apps to connect.** There are numerous appsas well as other parent portals that allow teachers to share quick messages, along with photos or videos of individual students or the entire class. Check your school's policy on using such platforms, and utilize these tools as an additional way to connect briefly with families by providing snapshots of classroom events and activities.

Special Concerns of Fifth Grade Parents

The transition to middle school can be scary for both fifth grade students and their families. Fifth grade teachers often have to place students in leveled classes for the first time. In addition, the middle school format will most likely look very different from the elementary school format. For parents whose oldest or only child is in fifth grade, this time of uncertainty can make them feel particularly anxious.

Consider holding individual conferences or a whole-class session to provide information about what the middle school transition will entail. During these meetings, it is helpful to acknowledge parents' feelings, invite questions or concerns, and provide information about the process. This will support parents in staying involved throughout their child's transition from elementary to middle school. Schedule these individual or whole-group meetings before the transition process begins. Doing so helps to clarify steps families will need to take and alleviates the need for individual meetings later on.

Many middle schools plan events for elementary students and their families, such as open houses, meet and greets, and mini field trips to allow them to become familiar with their future school. Informing families about these events well in advance, including when and where they will be held, will help ease the transition. Be available to answer parents' questions and concerns, and recognize that this can be a challenging time of uncertainty for many fifth grade families.

Communicating With Parents

Here are some ways to support your communication with parents as students begin to make the important transition into middle school:

- **Send positivity notes.** In Chapter 1, the idea of writing positivity notes to individual students, recognizing their demonstration of a specific skill, was discussed. Whether the note identifies an academic skill or a social skill, this practice can extend to connecting with parents as well. Make a point to send an email or a handwritten note to students' families at various times throughout the school year as an additional way to connect with them. An authentic, sincere message that highlights a child's positive contributions serves as a meaningful reinforcement that helps to promote a positive relationship among parents, teachers, and students. Strive to send at least one positivity note to each student's family at least once in a marking period, which equates to just a few messages during a given week. To help manage this process, keep a class list and check off the names of students who receive positivity notes. Keeping a record of who has received the messages serves as a good reminder to find positive attributes for all students in your class.

- **Choose the appropriate communication method to address academic and behavior concerns.** When academic and behavior concerns come up during the school year, it is important to keep students' parents informed. For small matters, such as missing an assignment, a simple note home or email usually works well. For more complex matters, such as social dilemmas or chronic misbehavior, email is often not the best tool. Because they lack the nonverbal aspect of communication, such as tone of voice and body language, emails can easily be misinterpreted. When trickier situations arise, scheduling a parent phone call, video meeting, or in-person meeting tends to work best. Having a conversation in real time, as opposed to back and forth through email, allows you to speak directly to the parents. Use a matter-of-fact tone of voice, be specific with the matters you are sharing, and convey empathy with the words you say and the way you say them.

- **Keep a communication log and use email subfolders.** It is essential to track all communication with families. Before school starts, design a communication log that you can maintain throughout the year. An efficient communication log could consist of the following: a copy of the class list, binder tabs that are labeled for each individual student, and a log sheet that can be used to keep notes when having parent phone calls or meetings. These notes are often useful to refer to in future meetings with parents and administrators. To keep accurate records of parent-teacher correspondence, create a binder to store copies of letters. Many teachers also find it beneficial at the beginning of the school year to create a subfolder in their email drive for each student. Creating a subfolder and labeling it with the student's name makes it easy to store and retrieve previous email messages when necessary. Spending a few minutes creating these subfolders at the beginning of the year can save you time later in the year by keeping parent-teacher email communications organized and easily accessible.

Holding Productive Parent-Teacher Meetings

During a given school year, there are many different types of meetings that teachers will have. Throughout the year, teachers will participate in IEP and 504 meetings, as well as individual conferences with parents. You may also have phone calls or videoconferences throughout the school year, as well as middle school transition meetings during the spring season. For all types of meetings, it is helpful to take notes and add them to your communication log. If you plan to share data or other information with parents, be sure to have a copy of the information ready to give to them. You may also wish to consider emailing this information to parents prior to the meeting. This allows them to review the information ahead of time and can assist with having a productive conversation. Lastly, when appropriate, follow up with the parents through email. In this message, summarize the key points from the meeting, thank the parents for their time, and remind them that you are available for any follow-up questions or concerns. These steps, along with the tips listed below, will help set you up for productive parent-teacher meetings.

Tips for Success

In the busyness of preparing for a meeting with parents, some simple things can be overlooked by teachers. Keep in mind the following when setting up for a parent meeting:

- Use adult-size chairs.

- Sit at a round table, if possible, to convey the message of everyone being an equal member of the partnership.

- To minimize interruption, put a sign on the outside of your class-room door letting students, colleagues, and others in the building know that a meeting is in progress.

Characteristics of Teacher Language

The characteristics of teacher language discussed in Chapter 3 apply to parent-teacher meetings as well. Be direct and genuine when speaking with parents, using a respectful, matter-of-fact tone. Next, convey faith in children's abilities. Keep statements brief, and if possible, include a typed summary to give to parents. Having a paper copy is particularly helpful when discussing report cards, testing results, or other items including data, or when reviewing an IEP or 504 plan. It is also especially important to know when to be silent, recognizing the importance of parents' input.

Scheduling Tools

Consider using an online scheduler when inviting all of your students' families to meetings, such as a before-the-school-year meet and greet, end-of-the-grading-period conferences, or a middle school transition meeting. This is especially helpful when scheduling an entire class's worth of parent meetings, such as midyear parent-teacher conferences, during a single day or week. Many of these scheduling tools also have settings that you can use to autogenerate reminder emails that usually result in greater parent turnout. A point of caution: be sure to know the parents in your class before implementing such a system. If parents have limited access to email, rarely respond to email, or speak a different language from the one used in the online scheduler, use an alternative method to schedule conferences.

Online Meeting Room Etiquette: Tools and Waiting Rooms

Virtual meetings have become more prevalent in classrooms, especially since the COVID-19 pandemic. For some parents, virtual meetings may become the preferred method of meeting with their child's teacher. As a result, it's a good idea for you to become familiar with how to navigate online meeting platforms. Set up a place with good lighting and audio that will allow you to have a meeting similar to a face-to-face one. Practice screen sharing if you plan to share data with parents so they can view this information during the meeting. Also, learn how to utilize meeting waiting rooms. This is particularly helpful if you are having back-to-back conferences with multiple families in a given day. When you become comfortable with using a waiting room, you can send the same meeting link to all parents in your class community and save yourself the time necessary to create multiple meeting links. This will also ensure that each parent-teacher meeting is private.

Involving Parents in Events and Activities

Encouraging parents' involvement in the classroom strengthens your connections with families and benefits your class as a whole. There are many ways that parents can be involved, including sharing their interests and expertise, observing or helping in the classroom, and viewing their child's work.

Parent Surveys

In one of the initial connections you make with them—whether in a class newsletter, during back to school night, or as part of an individual meeting—survey parents about their hobbies, interests, and areas of expertise. Find out what special talents or skills they have. For example, some parents may have background or training in an academic area that you will study during the year. If a parent works in the field of microbiology, see if they would be willing to share information about their work when the class is studying microworlds during science class. Tap into parents' areas of expertise to make real-world connections with students' learning.

Use this survey as an opportunity to find out about any special traditions or holidays that the family celebrates during the school year as well. This information can be important to have when planning assignments, so you can be mindful of times when students will be busy outside of the school day. It can also be useful to have when arranging special classroom events. For example, if a student in your class celebrates Lunar New Year, consider having the student and their family share about this holiday with the class during a Morning Meeting or another special time in the classroom.

Classroom Visits

Many public and private schools around the country recognize American Education Week. This week, typically held during the month of November, recognizes the importance of education. Consider using this week, or other times throughout the school year, as an opportunity to invite parents into the classroom.

Parents could take on a number of different roles during a visit—an observer, a participant, a sharer, or a helper. For example, you could have parents come in and observe or participate in an activity such as a Morning Meeting or a class project. If you have a parent in the classroom who has special expertise, invite that parent to be a guest sharer for a class period. A parent might be very skilled with video editing software; ask that parent to show students how to create a video. Students could then use this skill at the end of a research project to show what they researched by using a modality they have learned from an expert. On the other hand, you could have parents serve in the role of helper by assisting with the peer editing and publishing processes during writing workshop. It is also helpful and necessary to remind parents about maintaining confidentiality when supporting students in the classroom.

Regardless of what role parents will take on, ensure that all parents have an opportunity to participate throughout the school year. Scheduling multiple opportunities for classroom visits helps to accommodate parents' schedules while providing all parents with the opportunity to be connected with their child's education.

Portfolio Share

Portfolios are an effective way to increase student engagement, as discussed in Chapter 4. In addition to providing this benefit, student portfolios serve as a way to keep parents connected to their child's education. Toward the end of the school year, set up a portfolio share, an opportunity for students' families to visit the classroom to view the work artifacts their child has collected during their time in fifth grade. Before parents visit, have students identify some specific work samples they would like to share with their family. Students can consider sharing something they are extremely proud of, something they enjoyed doing during the year, and something they found challenging and succeeded at as the result of hard work and perseverance. To accommodate parents' schedules, consider having more than one portfolio share session—perhaps one during the school day and one before or after school. Having students create a shareable link or drive for a digital portfolio is an alternative to having an in-person portfolio share.

Advice for Tricky Situations

Communication is a two-way street. This is especially true when communicating with parents about tricky situations such as behavior issues, questions about a grade, or misunderstandings. Before approaching a tricky situation, think about the speaking and listening skills you will need to use for effective communication.

For speaking skills, refer to the five characteristics of teacher language outlined in Chapter 3. Think about the most important message you want to share with parents and how that message can be delivered in a brief, matter-of-fact tone. Also, consider using inclusive language, such as "we," which will demonstrate your view of parents being partners in their child's education. For example, questions like "What can we do to help Ryan develop his study skills?" send the message that you want to work together with families. It is helpful to have a few ideas in mind that you can share with parents if they are not sure of ideas to address the problem being discussed.

To exercise your own listening skills when addressing tricky situations, it is helpful to ask parents for their perspective before suggesting advice. For example, if a student consistently forgets homework, ask parents what they notice on their end. Often, a parent's answer will provide information that is helpful to the teacher. When asking for a parent's point of view, demonstrate empathy with your tone of voice and body language in addition to the words you say. Thank parents for their perspective and ideas at the end of the conversation as well. These practices help to maintain a trusting parent-teacher partnership.

Lastly, consider making a mindset shift when preparing for a tricky situation. You may start out by thinking, "I have to have a difficult conversation with a student's parents." As you prepare to address a tricky situation, however, consider changing your outlook so that you think, "I have the opportunity to have a critical and necessary conversation with a student's parents." Critical conversations, although challenging and possibly intimidating, are necessary to support a student's academic, social, and emotional growth in partnership with parents.

The following checklist may help in preparing for critical conversations with students' families about tricky situations:

- **Make an initial contact once there is a pattern to problematic behavior** (or immediately, depending on the severity of the behavior). Consider using the phone instead of email—often, you can address the situation more effectively and in a more personal manner in a brief phone call than you can through a back-and-forth exchange of emails. Speaking in person allows all parties to hear each other's tone of voice, which can make it easier to convey and listen to a difficult message. Also, if anything is said that is misunderstood or gives offense, it can be addressed right away instead of through an exchange of emails.

- **Call again or send another note if the problem persists.**

- **Meet with parents in person if the problem continues.**

- **Have a problem-solving conference with the student and tell parents about it.** Inform parents of a check-in date (usually about one week) to communicate again, to determine if the problem has been resolved or to plan the next steps.

- **Know when to get support.** It may be helpful to have a colleague, such as a counselor, another teacher who works with the student, or an administrator, present for a meeting. Consider having only one colleague support you during a difficult meeting, so as to not over- whelm the parents.

Pause and Ponder

- What proactive communication strategies can you add to your repertoire?

- What are some common concerns of fifth grade parents in your school community, and what can you do to address these concerns?

- What method(s) of communication work best for the parents in your class?

- What advice will you use to hold productive parent-teacher meetings?

- What activities during the school year lend themselves to involving parents? Map out some special projects for which you can solicit parent volunteers.

- What tips for tricky situations are applicable to your work with students' parents?

Final Thought

A positive teacher-family relationship based on mutual respect and cooperation sets students up for a successful school year. Recognizing that this is true, teachers need to dedicate time to connecting with parents, using a variety of methods—newsletters, websites, formal and informal meetings, and more—to partner with parents in their child's education. When strong connections are in place, a productive school year is likely.

Chapter 6
Healthy Teachers, Healthy Classrooms

• •

Overview

In the first five chapters of this book, we discussed significant topics in the field of education: how to respond to students' developmental needs, manage classrooms effectively, build positive communities, engage students in meaningful academics, and connect with families to support students' success. We know from experience and from research that these five areas are crucial for teaching and learning, and taken together, they create classrooms where all students feel safety, significance, and a sense of belonging—just what they need to make academic, social, and emotional progress and find success in the classroom and beyond. But there is one element of education that we haven't mentioned yet, and while it's by far one of the most impactful areas of any educational setting, it's often given the least amount of time (if any time at all) in teacher preparation programs, professional development, school schedules, and more: teacher health and well-being.

Everyone should take steps to support their own health and well-being, but it's a particularly important habit for people in high-stress professions. In a Gallup poll on occupational stress, teachers and nurses tied for the highest reported levels of daily stress (Gallup 2014)—and that was before the toll of the COVID-19 pandemic in 2020 and 2021. While the pandemic changed and complicated teachers' experiences in many stressful ways, it's important to remember that the teaching profession has always had its challenges. According to a 2017 survey from the American Federation of

Teachers and the Badass Teachers Association, 61 percent of teachers described their daily work as often or always stressful.

What Is Stress?

Lisa Dewey Wells, coauthor of *Empowering Educators*, grades K, 1, 2

Stress is the body's way of responding to anything that requires our attention or action, including physical, psychological, or emotional strain. The human body has a two-part nervous system, the sympathetic and parasympathetic systems, that help us respond to stress.

The sympathetic system's job is to help us respond quickly to danger, such as an approaching lion or a child who darts across the street to get a ball as we're driving. This system allows our bodies to rev up, gather energy, and respond quickly, and it also makes us sweat, breathe quickly, and then sometimes have that shaky feeling when the threat dissipates. The parasympathetic system helps our body rest and digest. It calms our breathing, heart rate, and mind. It lets us process information and emotions and restores a sense of calm.

Stress itself has benefits as well as drawbacks. Good stress, called eustress, can help us be more creative and productive and even boost our mood. Bad stress can be overwhelming and often makes it hard to handle the situation at hand. It's important to have time to reflect on stressors and how you handle them. Take a moment to jot down a few of your current stressors. Naming our stressors can help us begin to identify if they create good stress or bad stress and then choose how we want to respond and manage these stressors.

So what is it that makes teaching so stressful? While there are different factors at play for everyone, common themes for many educators include the amount of time and effort they dedicate to their work—far more than forty hours a week (Diliberti, Schwartz, and Grant 2021)—and how effective they feel they are able to be within their classrooms, schools, and districts. Educators are deeply invested in their work and in seeing their students succeed, and feeling ineffective is a significant source of stress and worry among teachers.

Stressing Student Success

Teachers' remarkable dedication to their work and their deep desire to make a difference in students' lives are two of the causes of educator stress. It's a vicious cycle: teachers work so hard to support their students that they can become burned out, which in turn makes them less effective in the classroom, so they need to work even harder! According to Jones and Bouffard (2012), teachers who have strong social and emotional competence themselves are better able to build positive relationships with students, manage their classrooms successfully, and teach social and emotional learning skills effectively. That means that educators dedicated to meeting their students' needs and helping them succeed may find the most success by starting with themselves. In order to be an effective educator, you need to find ways to support your own social and emotional needs. Healthy teachers make healthy classrooms!

In addition to educators' own social and emotional learning skills, there's another powerful, teacher-focused element that contributes to student success. Collective teacher efficacy, or teachers' mutual belief that they are successful in their shared work in their school, is the most signficant factor influencing student achievement. Collective efficacy has more than three times the impact and ability to predict student success than socio-economic status, home environment, or student motivation (Hattie 2016). That's remarkable to think about: a group of educators who share a strong belief in the collective work they do in their school can make more of a difference in student success than even the students' own motivation or home life! There is real power in shared teacher beliefs and in the community that teachers find with their colleagues.

These studies about the impact teachers have on students may come as no surprise to you. Anyone who has seen the progress that students make over the course of a school year, the way that educators collaborate to create meaningful learning experiences, and the challenges that both students and teachers can overcome together won't bat an eye at these findings. The powerful impact teachers make doesn't happen magically; it comes from deep commitment, tireless effort, and ceaseless collaboration.

This work takes a toll, and so it's worth restating two important points: healthy teachers make healthy classrooms, and no one can do it alone.

In this chapter, we'll delve into:

- What it means to be a socially and emotionally healthy educator.

- How you can become a strong leader in your classroom and beyond.

- Why it's important to understand your implicit beliefs.

- How you can keep growing and learning as a teacher, colleague, and leader.

- How to take care of yourself so you can take care of your students.

● ● ● ● ● ● ● ● ● ●

Adult Social and Emotional Learning

In Chapter 1, we discussed developmentally responsive teaching and the four principles of child and adolescent development. Social and emotional development adheres to those same principles, following a reasonably predictable pattern that individuals progress through at their own pace and at a varying rate over the course of their lives. Social and emotional growth, like all human development, is uneven. There are periods of intense growth and change followed by relatively quiet periods, a spiraling pattern that continues throughout our lifetimes.

That last part is the key, and it's a fact that is often forgotten: human development continues throughout adulthood! Social and emotional growth, in particular, lasts for a lifetime, with readiness to demonstrate social and emotional skills influenced by a variety of circumstances, including sociocultural and economic factors as well as individual personality and experiences.

Lifelong Social and Emotional Learning

These truths about social and emotional development mean that it's possible, and important, for adults to continue learning and demonstrating new social and emotional skills. How many times have you used the phrase "lifelong learner" as an educator? Effective teachers are often the most committed learners, deeply curious about the subjects they teach and the best ways to reach their students. You've probably been focused on your own social and emotional growth throughout your life without even realizing it. Have you ever intentionally focused on being effective while working with others, standing up for yourself, taking responsibility for something in your community, listening and caring for others, or persevering through a difficult time? You've been honing your social and emotional competence throughout all of those actions and more.

Everyone relies on social and emotional skills to be successful in life. Teaching is a deeply social and emotional profession, so it requires educators to call on those skills every minute of every day. The emphasis on these two types of skills is another reason why professions like teaching can be so exhausting and stressful at times; it takes a toll not only on your physical and cognitive energy but also on your social and emotional energy. When you understand more about your social and emotional strengths and tendencies, you are better able to develop the skills you need to be calm, focused, successful, and happy.

Social Competence and Emotional Competence

Social and emotional learning is often talked about as if it's one idea, but there are two crucial parts: social competence and emotional competence. *Social competence* is the ability to make positive contributions to the community and society and to cooperate well with others; it encompasses interpersonal skills like relating to others. *Emotional competence* is the ability to understand your emotions and how those emotions impact the way you feel, think, and act; it encompasses intrapersonal skills like managing your emotions.

Developing Social and Emotional Learning Skills

While that goal may sound lofty, it's possible for anyone to achieve. Like any skill, social and emotional skills can be explicitly taught and intentionally learned. It takes time, practice, and patience to improve your skills, but it makes a difference, not just in your own life, but in the lives of the people around you, from your family to your colleagues to your students. If we don't model, live by, and believe what we say, nothing will change for our students. We know that social and emotional skills are crucial for our students, and they are just as important for us.

Just as we would do with our students' learning, when we focus on our own learning, it's helpful to start with a sense of the skills and competencies we aim to develop. Over time, there have been many different definitions and terms applied to these skills and competencies. Two organizations that have been committed for decades to bringing social and emotional learning to the forefront of education are Center for Responsive Schools, founded in 1981, and the Collaborative for Academic, Social, and Emotional Learning (CASEL), founded in 1994. Both organizations have identified five core social and emotional learning competencies, and while the two organizations use different terms to describe these competencies, the terms correspond closely to each other.

The chart that follows provides definitions of each of the terms and shows how the Center for Responsive Schools competencies (in the left-hand column) and the CASEL competencies (in the right-hand column) connect to each other. In the center column are anchor standards that connect to each one of the Center for Responsive Schools competencies. These standards encompass the abilities an individual needs to exhibit to successfully demonstrate social and emotional competence. They provide a solid grounding for considering learning goals for your students as well as yourself.

C.A.R.E.S.

Competencies	Anchor Standards	CASEL Core Competencies

Cooperation

The ability to establish new relationships, to maintain positive relationships and friendships, to avoid social isolation, to resolve conflicts, to accept differences, and to be a contributing member of the classroom and community in which one lives, works, learns, and plays

- Able to make and keep friends
- Works with others toward a common goal
- Resolves differences quickly
- Cooperates as a group leader or a member of the group
- Exhibits helpfulness

Relationship Skills

The abilities to establish and maintain healthy and supportive relationships and to effectively navigate settings with diverse individuals and groups

---

Assertiveness

The ability to take initiative, to stand up for one's ideas without hurting or negating others, to seek help, to persevere with a challenging task, and to recognize one's individual self as separate from the environment, circumstances, or conditions one is in

- Expresses strong emotions and opinions effectively
- Able to seek help
- Shows openness and honesty
- Persists through challenging events
- Takes the initiative to do what is right, fair, and just
- Makes choices one feels good about later

Self-Awareness

The abilities to understand one's own emotions, thoughts, and values and how they influence behavior across contexts

---

Responsibility

The ability to motivate oneself to act and follow through on expectations; to define a problem, consider the consequences, and choose a positive solution

- Selects the best option among choices for a suitable outcome
- Holds oneself accountable
- Demonstrates social, civic, and digital responsibility
- Takes care of property

Responsible Decision-Making

The abilities to make caring and constructive choices about personal behavior and social interactions across diverse situations

---

Empathy

The ability to recognize, appreciate, or understand another's state of mind or emotions; to be receptive to new ideas and perspectives; and to see, appreciate, and value differences and diversity in others

- Recognizes and manages one's own emotions and recognizes the emotions of others
- Respects and values diversity in others
- Respects differing cultural norms
- Aware of the impact of one's actions on others

Social Awareness

The abilities to understand the perspectives of and empathize with others, including those from diverse backgrounds, cultures, and contexts

---

Self-Control

The ability to recognize and regulate one's thoughts, emotions, and behaviors in order to be successful in the moment and remain on a successful trajectory

- Adheres to social, behavioral, and moral standards
- Manages overwhelming thoughts or emotions
- Controls impulses and delays gratification
- Shows hope and perseverance

Self-Management

The abilities to manage one's emotions, thoughts, and behaviors effectively in different situations and to achieve goals and aspirations

Demonstrating Readiness

As you read the anchor standards listed in the chart you might have found yourself pausing on certain skills and thinking, "I do this most of the time, but not all the time." For instance, you might usually work well with others toward a common goal, but if your strong feeling about how to achieve that goal clashes with someone else's, you might choose to stand your ground. Maybe you make choices you feel good about most of the time, but every so often, there's something you regret in hindsight. That just means you're human! This back and forth is all part of social and emotional learning.

There is no such thing as complete mastery of social and emotional skills. No one can make the right choice all the time, or resolve every single difference quickly, or show hope and perseverance every minute of every day. But we can strive for readiness to demonstrate these skills most of the time, and we can learn more about ourselves and deepen our skills when we encounter moments that challenge us.

Learning About Yourself

It's also important to emphasize that developing social and emotional competence means coming to understand yourself and the ways you tend to feel, think, and behave. There is no one right way to demonstrate the five core social and emotional competencies of cooperation, assertiveness, responsibility, empathy, and self-control. There are many possible ways to be assertive, for instance; some ways work for certain people or in certain situations, but not in others. Understanding your social and emotional tendencies—the way you usually approach situations involving these competencies—can help you manage your emotions, thoughts, and behaviors.

One way to think about your tendencies is to consider your own range of possible reactions within the competencies. Each of the five social and emotional learning competencies encompasses a spectrum of behaviors. At the end of each spectrum are two dichotomous sets of behavioral tendencies for demonstrating social and emotional competence. Within each spectrum, there are many variations and possibilities. For example, under the social and emotional competency of cooperation, at one end of the spectrum we have the Synergist, whose tendency is to be highly collaborative, and at the other end we have the Insulator, who will engage in group work if invited but whose tendency is to view people's roles separately rather than collectively. Each of the dichotomies, and the variations in between, can represent a meaningful and valid way to behave and to react in academic and social settings. The key for us as teachers is to understand where our tendencies lie within this spectrum.

Understanding Your Social and Emotional Type

The dichotomies for each of the five social and emotional learning competencies were developed through research done at Center for Responsive Schools as part of the development of Fly Five, a social and emotional learning curriculum for kindergarten through eighth grade. Part of the Fly Five program includes the Social and Emotional Type Inventory, a typological assessment for adults to help educators better understand their own social and emotional competence as they teach social and emotional learning skills to their students. Scan this QR code for more information about Fly Five.

As your social and emotional skills grow and change over the course of your life, where you fall along each continuum can and will shift. Take a look at the traits for each dichotomy in the five social and emotional learning competencies to get a sense of your tendencies.

C.A.R.E.S. Competency Traits

Cooperation	
Synergists:	Insulators:
• Are highly collaborative and want to hear all ideas and suggestions. • Are quick to help resolve conflicts. • Develop long and lasting friendships. • Are highly collaborative no matter the situation.	• Engage meaningfully in group work when there is a clear benefit to it. • Consider everyone's role separately rather than collectively. • Are not interested in conflicts, either resolving them or starting them. • Develop shorter, intense friendships.

Assertiveness	
Expectors:	Hypothesizers:
• Express their ideas, feelings, and emotions clearly while acknowledging those of others. • Are usually open to receiving help or feedback. • Are confident in their ability to succeed at new or challenging tasks.	• Carefully analyze situations. • Can sometimes hesitate to express their own ideas, feelings, and emotions for fear of hurting others. • Are quick to think for others, but tend to doubt themselves. • Don't always trust others to do things, so they take on extra responsibility themselves.

Responsibility	
Navigators:	Traversers:
• Are intrinsically motivated as they want to be seen as trustworthy and dependable. • Work hard to manage their emotions in order to modify their behavior and consider the consequences of their actions in order to best align with expectations. • Tend to be careful and consistent.	• Rely on extrinsic cues, prompts, and reminders to help them make good choices. • Often make decisions by choosing a preferred option, which can sometimes lead to unforeseen consequences. • Tend to be spontaneous and impulsive.

Empathy	
Associates:	Limiters:
• Can read and understand the emotions and behaviors of others.	• Make decisions based on their own feelings and emotions.
• Value the diverse perspectives they gain from connecting with others.	• Do not always consider the impact of their actions on others.
• Consistently act on their feelings of empathy to care for others.	• Show compassion and caring for those similar to themselves but do not always extend that empathy to those who are significantly different.

Self-Control	
Regulators:	Adventurers:
• Like to be in control.	• Do things differently and think outside the box.
• Hold themselves to high standards.	• Live in the moment without thinking about the consequences of their actions.
• Are motivated to see their goals through to the end.	• Seek strategies, resources, and help outside of themselves to solve problems.
• Use their willpower and confidence to stay hopeful and persevere through difficulties.	

Cooperation, assertiveness, responsibility, empathy, and self-control are vital skills for everyone, especially those in professions like education that require strong social and emotional skills. As teachers, we connect with a wide range of colleagues, families, and students all day every day, and inevitably, we find ourselves in situations with people who react differently than we do. Recognizing our own social and emotional tendencies and those of the people around us can help us better understand ourselves and others.

Imagine, for instance, that you tend toward the Regulator end of the self-control spectrum and like to plan in advance and stay in control of a situation, and you work with a grade-level partner who tends to be more of an Adventurer, someone who spontaneously changes direction and is guided by what's happening in the moment. How would you approach that partnership compared to one with another Regulator? What challenges would that pairing present, and what strengths would it bring forward? Now imagine that you tend to be more of an Expector in the realm of assertiveness; you are eager to try new approaches and thrive on immediate feedback. Your supervisor is more of a Hypothesizer, someone who meticulously reviews a situation before responding and is tentative about delegating. How would your awareness of your own approach and your supervisor's approach change how you might assert yourself in this situation?

Growing Pains

Linda Berger, coauthor of *Empowering Educators,*
grades 6, 7, 8

Recently, I led a four-day workshop at a middle school with a primarily Black student population and a primarily white teaching staff. The workshop took place at the end of the school year, at a time when the educators were exhausted from a demanding year yet deeply committed to returning in the fall with a renewed passion for equity and relationships.

Our discussions often revolved around how to foster authentic connections with students who desperately need and want to be seen. How can we reach students with academic challenges that reflect not only the reality our students live in but also their aspirations for the future? Where can we find meaningful, culturally responsive materials to teach the required curriculum? Does our teaching truly come from a place of empathy and understanding?

As we questioned our beliefs, our practices, and our resources together, we recognized that we all have room to grow. That knowledge can be uncomfortable. But when growth comes from a place of true compassion, the results elevate us all and help create a better world for our students.

As you consider your own social and emotional competence and grow more aware of the skills and tendencies you recognize in the people around you, it's important to keep in mind that there are no right or wrong reactions to emotions. There is no one way that you, or the people you encounter, should feel. Developing your skills in and understanding of the C.A.R.E.S. competencies allows you to gain insight into how you feel, how others might be feeling, and how you can respond to those emotions so that you stay on a successful path.

Awareness of your social and emotional strengths and areas of growth is the first step in developing skills in social and emotional competence. As you become more aware of your emotions, thoughts, and behaviors, you can embark on your own natural learning cycle and learn more, set goals, practice skills, and continue your social and emotional development.

Teacher Leadership

Teachers wear many hats: instructor, coach, cheerleader, referee, entertainer, mentor, and so much more. A particularly important role is that of leader. You might think of yourself as a leader in your classroom, but it's important to remember the leadership role you occupy in other areas as well. As educators, we usually think of ourselves in relation to our students, but we are also part of a crucial community of adults within our school. How we work together as adults to create a safe, joyful, and inclusive environment is as important as our individual contributions or competence. No matter how effective an educator you are within the walls of your classroom, the environment outside your classroom is just as important for your students. It's vital that we work together with other adults in our school, in our students' families, and in our community to support student success. You are not just a leader among your students; you are a leader for your students.

Understanding yourself as a leader starts with thinking about your leadership style. Your teacher leadership style impacts the community you build in your classroom, how you manage your classroom, and how you relate to others, including your students, their families, and your colleagues. Think back to the C.A.R.E.S. competencies and dichotomies we were just discussing. The way you firmly yet fairly understand, manage, and balance your classroom community connects with every one of the five social and emotional competencies. The professional way you conduct yourself with your students, their families, and your colleagues sends an important message about who you are as a leader and your implicit beliefs about students and their potential.

What we say and how we say it are also part of who we are as leaders. Our words reveal what we believe. We all have implicit beliefs and biases that we have to learn to recognize, and the words we choose can give light to those implicit beliefs. We've talked a lot in this book about teacher language and how powerful our words are. Your leadership style is reflected in what you say and also in how you act, two crucial aspects of effective classroom management and behavior management. Your approach to discipline comes out of your leadership style. (See Chapter 2 for more information about these topics.) Your words and actions are impactful outside the classroom, too, and they send important messages to the adults in your community about who you are and what you believe. Thinking about your current leadership style and how to grow to become the type of teacher leader you want to be can also help you clarify your beliefs and approach to teaching and learning.

Leading In and Out of the Classroom

Amanda Stessen-Blevins

Recently, I was in an adult meeting in which people were talking over each other, making it difficult to hear the ideas of those trying to share. Frequently, the loudest person kept interrupting and bulldozing over everyone else's ideas until they were the only one speaking. We've all probably been in a meeting like this at one point or another; it's unproductive and incredibly frustrating.

In this particular meeting, it suddenly occurred to me that had this behavior occurred in a classroom setting where I was the teacher, it would have played out very differently:

- I would have stepped in to make the space safer for all voices to be heard. I would have authoritatively supported students to take turns talking if students were not yet able to do that themselves.

- I would have supported students who were learning to be more assertive by asking, "Could you say more about that, _____? It didn't sound like you were finished sharing your idea."

- For students having difficulty leaving space for others' ideas, I would encourage their developing skills in self-control, empathy, and cooperation by reminding them of our classroom norms, incorporating visual cues to activate their listening skills, and using redirecting language to guide their behavior.

- In my role as the teacher, I would have scanned the space and challenged my implicit biases, asking myself, "Are there voices that have been heard more than others? Do I observe anyone who looks like they want to say something but hasn't yet?"

As I was processing my realization of how differently I would have managed the situation with children compared to adults, I had to ask myself some challenging questions: "Why do I feel more comfortable supporting students with this common conflict? Why don't I feel comfortable to assert myself in the same way when I'm in a meeting with adults?" I realized that the same skills I teach my students and strive to model in the classroom are also strategies I can apply outside of the classroom with family, friends, and yes, even with colleagues in a professional meeting. Just as we support students with curiosity and compassion, we must give the same grace to ourselves and our own learning.

The following leadership styles represent broad categories of what teacher leaders can look like in a classroom. While the styles are described from a classroom perspective, imagine how it might feel to work with someone who models each of these styles. What type of colleague would you prefer to work with?

Teacher Leadership Styles

	Autocratic	Permissive	Flip-Flop	Authoritative
Sounds like . . .	"Because I said so."	"Can you please cooperate now?"	"I said no. Okay, one more chance. This time I mean it! Actually . . ."	"Let me show you . . ."
Looks like . . .	The teacher tends to rely on external means—punishments and rewards—to get students to behave.	The teacher tends to rely on ignoring and bargaining to keep students happy.	The teacher bounces back and forth between autocratic and permissive approaches.	The teacher uses strategies like Interactive Modeling, teacher language, and logical consequences to shape positive behaviors.
Sends the message that . . .	Children are naturally unruly and impulsive, requiring strict rules to keep them quiet and obedient.	The most important thing is to be liked, which is achieved by being nice, offering praise, and ignoring undesirable actions.	The teacher's reactions are inconsistent, and it's not clear to students what the expectations are.	The teacher believes students want to do what's right and supports that goal with clear guidance and expectations.
Leads to students feeling . . .	Anxious, angry, and resentful.	Tense, unsure, and emotionally unsafe.	Confused, frustrated, and anxious.	Empowered, confident, and successful.

You may recognize the authoritative leadership style as the one we have described throughout this book: firm, fair, professional, respectful, kind, and empathetic. Just as social and emotional growth takes time, so does growing as a leader. Being aware of the message your words and actions send is the first step to becoming an authoritative leader. The second is coaching yourself when you make a mistake and rehearsing alternative choices. Your leadership style is an important tool for your work with students and adults alike. As you become aware of your current leadership approach and set goals for developing your authoritative approach, you will have opportunities to consider what you believe about education and how your words and actions can support those beliefs.

Power of Teacher Beliefs

Our individual and collective beliefs have a huge impact on our work in schools and our effectiveness as educators. When our beliefs are conscious and healthy, like the collective belief in teacher efficacy described in the overview of this chapter, then the results are often positive and productive ones, such as improved academic outcomes for students and high morale for teachers. But we all have implicit biases, attitudes, or stereotypes we hold outside of our conscious awareness. Those implicit biases can get in the way of our conscious dedication to equity in education and impact our words, emotions, and actions.

Extensive research, particularly in K–12 school settings, has shown that implicit bias has a significant impact on discipline in schools, perceptions of behavior, and even teaching practices and leadership styles (Kirwan Institute for the Study of Race and Ethnicity 2018). It's crucial for educators to recognize their individual beliefs and biases, but the work doesn't stop there. The next step is to consciously let go of biases and of the beliefs that do not serve educators or students well, and cultivate or hold on to beliefs that are beneficial.

Identifying Implicit Biases

A first step is bringing awareness to implicit biases by intentionally pausing and asking yourself questions to get below the surface of your actions and words (Kirwan Institute for the Study of Race and Ethnicity 2018). Three simple questions, recommended by the National Education Association (n.d.), that you can ask yourself are:

1. What is true for you? Consider what past experiences you've had that you may carry with you.

2. What do you value? Think about what's most important to you and identify what your priorities are.

3. What's your privilege? Bring your awareness to the advantages you have had in your experience that others have not.

Another step in growing your awareness of implicit or unconscious biases is to explore an implicit association test, or IAT, like the ones developed by psychologists at Harvard University, the University of Virginia, and the University of Washington at Project Implicit (Project Implicit 2011). These IATs examine the link between hidden biases and observable behavior. There are several IATs available through Project Implicit that measure implicit associations about a wide range of topics. The IATs are available for free and may be taken easily online. These tests may not provide all of the nuanced data that an individualized, in-person assessment might offer, but they do give useful initial insights into biases you may not have been aware of. As you explore your own beliefs and biases, you can increase your awareness and work on changing your beliefs by building empathy for those with different perspectives and building connections with people who are different from you (Kirwan Institute for the Study of Race and Ethnicity 2018).

As you bring your focus to your implicit beliefs, you can also think about your explicit beliefs and ensure that they serve you and your students well. Some beliefs contribute to our collective efficacy and to students' growing social and emotional learning skills. Those are beliefs we want to embrace, develop, and share with others. Shared teacher beliefs don't develop overnight, but they improve through strong instructional leadership and consistent opportunities for teacher collaboration, like structured professional learning and opportunities to observe colleagues. In turn, these shared beliefs can lead to improved student achievement (Goddard et al. 2015).

Putting Student Behavior Into Perspective

Brian Smith, coauthor of *Empowering Educators*, grades 6, 7, 8

Often, teachers are the first adults that students see each day besides their family members. Sometimes, they may see their teachers even more than certain family members! Young people will often lash out at the ones closest to them, and so we often find ourselves at the center of a young person's life when they need to vent. This behavior can be hurtful and feel personal, but it's important to remind yourself that student behavior usually has very little to do with your classroom or your teaching. Most of the time, in fact, students are often not even aware of the impact their behavior has on their teachers or others around them.

The sooner we realize that we are not the target of student behavior, even if it appears that way, the sooner we are able to get students the help and support they need. Keep these tips in mind:

- **Stay calm.** We must maintain a professional and kind front no matter how a student behaves.

- **Remind them you care.** When the student is ready, take a quiet moment one-on-one to talk and determine how you can help them.

- **Use your resources.** If you feel overwhelmed by the situation, take the student to another adult who can offer a fresh perspective.

- **Be firm yet kind.** Our students rely on us for a stable and consistent environment. Once a student has calmed down, they should be able to rejoin the class and maintain their sense of belonging in the classroom community.

Teacher Beliefs That Promote Social and Emotional Learning

Teacher beliefs are a set of principles, assumptions, values, and convictions that educators hold true regarding students, the classroom, education and educational concepts, curriculum, pedagogy, and discipline. This belief system guides and informs their thoughts, actions, and classroom behaviors, forms the basis for decision-making, and helps to sort, organize, and prioritize information. Center for Responsive Schools has identified eight teacher belief domains that are critical to teachers' approach to education. These eight domains lie at the heart of social and emotional learning in the classroom and the school.

Conditions for Learning	Belief that students learn best in environments of high expectations that are student centered, developmentally responsive, academically challenging, and safe to make learning mistakes.
Conditions for Effective Teaching	Belief that teaching is most effective when lessons are planned and designed with knowledge of students, including evidence-based practices and strategies, and offer learning goals and instructional activities that are directly related to expectations for what a student should know and be able to do at the end of the instructional chunk.
Goal of Discipline	Belief that the goal of discipline is to teach students to be in control of themselves and to choose socially and morally responsible behavior because it is the right thing to do, not because of fear of punishment or hope of reward. Belief that teaching students self-discipline and self-control develops goal-setting, problem-solving, and critical thinking skills and helps them to become good citizens who exhibit prosocial behaviors and demonstrate respect for self, others, and property.
Goodness of Student Intentions	Belief that educators should hold and communicate positive beliefs and expectations for all students, including those who may have different values than they do; are culturally, racially, or socioeconomically different from them; who appear disengaged and unmotivated; or who struggle and misbehave. Belief that problem behaviors result from unmet needs or lack of skills rather than the student's character, family background, or intention to do harm.

Nature of Learning	Belief that learning is cognitively constructed and relies on social, emotional, and cooperative processes. Belief that learning builds on prior knowledge, is facilitated through choice and through understanding of students' context and interests, and becomes transferrable to a new context when there is an emphasis on process as well as outcome. Belief that changes in the learner happen because of the learning experience.
Purpose of Education	Belief that the purpose of education is to build in students a social consciousness and a strong sense of self, to cultivate the attitudes and dispositions of good citizenship, and to teach students to participate in the democratic process. Belief that education should provide new experiences and open windows for students to see and pursue a bright future for themselves, their families, and their local and global communities. Belief that the purpose of education is to enable students to read, speak, write, and listen well; to work well with numbers and technology; to think, reason, wonder, and be curious; to appreciate and value music, art, culture, movement, and athletics; and to manage themselves and know how to cooperate well with others.
Role of Social and Emotional Skills in Learning	Belief that the social and emotional curriculum has equal weight as the core academic curriculum and that social and emotional learning includes (a) school and classroom environments that support the development of social and emotional learning skills and (b) time and resources given for explicit instruction in social and emotional skill development.
Role of School and Classroom Environment	Belief that the school and classroom are a community in which all students belong, can operate autonomously and responsibly, and feel represented, welcome, and accepted as members of the school and academic community.

Imagine the power of a school community in which all educators consciously share these eight powerful beliefs and strive to ensure that their words and actions align with those beliefs. That kind of community would need to commit to continued exploration, collaboration, and reflection—an ongoing learning cycle that supports these shared beliefs and the teachers who hold them.

Building Shared Beliefs

Collective efficacy doesn't happen overnight. It's something school communities have to work toward and constantly fine-tune. You might find yourself in a school community where you have a different mindset or belief system from those around you. Feeling alone or different from your colleagues can be frustrating and discouraging. How do you create a community of colleagues from the ground up? Start by making a connection with one person from your school. See the next section, "Professional Growth," for ideas that can help build these bonds.

Exploring your own implicit biases and beliefs is deeply personal work, and it can have powerful results for you and your students. It's not easy, and it is a particular challenge to address in isolation. Finding colleagues or, even better, a whole school community committed to embracing this work will make it even more engaging and effective. Remember to have empathy for yourself as you go through this reflective process. You will be learning new ways of thinking about the world and your place in it, and there will be moments of discomfort and disquiet. That's an important part of the learning process, and going through it allows us to make stronger, more meaningful connections on the other side. Give yourself the same grace and patience you offer your students. Just like them, you are learning, growing, and changing through this work.

Professional Growth

Whether it's learning more about your students and their families, discovering new books and resources to bring into the classroom, honing instructional approaches, exploring new information in a content area, or finding the answer to a student question, there is always more to learn when it comes to teaching. The most effective teachers are those who are eager to delve more deeply into the art and practice of teaching, and who are always ready to try something new or consider an idea from a new perspective.

In the same way that we encourage our students to take the initiative to ask questions and seek answers, it's important to support our own continued growth and learning. Professional growth feeds your curiosity, challenges your brain, and makes you a better teacher. It's also a great opportunity to model your own learning for your students. Learning more about new approaches can ultimately help you work smarter, not harder! However, with school schedules only getting busier and busier, professional learning is often something many educators put off until another time. So how can you make time to dive more deeply into a topic when your daily schedule barely has time for lunch?

The Gift of Time

Kirsten Lee Howard, coauthor of *Empowering Educators*, grades K, 1, 2

Years ago, my partner and I were brand-new parents to a tiny baby. We were overwhelmed navigating our new life as parents. We'd already figured out how to be full-time working adults, but we suddenly had a tiny person we wanted to spend time with, so staying an hour or two late at work or going out of town for a workshop were no longer attractive options.

One night, as I was trying to get work done at 10:30 p.m. after an evening of family time and rocking the baby to sleep, I lamented, "I just need five full hours to get stuff done!" At first, that seemed like an impossible wish, but the more we talked about it, the more realistic it became. It turned out that if we took time to plan for it, each of us could have one monthly catch-up night.

That night became a gift of time. I worked it out with the administration and the custodial staff at my school so they knew to expect me. Once a month, I'd either order dinner or pack one, say goodbye to my students at dismissal, shut my classroom door, and have several uninterrupted hours to accomplish what I needed to do. Some nights, that meant organizing the space and rotating stations, while other nights, it was deeper learning and planning for the future.

Because I would schedule the time in advance, I could keep a running list of tasks for my catch-up night, which also helped me prioritize valuable time during the school day for planning lessons and making adjustments to the learning my students were doing. It was so freeing to keep a small bin in the classroom for catch-up night and give myself permission to focus on other tasks until then. By the end of the night, I would be exhausted but exhilarated. Walking into the classroom the next morning and seeing all I had accomplished the night before gave me such satisfaction.

In the grand scheme of things, I don't always advocate for teachers spending long nights at school—we often do too much of that—but for me, planning for one long night every four to five weeks gave me a sense of balance. When I was at home, I could focus on my family, and when I was at school, I could use my time fully and well.

When we think about professional growth and development, we often think of formal opportunities like doing graduate work, taking a course or workshop, or participating in schoolwide learning. These options are valid, useful, and interesting, but they also require an investment of time and money that means they are not choices we can make every day. Luckily, there are many other, informal ways to incorporate professional learning and growth into your busy schedule.

You don't need to wait for scheduled professional development days to begin exploring the options available to you for learning and growth. Informal opportunities for professional growth are all around us, from free webinars to meaningful reading material to insightful colleagues. The following are some easily accessible and often free ways to support your own growth as an educator that can work with your schedule and that you can tailor to your particular needs and interests:

- **Find a mentor.** Perhaps, as a new teacher, you were lucky enough to be assigned a mentor teacher—someone to guide you, answer questions, offer advice and insights, bounce ideas off of, and more. If not, don't let that stop you! A professional mentor can be a colleague you have worked with, a match through your college alumni network, a connection you make at a workshop or conference, or even someone you've never met but find through mutual friends, shared interests or experiences, or social media. Wherever they come from, mentors are an invaluable resource for building confidence, offering guidance, and supporting your growth.

- **Observe other classrooms—and welcome observers into your own.** Watching other teachers in action is one of the best ways to learn. You might choose to observe your own students with a special subject teacher, visit the classrooms of colleagues who teach in the grades above and below you, seek out grade-level colleagues, or even observe someone who teaches content completely different from yours. Classroom observations don't have to be long—just ten or fifteen minutes can often be enough. If peer observations aren't already part of your school's routine, you can suggest this practice to your administrator as a free and effective way for colleagues to learn from one another. If you have breaks during your teaching schedule, you might be able to work in an observation or two each term on your own. Most colleagues will be flattered that you are interested in observing them, and they may want the chance to see you in action, as well. It's a great opportunity to discuss your practice with a trusted colleague and learn from their insights.

- **Read, listen, and watch.** There are more amazing books, podcasts, videos, and webinars available to educators now than ever before. Many are free, but many of those that aren't are affordable and worth the investment. Whether it's social and emotional learning, culturally responsive teaching, brain-based strategies, approaches for different content areas, or something else, the resources are robust and readily available. You can read, listen, and watch independently, or find a colleague or two to start an informal book group or discussion to further build on your learning.

- **Think outside the box.** Learning a new skill, delving more deeply into a hobby, or reading about something completely outside of education can inform your teaching in unexpected ways. When you take on the role of the learner rather than the teacher, you have the chance to experience your own natural learning cycle, understand your cognitive approach in different ways, and develop empathy for what your students experience on a daily basis in your classroom. Plus, it's fun to learn something new and to make connections to your prior knowledge and experience.

- **Intentionally seek others' perspectives.** Whether it's on social media or in real life, we can easily find ourselves in a bubble with people who share our viewpoints and backgrounds. Consciously reaching out to people outside that bubble can be an eye-opening experience. A first step toward this goal could be diversifying the media you consume—those you follow on social media, what you watch and listen to—to include new voices and perspectives that could add to your learning.

- **Look at your curriculum through a new lens.** At some point in your planning for the next school year, term, or unit, you will likely take some time to review the lesson plans and student-facing resources that you use in your classroom. That's the perfect moment to look at your lessons and curriculum through a new lens. You might ask yourself:

- "How can I link this content to current events to make real-life connections?"

- "What perspectives are missing from this lesson? Whose stories aren't being told?"

- "Where can I add opportunities for students to engage with each other and learn both actively and interactively?"

- **Create your own professional learning community.** Many schools build professional learning communities, or PLCs, into their annual professional development work. PLCs can be a wonderful way to connect with colleagues and explore resources relevant to your school or district. You can also build your own PLC with colleagues who share interests, goals, and questions that are similar to yours. With so many online resources and connections available, your PLC can be local or global, in person or virtual, and short or long term. Learning alongside other practitioners can be an effective way to add to your teacher toolbox.

- **Set and track professional goals for yourself.** There are so many opportunities for professional learning out there that it's easy to become daunted. Identifying one or two professional goals to focus on each year, and then breaking those goals up into actionable steps, is one way to approach your professional learning. Sharing these goals with a mentor or a PLC can also be an effective way to collaborate on, and stay on top of, achieving these goals.

No matter how many years you have been teaching, there is always more to learn. Sometimes it seems like the more you learn, the more you realize there is to learn! Professional learning is also a wonderful way to expand your interests, connect with colleagues all over the globe, and of course, better meet the needs of your students. In addition, the knowledge and resources that come with that learning can go a long way to helping you feel confident, effective, and hopeful in your teaching practice, even when facing a challenge.

Taking Care of Yourself

Teaching is one of the most challenging and rewarding professions out there. Educators take on and deal with so much each and every day. We stay up late thinking of ways to help struggling students, stay after school planning engaging activities, and spend our free time reading books like this one—all in an effort to be the best teachers we can be for our students.

This work can take a physical and emotional toll, and summer break is simply not enough time to recharge batteries that are fully drained after an intense school year. You know yourself and what you need to be at your best. Think about what you already do to take care of yourself. Are you someone who needs a solid eight hours of sleep every night? Do you need to take a walk every day? A quiet cup of coffee in the morning? A few minutes to unwind with a favorite podcast? Everyone rejuvenates in different ways; what's important is that you find a way that works for you.

What Is Self-Care?

Lisa Dewey Wells, coauthor of *Empowering Educators*, grades K, 1, 2

Self-care tends to get a pretty shiny, exciting, and enticing reputation. But it doesn't have to be about a spa day, massage, or weekend with your best friends (unless that's what works for you!). A simple, practical, and nourishing way to think about self-care revolves around two key elements: it's something you do just for yourself, and it's intentional.

I know a parent who uses dinner prep time to put on headphones and listen to a favorite podcast. For her, that's self-care. I know countless people who get up early to run or swim, and that's their self-care. It doesn't matter what you do to refill your cup and nourish yourself, but devoting just a few minutes each day to intentionally doing something just for you can help strengthen you for the heavy lifting of teaching and caring for others. Self-care can be as simple as:

- Moving (walk, swim, yoga, tennis, dancing)
- Resting (a quick nap in the afternoon or cutting back on binge-watching or social media scrolling to get just a few more minutes of sleep)
- Laughing (alone, with friends, with your students)
- Creating (knitting, building, painting, preparing a meal)
- Breathing (slowly and deeply on your own, with an app, or in a class)
- Connecting (being truly present with just yourself or with someone you care about)

If you're looking for more ideas for self-care routines, the following are some tips we've compiled for practices you can embed in your daily life so that self-care is something you do every day:

- **Take care of your physical body.** Simple things like replacing soda with water, choosing healthy snacks, decreasing your sugar intake, adding more water to your diet, or getting enough sleep can make a huge difference in how you feel physically. When your body feels energized, it has a positive impact on your thoughts and feelings.

- **Talk about it.** It's important and healthy to talk about your thoughts, feelings, and experiences. Think of it like a balloon; if we don't let air out of our balloons by talking about things, eventually we pop. Make and take time to talk to someone (family member, friend, colleague) about your work. Sometimes a colleague who doesn't teach what you teach can be the best sounding board. When you have a trusted relationship, it provides the ability to brainstorm, discuss, and confide, supporting your own emotional well-being. There is also an active and enthusiastic online community of educators on social media platforms that offers valuable connection, support, and ideas no matter where you are. Now more than ever, we're recognizing the part mental health plays in overall wellness. If you're feeling overwhelmed, distressed, or anxious, consider consulting a healthcare professional. Many schools offer employee assistance programs with counseling, and your insurance provider or local community will also have resources. You don't have to go it alone.

- **Look for ways to bring joy to your day.** Even in a job you love, there will be days that are less exciting and happy than others. When those days happen, it is important to have a few strategies to call on to boost yourself up. You might need to step outside to get some fresh air on days that are particularly stressful or run to the local coffee shop during lunch. Maybe you need to set aside a few minutes to do a quick mindfulness exercise. On days that are hard, ask yourself, "What can I do today to take care of myself? What will bring me joy today?"

- **Use energizers.** Consider incorporating a fun energizer into your teaching when things feel tense. These activities only take a short time, but often those few minutes of fun and activity are all it takes to bring a smile back to your face. Using this strategy can also be a teachable moment for your students. On a demanding day, for instance, you might say, "I'm noticing that my mind is wandering. I think I need a quick break to refocus and recharge. Let's play Double This, Double That together."

Finding a Healthy Balance

Andy Moral

A few school years ago, I struggled with maintaining a healthy balance between my professional life and personal life. Many days, I would come home after a long day feeling exhausted, emotionally drained, and irritable. These feelings, coupled with what seemed like a never-ending to-do list, had me questioning whether I was nearing the point of teacher burnout.

I spent the following summer identifying ways to recalibrate my mental health. With time to recharge and reenergize, I felt great heading into the next school year, but I worried about supporting my well-being as the year progressed. I knew I couldn't wait until summer break to rejuvenate; I needed to dedicate time to taking care of myself throughout the school year and even during the school day. That year, I set a few goals for myself. I tried to:

- **Focus on the five senses.** When you set up your classroom space, be sure to incorporate homey touches that make your workspace a welcoming, comfortable environment. A favorite water bottle, a beautiful plant, or a funny family photo will bring a sense of calm or a smile to your face during the day.

- **Support the need for social interaction.** Teachers share the same needs for social interaction their students have! Connect with teammates and colleagues in your building—have lunch together, join a committee together, or work together on planning a student project.

- **Practice being grateful**. At the end of the school day, maybe before you leave your classroom or during your commute home, identify something you are happy about from that day with students. You could even jot a note about it in your plan book to keep a record of these important moments.

- **Create healthy boundaries.** Be cognizant of the amount of time spent outside the school day working on school tasks. Taking steps like setting a time at night when you no longer check email until the following morning will preserve a healthy separation between home and work.

Incorporating these strategies into my days has helped me stay better calibrated in my professional and personal life. Find out what works best for you to support your well-being, avoid teacher burnout, and be the best teacher that you can be.

- **Put quiet time on the schedule.** Quiet time is an after-lunch practice that allows students to make a quiet, independent choice. Teachers look forward to those five to ten minutes to take deep breaths, relax, and prepare for the afternoon possibly more than the students! Try allowing for quiet time after lunch or lunch recess if you feel a small break might benefit you in taking care of yourself during the school day.

- **If you need a break, take a break.** With some preliminary arrangement, you can lean on your colleagues for support and let them lean on you. If you need a break, you can let your colleagues know, and they can step in for you for a moment while you grab a drink of water, make a cup of coffee, or go outside for a few seconds.

- **Notice the positives.** We often focus on the negatives—what didn't go well, what we shouldn't have said—and skip over the positives. There's great benefit to dwelling on those positive moments and reminding ourselves of all the good and growth we witness in our daily work. You can build this practice into your weekly schedule with a routine like jotting down your "wins of the week" (WOW) in your planner to help develop the habit of identifying and reflecting on the positives. Another positive practice is creating a smile file, a place to stash those one-of-a-kind, tug-at-your-heart notes, artwork, and messages from students, families, or even administrators and colleagues. On difficult days, you can pull out your smile file and remember why you do this, that you can do this, and that there are always better days ahead.

- **Step away.** In the evenings and on the weekends, it's easy to be tempted to keep working. There are always lessons to prepare, emails to respond to, and assignments to review. Remember, though, that taking care of yourself so you can be there for your students is what's most important during those off-duty times. Take time to step away so that you can return with renewed strength and perspective.

Focus on Ta-Das, Not To-Dos

Kirsten Lee Howard, coauthor of *Empowering Educators*, grades K, 1, 2

I have a former colleague and good friend with whom I have a lot in common. We're both wildly energetic, very positive, and truly love teaching. We also both used to have way too much stuff, and packing up our classrooms at the end of the school year was quite a process. It took us both longer than we would have liked.

It was difficult, too, being around others that were quite efficient and quick at packing up. Well-meaning colleagues would stop by to say goodbye for the summer and might comment, "Oh, you still have quite a lot to do."

After one of those experiences, I appeared in my friend's doorway in tears. I knew I still had a lot to do. Being reminded of it had shaken me out of my can-do mindset, and I was overwhelmed.

She empathized because she'd been in that situation, too. We walked back to my classroom and looked around. She pointed out everything she could see that I had already done. It helped a lot to be able to focus on what I had done: my ta-das rather than my to-dos. We went back to her classroom and pointed out all of the things that she had done, as well. We both jumped back into packing up with a better mindset and a lighter heart.

It became an end-of-the-year tradition for us to stop by each other's rooms and say, "Wow! Look how much you have done already!" We don't even live in the same state anymore, but to this day, more than fifteen years later, one of us always texts the other sometime in June to say: "Your classroom looks great! You're almost finished!"

Communication Self-Care

Becky Wanless, coauthor of *Empowering Educators*,
grades K, 1, 2

It was around 10:00 p.m. and I was getting ready to call it a
night when I heard my phone ding. It was an email from a parent,
who was clearly very upset over a situation that had happened at school
that day. She gave few details about the situation and demanded
I call her immediately. I was left wondering what she was talking about as
I reread her email countless times. Needless to say, I couldn't sleep at all that night.

I arrived at school the next day bright and early, an extra-large coffee in hand, having had little sleep and feeling nervous. I took a deep breath, reminded myself to be curious, and made a
call to the parent. There had been a situation at lunch that involved another student in a different
class. The situation had ultimately been resolved by a lunch teacher, but it hadn't been shared
with me. The parent had been taken aback when her child shared what had happened and
was upset that she had not been contacted. I listened to her concerns and reassured her that I
would gather more information and call her back later that day so we would both have the full
story. We ended the conversation on a positive note, and later that day I was able to provide
more details about what had happened.

While this situation was ultimately straightforward to resolve, I literally lost sleep over it. I'd
spent ten hours in a panic, and I wasn't going to let that happen again. That was the moment I
set up some healthy communication boundaries. I immediately removed my school email from
my cell phone.

While it is tempting to check or respond to emails at night or make a quick parent phone call,
you also need to unplug from the school day and allow yourself time and permission to
recharge and take care of yourself. You spend the day giving your all to families, students, and
colleagues. Whatever emails are in your inbox after the school day is done can wait.

Removing your school email from personal devices and setting clear communication boundaries with families (and colleagues) about availability can be two of the best things for your mental well-being. Here are some tips for communication self-care:

- **Communicate your hours of availability.** "I will respond to emails from 9:30 to 10:00
  a.m. and from 3:30 to 4:00 p.m. I am busy teaching during other hours of the day. If you
  have an emergency, please call the office at . . ."

- **Let families know that you are unable to respond to emails during the evening.** "I
  am unable to respond to emails after 4:00 p.m. as I am spending time with my family" or "I am
  unable to respond to emails after 5:00 p.m., as I am likely resting and rejuvenating from a day
  full of joy and learning."

- **Give families a time frame in which to expect a response.** "While I try to respond to all
  emails in a timely manner, it might take twenty-four hours for you to receive a response."

In the same way that we work so hard each and every day to make sure our students have what they need to be successful academically, socially, and emotionally, we also need to make sure we have the same support in place for ourselves. To best help our students, we need to take care of ourselves first. When educators are empowered to create healthy classrooms that are developmentally responsive and effectively managed, with positive communities and engaging academics, all students can succeed.

Pause and Ponder

- Where do you see yourself in the C.A.R.E.S. competency spectrums? How does that help you understand your social and emotional tendencies?

- How will you maintain your awareness of your teacher leadership style and the message it sends to others?

- Which one of the eight teacher beliefs that promote social and emotional learning do you feel most connected to? Which one would you like to spend more time with?

- What goal do you have for your professional growth for this school year? How can you plan backward from that goal to set smaller, incremental goals throughout the year to help yourself reach that milestone?

- Which everyday tip for self-care would you like to work into your routine?

Final Thought

"Our words can shape identities. What we say to others can deeply affect their sense of who they are and who they might become. The words of a teacher may have special power in this regard."

—Paula Denton, *The Power of Our Words*

Appendix

Closing Circles

A closing circle is a strategy for bringing a peaceful end to the school day. It doesn't take very long—students gather for five to ten minutes to do a brief activity or two—but it has a big impact on students' learning and behavior and the classroom climate.

What takes place during the few minutes of a closing circle can vary from class to class and from day to day. A closing circle can help build trust and cooperation in the classroom, which in turn sets the stage for students to do their best learning. Here are just a few things a class might do:

- Sing a song together
- Think about an accomplishment from their day
- Set a personal goal for the following day
- Play a game
- Send a friendly goodbye around the circle

The common thread that runs through these activities is their focus on the positive. It's a time to wrap up the day in a way that leaves students feeling calm, competent, and upbeat about their learning.

Energizers

Energizers are quick, whole-group activities that can be done anytime in the school day. Energizers are a playful, purposeful way to incorporate physical exercise and mental stimulation into even the most tightly scheduled classroom days. Here are some of our favorites for students in third, fourth, and fifth grades.

Double This, Double That

Preparing Students for Success

- Practice saying the chant together.

- Model and practice actions for each motion with a partner, emphasizing that all motions need to be gentle.

- Begin slowly!

- Talk about respectful ways to support partners who need help learning the words and motions.

Words and Actions

Hold hands in loose fists up in front of you at about chin level.

Double Double	Tap pinkie side of fists twice against pinkie side of partner's fists.
This This!	Tap palms twice against partner's palms.
Double Double	Tap pinkie side of fists twice against pinkie side of partner's fists.
That That!	Tap back of hands twice against back of partner's hands.
Double This!	Tap fists once against partner's fists and then palms once against partner's palms.
Double That!	Tap fists once against partner's fists and then back of hands once against back of partner's hands.
Double Double	Tap pinkie side of fists twice against pinkie side of partner's fists.
This That!	Tap palms once against partner's palms and then tap back of hands once against back of partner's hands.

Human Protractor

Actions

Begin with everyone standing, arms stretched straight up in the air. Then have the group touch their toes. Tell the children they're going to straighten up gradually, keeping their arms straight out in front of their bodies. At the same time, you'll be calling out numbers between one and twenty. When you reach twenty, the children's arms will again be straight up in the air. Tell the children to try to remember where their hands and arms are for each number.

Now randomly call out numbers between 1 and 20 as the children raise their bodies to roughly the same position they used for each number the first time through.

When the children are confident with the activity, invite one of them to lead it.

Note: If you decide to do math problems, remember energizers are intended to be playful and fun, so don't get too caught up in the problem-solving process. Be sure to include easy problems or call out plain old numbers in between the problems.

Silent Birthday Lineup

Challenge students to line up according to their month and day of birth, without any talking.

Shake It Down!

Preparing Students for Success

Invite students to share ways to maintain balance and self-control while staying in one place.

Words and Actions

Chant and count with vigor!

1, 2, 3, 4, 5, ... 16!
Stand and lift your right hand up high and shake it sixteen times
Repeat three times—with left hand, right foot, left foot

Cut!
Slice or cut right hand down on left palm

1, 2, 3, 4, 5, 6, 7, 8!
Lift your right hand up high and shake it eight times
Repeat three times—with left hand, right foot, left foot

Cut!
Slice or cut right hand down on left palm

1, 2, 3, 4!
Lift your right hand up high and shake it four times
Repeat three times—with left hand, right foot, left foot

Cut!
Slice or cut right hand down on left palm

1, 2!
Lift your right hand up high and shake it twice
Repeat three times—with left hand, right foot, left foot

Cut!
Slice or cut right hand down on left palm

1!
Lift your right hand up high and shake it once
Repeat three times—with left hand, right foot, left foot

Cut!
Slice or cut right hand down on left palm

Shake it down!
Shake whole body from top to bottom!

Sparkle

How to Do It

Students should form a circle. One student will be the spelling word list holder.

1. The list holder chooses a word from the list and says it aloud.

2. A volunteer from the circle begins spelling the word by saying its first letter.

3. The next student in the circle says the second letter, the next student says the third letter, and so forth. The list holder keeps an eye on the word list to make sure the word is being spelled correctly.

4. If anyone makes a mistake, the list holder calls out "Check!" (If the list holder misses the mistake, anyone else in the circle can say "Check.") The student who made the mistake either corrects it or asks for a "lifeline"—help from the group.

5. When the entire word has been spelled correctly, the next student in the circle says "Sparkle" to indicate that the whole word has been spelled correctly.

6. Repeat steps 1–5 for four or five more words.

Guided Discovery

Guided Discovery is an inviting way to introduce students to materials, classroom or school areas, or activities. A teacher might use Guided Discovery to introduce a learning center, such as the library or computer area; a specific material, such as crayons or a compass; or an activity, such as journal writing or quiet time.

A Guided Discovery consists of five steps:

1. **Introduction**—The teacher names the material, area, or activity in a way that piques students' curiosity.

2. **Generating and modeling ideas**—The teacher asks for children's thoughts on how they might use a material or area or do an activity, and then models a few of their ideas.

3. **Exploration**—Children actively explore and try out various ideas while the teacher observes, reinforces, and redirects if necessary.

4. **Sharing**—Children share their explorations and observations in response to a focused question from the teacher.

5. **Cleanup and care of materials**—When the Guided Discovery is complete, the teacher asks children for ideas on how to put away materials and clean up work areas.

Working with the whole class, small groups, or individuals, teachers can use Guided Discovery both to introduce new materials, activities, and areas, and to help children explore new ways to work with those that are familiar. Offering a Guided Discovery for every material or activity is unnecessary; instead, teachers use it selectively in situations where they want to encourage creative exploration and elicit a wide variety of ideas from students about how to use a material or area or do an activity.

Interactive Learning Structures

Interactive learning structures promote maximum learning because they are both active and interactive. From simple partner chats to more involved small-group discussion formats, these learning structures support students in working together effectively and building up their knowledge base and skill sets. Interactive learning structures give students practice in essential listening, speaking, and thinking skills and in key social skills such as cooperation.

Inside-Outside Circles

This conversation structure is a good way to share information that doesn't require in-depth discussion or to do a quick reflection on an activity or topic.

Skills practiced:
Listening, turn-taking, staying focused and brief when speaking

Directions

1. Students count off by 2s. Ones form a circle, facing out; twos form a circle facing the ones so everyone has a partner.

2. Give a topic for discussion. Partners take turns speaking—allow about one minute for each partner.

3. Give a new topic. Direct students in one of the circles to take a step to their right or left so that everyone has a new partner with whom to discuss the new topic.

Tips for Success

- Model how to move safely into the circles.

- Use an established signal for quiet to get attention before directing students in one of the circles to move.

- Give students the next topic to discuss before directing them to move so they can immediately begin talking with their new partners.

Fishbowl

To reinforce skills the class is learning or knowledge they're gaining, a few students hold a brief mock discussion or demonstration while the rest of the class observes. Afterward, students note key words they heard or actions they observed.

Skills practiced:

Speaking and listening skills, using multiple skills at the same time (such as paraphrasing and expressing partial agreement), using skills learned in one context (such as how to describe a sequential process in language arts) in another (such as math or science)

Directions

1. Prepare the students who will be in the Fishbowl to make sure they can demonstrate the skills or share the knowledge you want to reinforce.

2. Tell the class what to observe. For example: "Watch how your classmates demonstrate backing up their ideas with reasons and evidence."

3. Students demonstrate and classmates watch while you coach as needed.

4. After the demonstration, guide the class discussion to make sure all key points are covered.

5. Give the whole class a chance to discuss what they've heard or to practice the skills they've seen demonstrated, or invite volunteers to do another Fishbowl.

Tips for Success

- Choose a topic that students are interested in or familiar with so they can more easily focus on what they're seeing and hearing.

- Keep it brief—no more than five minutes.

- Choose students purposefully, but be inclusive over time.

- Take part if needed to ensure key skills are included and the conversation or demonstration flows smoothly.

Four Corners

Grouping students according to their preferences or opinions can spark discussions, help students reflect about a variety of topics, and give them a chance to share ideas on topics they care about.

Skills practiced:
Making connections, making a choice, sharing ideas with others

Directions
1. Pose a question to the group and provide four possible responses. Designate one corner of the room for each response.

2. Students move to the corner of their choice.

3. In the corners, students discuss the response their corner represents. They can do this as a small group or in pairs.

Tips for Success
- Decide on the question and possible responses.

  - You might ask a question about aspects of a topic they're studying. ("Which type of fiction do you like best—historical, mystery, fantasy, or humor—and why?")

  - You might present a current event and possible opinions. ("Which environmental issue should be a priority for our city to research and invest in—recycling, alternative forms of transportation such as bicycles or electric cars, alternative forms of energy such as solar or wind, or water conservation?")

- Give students some think time before releasing them to choose a corner.

- Model safe movement.

- Before students go to their chosen corner, let them know whether they'll discuss their response with a small group or a partner.

- Give a focus question for discussion within each corner group; for example, "What's the one big reason you love the genre you chose?" or "What's one book you think might convince other classmates to like your favorite type of fiction?"

Maître d'

The teacher invites students to "tables" of various sizes, where they exchange ideas on a topic. This is a good activity for helping students share a range of ideas or opinions.

Skills practiced:
Listening, turn-taking, staying focused and brief when speaking, moving carefully

Directions
1. Activity begins with students standing in a circle. You call out a grouping (for example, "Table for two") and students form groups with the specified number of members.

2. Give a topic for discussion. Let students know how long they'll have to share.

3. When time is up, announce a new table grouping and new topic.

Tips for Success
- Create your list of discussion topics for the different groupings.

- Use a signal to get attention when it's time to move to a new group.

- Consider giving a thirty-second warning before inviting students to move to a new group.

- Model how to move safely and efficiently into new groupings.

Mix and Mingle to Music

In this lively activity, students have a chance to gather ideas and information from several partners. This is a useful way to share learning about a topic—and to get children moving.

Skills practiced:
Listening, turn-taking, staying focused and brief when speaking, moving carefully

Directions
1. Before doing the activity, students gather information, examples, techniques, or strategies related to a topic.

2. With notes in hand, students move around the room while music plays.

3. When the music stops, they find a partner and each shares one idea or piece of information.

4. Repeat for several rounds.

Tips for Success
- Give students time to consolidate key learning, facts, and ideas before doing the activity.

- Consider providing a note-taking sheet.

- Choose music that's lively enough to energize but not so lively that self-control is challenged.

- Model safe and efficient movement.

Interactive Modeling

Interactive Modeling is a straightforward technique for teaching procedures and routines, such as lining up safely in the classroom, and social and academic skills, such as taking turns speaking and looking up a word in the dictionary. It's a great way to teach any routine or skill that needs to be done in one specific way (for safety, efficiency, or other reasons).

Instead of assuming that if we tell children how to do something enough times, they'll "get it," Interactive Modeling shows students exactly how to do what we expect and gives them a chance to practice meeting those expectations. It has built-in steps that help students notice for themselves the details of how a routine or skill looks and sounds in action, and it provides immediate teacher feedback. This powerful combination of noticing, practicing, and timely feedback enables students to engage more deeply in their learning and to remember more of what they've learned.

Steps of Interactive Modeling:

1. Say what you will model and why.

2. Model the behavior.

3. Ask students what they noticed.

4. Invite one or more students to model.

5. Again, ask students what they noticed.

6. Have all students practice.

7. Provide feedback.

Helpful routines to teach in grades 3, 4, and 5 include:

- Morning Meeting
- Bathroom
- Recess
- Lunch
- Reading/writing workshops

- Student-led recess games
- Individual projects
- Homework
- Group projects
- Cross-grade buddies
- Schoolwide jobs
- Research projects
- Leadership roles

Morning Meeting

Morning Meeting is a twenty- to thirty-minute whole-class gathering at the beginning of each day. The purpose of these meetings is to set a tone for engaged learning in a climate of trust, to build and enhance connections among class members through meaningful interactions and lively activities, and to give students practice in academic and social-emotional skills. Morning Meeting addresses students' basic need to feel a sense of belonging and significance and warms them up for the day of learning ahead.

The four sequential components of Morning Meetings are:

1. **Greeting.** Each child is greeted by name, the most basic way of providing a sense of belonging.

2. **Sharing.** Children share news or information about themselves, which helps them get to know one another and strengthen communication skills.

3. **Group activity.** A whole-group activity reinforces learning and encourages cooperation and inclusion.

4. **Morning message.** A brief note from the teacher to the class further reinforces skills and sparks children's excitement about what they'll be learning that day.

Although the Morning Meeting format is intentionally predictable, there's plenty of room for variation within this format. Meetings vary from class to class, with each meeting reflecting the different styles and goals of individual teachers and classes.

The Birthday Cluster Exercise

(from *Yardsticks* by Chip Wood)

You can use the Birthday Cluster exercise to get an idea of the overall developmental abilities and behaviors you're likely to see in a class. While chronological age does not always correlate directly to developmental age, this exercise is a good place to start in understanding the needs of your students.

Step 1: Create a chronological roster by listing students in the class from youngest to oldest using a "year, month" format (for example: 9 years, 2 months). This will help you easily see the range of ages you will be teaching.

Step 2: Calculate the age of each student on September 1 (beginning of the year) and six months later on March 1 (middle of the year) and add this age to your chart. To make this step a bit easier, consider using an online age calculator or the DATEDIF function in a spreadsheet program.

Step 3: Once you have a completed chronological age chart, take time to see where the birthday clusters lie. Once you've noted birthday clusters and unique scenarios (that is, students who are particularly young or old), begin to ask questions such as the following:

- "What impact might this age cluster have on the classroom?"
- "What do I need to be aware of as we go through the school year?"
- "How might the classroom dynamic change as students get older?"

Step 4: The final step is to use what you've learned to create an optimal learning space for all students. Here are a few tips to consider:

- Reference the birthday cluster document after winter break and in the spring to note any changes you might want to take into consideration. Ask yourself questions such as these:

  o "How might my class change?"

  o "What do I need to be aware of as we move into the next part of the school year?"

  o "Do I need to rethink our classroom space or the way students are partnered?"

- Use the birthday cluster document when problem-solving student behavior or struggles with learning. Consider these questions:

  o "Are the academic expectations I've set developmentally appropriate?"

  o "Is this behavior indicative of a seven-year-old or of an eight-year-old?"

  o "Is this student a young seven-year-old or an older eight-year-old?"

Think about sharing your birthday cluster document with other teachers who work with that group of students (aides, lunch teachers, special area teachers, school counselors).

Sample Schedules

Ideal Schedules for Grade 3

Time	Activity	Time	Activity
8:30–8:45	Arrival routine	8:30–8:40	Arrival routine
8:45–9:15	Morning meeting	8:40–9:00	Morning meeting
9:15–10:00	Reading workshop	9:00–9:45	Math
10:00–10:15	Word study, spelling, and snack	9:45–9:50	Math fact games and activities
10:15–10:30	Whole-class outside game	9:50–10:30	Reading workshop
10:30–11:05	Special	10:30–10:40	Outside whole-class game
11:05–11:20	Math fact games/activities	10:40–10:45	Snack
11:20–12:00	Writing workshop	10:45–11:30	Science and social studies
12:00–12:20	Recess	11:30–12:15	Recess and lunch
12:20–12:40	Lunch	12:15–12:40	Read-aloud
12:40–1:00	Quiet time	12:40–1:30	Writing workshop
1:00–1:50	Math	1:30–1:40	Energizer (movement break)
1:50–2:10	Read-aloud	1:40–2:00	Word study and spelling
2:10–2:15	Energizer (movement break)	2:00–2:15	Catch-up and extensions
2:15–3:00	Science and social studies	2:15–3:00	Special
3:00–3:10	Cleanup and packup	3:00–3:10	Cleanup and packup
3:10–3:15	Closing circle	3:10–3:15	Closing circle
3:15	Dismissal	3:15	Dismissal

Ideal Schedules for Grade 4

8:30–8:40	Arrival routine		8:30–8:40	Arrival routine
8:40–9:00	Morning meeting		8:40–9:00	Morning meeting
9:00–9:50	Writing workshop		9:00–9:50	Writing workshop
9:50–10:20	Word study		9:50–10:20	Word study
10:20–10:30	Outside whole-class game		10:20–10:30	Outside whole-class game
10:30–10:45	Snack		10:30–10:45	Snack
10:45–11:30	Math		10:45–11:30	Math
11:30–12:15	Recess and lunch		11:30–12:15	Recess and lunch
12:15–12:40	Read-aloud		12:15–12:40	Read-aloud
12:40–1:30	Science/social studies		12:40–1:30	Science/social studies
1:30–2:15	Reading workshop		1:30–2:15	Reading workshop
2:15–3:00	Special		2:15–3:00	Special
3:00–3:10	Clean up and pack up		3:00–3:10	Clean up and pack up
3:10–3:15	Closing circle		3:10–3:15	Closing circle
3:15	Dismissal		3:15	Dismissal

Ideal Schedules for Grade 5

8:30–8:40	Arrival routine		8:30–8:40	Arrival routine
8:40–9:00	Morning meeting		8:40–9:05	Morning meeting
9:00–9:55	Math		9:05–10:05	Science
9:55–10:05	Snack break		10:05–10:20	Recess
10:05–11:05	Reading workshop		10:20–11:30	Literacy*
11:05–12:00	Social studies		11:30–12:30	Special
12:00–12:45	Recess and lunch		12:30–1:15	Recess and lunch
12:45–1:05	Read-aloud		1:15–2:15	Math
1:05–1:45	Writing workshop		2:15–3:00	Social studies*
1:45–1:55	Snack break		3:00–3:20	Read-aloud
1:55–2:35	Science or socialstudies		3:20–3:30	Dismissal routine
2:35–3:20	Special		* Students may eat while working during these periods	
3:20–3:30	Dismissal routine			

Sample Parent Communications

Beginning-of-the-Year Survey

Dear Parent/Guardian,

Please take a few minutes to fill out this form and return it to school with your child when it is completed. Your information will help me learn more about your son or daughter. You may check more than one response for each question. Both the survey and your written responses will be strictly confidential. Thank you in advance for your help!

Sincerely,
Mr. Moral

My child usually approaches learning . . .
☐ with curiosity
☐ with confidence
☐ with excitement
☐ with anxiety
☐ with reluctance
☐ without interest

My child learns best . . .
☐ by listening
☐ by watching
☐ by doing
☐ I'm not sure

My child finds it challenging to . . .
☐ pay attention
☐ follow directions
☐ behave appropriately
☐ speak in front of others
☐ work neatly
☐ take risks
☐ work in groups

My child's favorite subject(s) is (are)...

_____

_____

How would you describe your child's reading habits? My child...
- ☐ enjoys reading with others
- ☐ enjoys reading alone
- ☐ reads well, but is reluctant to read
- ☐ does not read on his/her own

When it comes to writing, my child...
- ☐ loves to write
- ☐ dislikes writing
- ☐ writes well, but is reluctant to write
- ☐ has difficulty getting started

When completing homework assignments, my child...
- ☐ finishes quickly
- ☐ works at a good pace
- ☐ works slowly
- ☐ works without assistance
- ☐ works with some assistance
- ☐ works with much assistance
- ☐ becomes overwhelmed

When studying for a test, my child...
- ☐ works without assistance
- ☐ works with some assistance
- ☐ works with much assistance
- ☐ doesn't know how to study
- ☐ rarely studies
- ☐ never studies
- ☐ prepares in advance
- ☐ waits until the last minute

When completing homework or studying my child . . .

☐ works in his/her room
☐ sits at a desk
☐ works in a comfortable spot (bed, floor)
☐ works in the kitchen or den
☐ prefers background noise
☐ prefers silence

My child's organizational skills . . .

☐ are excellent
☐ are pretty good
☐ need improvement

When it comes to friendships, my child . . .

☐ has one or two close friends
☐ has many close friends
☐ finds it difficult to meet new friends
☐ finds it easy to meet new friends
☐ is worried about meeting friends in this class

My child's special talents, abilities, and interests include . . .

_____

_____

Parent Volunteer Checklist

Volunteer Name:
Child's Name:
Phone Number:
Email:

Circle the way(s) you would like to help our classroom:

- Copy
- Laminate
- Cut/Paste
- File
- Work on bulletin boards
- Work on projects from home
- Work with small groups
- Work with individuals
- Organize events
- Other:
- No preference

Circle the day(s) that work best for you:

- Monday
- Tuesday
- Wednesday
- Thursday
- Friday

Building a Diverse Classroom Library

To grow your classroom library, talk with other teachers, librarians, parents, and students to discover additional books and authors and to build your community of readers. Utilize social media and search the hashtags #classroombookaday and #WeNeedDiverseBooks for titles. The following websites are also a great resource for expanding any library:

African American Literature Book Club
https://aalbc.com/

Association for Library Service to Children (ALSC):
https://www.ala.org/alsc/

Caldecott Medal Books
https://www.ala.org/alsc/awardsgrants/bookmedia/caldecott

Colorín Colorado: A bilingual site for educators
and families of English language learners
https://www.colorincolorado.org

Coretta Scott King Medal Books
https://www.ala.org/awardsgrants/coretta-scott-king-book-awards

Lee and Low: Diverse book publisher for young readers
https://www.leeandlow.com/

Pura Belpré Medal Books
https://www.ala.org/alsc/awardsgrants/bookmedia/belpre

Robert F. Sibert Informational Book Medal
https://www.ala.org/alsc/awardsgrants/bookmedia/sibert

Bates College Diverse BookFinder
https://www.diversebookfinder.org

We Need Diverse Books
https://www.diversebooks.org

Social Justice Books: A Teaching for Change Project
https://www.socialjusticebooks.org/booklists

Recommended Books for Grades 3–5

Whether you are beginning to establish your garden of books or are weeding and adding to your collection, to your classroom library continues to grow each year. The following lists are recommendations for you and your students to consider—knowing that the students in each group you teach bring their own unique needs and interests that will inform your selection.

An asterisk next to the title indicates that the book is a title in a series.

Read-Aloud Books

Wishtree by Katherine Applegate

The Wild Robot by Peter Brown

Fish in a Tree by Lynda Mullaly Brown

Out of My Mind by Sharon Draper

Pax by Sara Pennypacker, illustrated by Jon Klassen

Wonder by R.J. Palacio

Ghost by Jason Reynolds

Charlotte's Web by E.B. White, illustrated by Garth Williams

A Wrinkle in Time by Madeleine L'Engle

Bridge to Terabithia by Katherine Paterson, illustrated by Donna Diamond

Charlie and the Chocolate Factory by Roald Dahl

Hatchet by Gary Paulsen

Holes by Louis Sachar

The Lightning Thief by Rick Riordan

Rules by Cynthia Lord

Walk Two Moons by Sharon Creech

Picture Books for Beginning of the Year and Hopes and Dreams

The Curious Garden by Peter Brown

All Because You Matter by Tami Charles, illustrated by Bryan Collier

Drum Dream Girl by Margarita Engle, illustrated by Rafael López

I Promise by LeBron James, illustrated by Nina Mata

Matthew's Dream by Leo Lionni

The Invisible Boy by Trudy Ludwig, illustrated by Patrice Barton

A New Alphabet for Humanity by Leesa McGregor, illustrated by Daniela Sosa

Because by Mo Willems

The Day You Begin by Jacqueline Woodson, illustrated by Rafael López

Rain School by James Rumford

The Most Magnificent Thing by Ashley Spires

The Dot by Peter H. Reynolds

Flight School by Lita Judge

What Do You Do With a Chance? by Kobi Yamada, illustrated by Mae Besom

What Do You Do With an Idea? by Kobi Yamada, illustrated by Mae Besom

What Do You Do With a Problem? by Kobi Yamada, illustrated by Mae Besom

I Can't Do That, YET by Esther Pia Cordova, illustrated by Maima W Adiputri

Your Fantastic Elastic Brain by JoAnn Deak, illustrated by Sarah Ackerley

How to Catch a Star by Oliver Jeffers

A Splash of Red: The Life and Art of Horace Pippin by Jen Bryant, illustrated by Melissa Sweet

Ruby's Wish by Shirin Yim Bridges, illustrated by Sophie Blackall

Graphic Novels

Knights of the Lunch Table: The Dodgeball Chronicles by Frank Cammuso

El Deafo by Cece Bell

The Baby-Sitters Club: Kristy's Great Idea adapted and illustrated by Raina Telgemeier, written by Ann M. Martin

Baby Mouse #1: Queen of the World by Jennifer L. Holm and Matthew Holm

Amulet #1: The Stonekeeper by Kazu Kibuishi

Lunch Lady and the Cyborg Substitute by Jarrett J. Krosoczka

*Dog Man series by Dav Pilkey

Sidekicks by Dan Santat

Smile by Raina Telgemeier

When Stars Are Scattered by Victoria Jamieson and Omar Mohamed

Drawn Together by Minh Lê, illustrated by Dan Santat

Historical Fiction

Bud, Not Buddy by Christopher Paul Curtis

Sarah, Plain and Tall by Patricia MacLachlan

Molly's Pilgrim by Barbara Cohen

Dragonwings by Lawrence Yep

Number the Stars by Lois Lowry

Out of the Dust by Karen Hesse

Roll of Thunder, Hear My Cry by Mildred D. Taylor

Sadako and the Thousand Paper Cranes by Eleanor Coerr, illustrated by Ronald Himler

The Breadwinner by Deborah Ellis

One Crazy Summer by Rita Williams-Garcia

Fantasy

The Magic Tree House Series by Mary Pope Osbourne

11 Birthdays by Wendy Mass

The Bad Beginning by Lemony Snicket

The Phantom Tollbooth by Norton Juster, illustrated by Jules Feiffer

Where the Mountain Meets the Moon by Grace Lin

Breadcrumbs by Anne Ursu, illustrated by Erin McGuire

Poetry and Novels in Verse

Out of Wonder: Poems Celebrating Poets by Kwame Alexander with Chris Colderley and Marjory Wentworth, illustrated by Ekua Holmes

*The Crossover by Kwame Alexander

*Love That Dog by Sharon Creech

*Like Pickle Juice on a Cookie by Julie Sternberg, illustrated by Matthew Cordell

*The Poetry Friday Anthology for Celebrations by Silvia Vardell and Janet Wong

Dictionary for a Better World: Poems, Quotes, and Anecdotes from A to Z by Irene Latham and Charles Waters, illustrated by Mehrdokht Amini

Inside Out and Back Again by Thanhhà Lai

The Dreamer by Pam Muñoz Ryan, illustrated by Peter Sís

Harlem by Walter Dean Myers, illustrated by Christopher Myers

Life Doesn't Frighten Me by Maya Angelou, paintings by Jean-Michel Basquiat, edited by Sara Jane Boyers

Informational Texts and Other Nonfiction

Counting on Katherine: How Katherine Johnson Saved Apollo 13 by Helaine Becker, illustrated by Dow Phumiruk

DK Eyewitness Books from Penguin Random House

Hidden Figures: The True Story of Four Black Women and the Space Race by Margot Lee Shetterly, illustrated by Laura Freeman

*Kid Scientists: True Tales of Childhood from Scientist Superstars by David Stabler, illustrated by Anoosha Syed

The Girl Who Drew Butterflies: How Maria Merian's Art Changed Science by Joyce Sidman

*Weird But True! series by National Geographic Kids

*Who Was? series by Who HQ

What Color Is My World? The Lost History of African American Inventors by Kareem Abdul-Jabbar and Raymond Obstfeld, illustrated by Ben Boos and A.G. Ford

Stamped (For Kids): Racism, Antiracism, and You adapted by Sonja Cherry-Paul, text by Ibram X. Kendi and Jason Reynolds, illustrated by Rachelle Baker

Paper Son: The Inspiring Story of Tyrus Wong, Immigrant and Artist by Julie Leung, illustrated by Chris Sasaki

References

American Federation of Teachers and Badass Teachers Association. 2017. *2017 Educator Quality of Work Life Survey.* Washington, DC: American Federation of Teachers. https://www.aft.org/sites/default/files/2017_eqwl_survey_web.pdf.

Bishop, Rudine Sims. 1990. "Mirrors, Windows, and Sliding Glass Doors." *Perspectives: Choosing and Using Books for the Classroom* 6, no. 3 (Summer).

Brown, Ellen. 2018. "Writing Is Third Career for Morrison." *The Cincinnati Enquirer*, September 27, 1981.

Cooperative Children's Book Center. 2019. *CCBC Diversity Statistics.* Madison, WI: Cooperative Children's Book Center. https://ccbc.education.wisc.edu/literature-resources/ccbc-diversity-statistics/.

Denton, Paula. 2008. "Watching and Learning." Responsive Classroom. https://www.responsiveclassroom.org/watching-and-learning/.

Denton, Paula. 2015. *The Power of Our Words: Teacher Language That Helps Children.* 2nd ed. Turners Falls, MA: Center for Responsive Schools.

Diliberti, Melissa Kay, Heather L. Schwartz, and David Grant. 2021. *Stress Topped the Reasons Why Public School Teachers Quit, Even Before COVID-19.* Santa Monica, CA: RAND Corporation. https://doi.org/10.7249/RRA1121-2.

Gallup. 2014. *State of America's Schools: A Path to Winning Again in Education.* Washington, DC: Gallup. http://www.gallup.com/services/178709/state-america-schools-report.aspx.

Goddard, Roger, Yvonne Goddard, Eun Sook Kim, and Robert Miller. 2015. "A Theoretical and Empirical Analysis of the Roles of Instructional Leadership, Teacher Collaboration, and Collective Efficacy Beliefs in Support of Student Learning." *American Journal of Education* 121, no. 4: 501–530. https://doi.org/10.1086/681925.

González, Norma, Luis C. Moll, and Cathy Amanti, eds. 2005. *Funds of Knowledge: Theorizing Practices in Households, Communities, and Classrooms.* New York: Routledge.

Goodenow, Carol. 1993. "Classroom Belonging Among Early Adolescent Students: Relationships to Motivation and Achievement." *Journal of Early Adolescence* 13, no. 1 (February): 21–43. https://doi.org/10.1177/027243 1693013001002.

Hammond, Zaretta. 2019. "Zaretta Hammond on Coaching and Culturally Responsive Teaching." Interview by Anthony Rebora. Turn and Talk. *Educational Leadership* 77, no. 3 (November): 12–13. http://www.ascd. org/publications/educational-leadership/nov19/vol77/num03/Zaret- ta-Hammond-on-Coaching-and-Culturally-Responsive-Teaching.aspx

Hattie, John. "Mindframes and Maximizers." Presentation at the 3rd Annual Visible Learning Conference, Washington, DC, July 2016.

Jones, Stephanie M., and Suzanne M. Bouffard. 2012. "Social and Emotional Learning in Schools: From Programs to Strategies and Commentaries." *Social Policy Report* 26, no. 4 (Winter): 1–33. https://doi. org/10.1002/j.2379-3988.2012.tb00073.x.

Kirwan Institute for the Study of Race and Ethnicity. *Implicit Bias Module Series.* 2018. The Ohio State University and the Schott Foundation for Public Education. Online course. https://kirwaninstitute.osu.edu/ implicit-bias-training.

Ladson-Billings, Gloria. 2009. *The Dreamkeepers: Successful Teachers of African American Children*. 2nd ed. San Francisco: Jossey-Bass.

National Education Association. n.d.. "Racial Justice." EdJustice. https://neaedjustice.org/social-justice-issues/racial-justice/.

New York State Education Department. 2017. *New York State Next Generation English Language Arts Learning Standards*. Albany, NY: New York State Education Department.

Project Implicit. 2011. "Implicit Association Test." https://implicit.harvard.edu/implicit/takeatest.html.

Style, Emily. 1988. "Curriculum as Window and Mirror," *Listening for All Voices*. Summit, NJ: Oak Knoll School.

Vygotsky, Lev S. 1978. *Mind in Society: The Development of Higher Psychological Processes*. Cambridge, MA: Harvard University Press.

Weiss, Heather B., M. Elena Lopez, and Margaret Caspe. 2018. *Joining Together to Create a Bold Vision for Next-Generation Family Engagement: Engaging Families to Transform Education*. New York: Global Family Research Project. https://globalfrp.org/content/download/419/3823/file/GFRP_Family%20Engagement%20Carnegie%20Report.pdf.

Wood, Chip. 2017. *Yardsticks: Child and Adolescent Development Ages 4–14*. 4th ed. Turners Falls, MA: Center for Responsive Schools.

Further Resources

All of the recommended practices in this book come from or are consistent with the *Responsive Classroom* approach to teaching—an evidence-based education approach associated with greater teacher effectiveness, higher student achievement, and improved school climate. *Responsive Classroom* practices help educators build competencies in four interrelated domains: engaging academics, positive community, effective management, and developmentally responsive teaching. To learn more, see the following resources published by Center for Responsive Schools and available at www.responsiveclassroom.org.

Classroom Management: Set up and run a classroom in ways that enable the best possible teaching and learning.

> *Interactive Modeling: A Powerful Technique for Teaching Children* by Margaret Berry Wilson. 2012.

> *Teaching Children to Care: Classroom Management for Ethical and Academic Growth K–8*, revised ed., by Ruth Sidney Charney. 2002.

Morning Meeting: Gather as a whole class each morning to greet each other, share news, and warm up for the day of learning ahead.

> *The Morning Meeting Book*, 3rd ed., by Roxann Kriete and Carol Davis. 2014.

> *80 Morning Meeting Ideas for Grades K–2* by Susan Lattanzi Roser. 2012.

> *80 Morning Meeting Ideas for Grades 3–6* by Carol Davis. 2012.

> *Doing Math in Morning Meeting: 150 Quick Activities That Connect to Your Curriculum* by Andy Dousis and Margaret Berry Wilson. 2010. (Includes a Common Core State Standards correlation guide.)

Doing Science in Morning Meeting: 150 Quick Activities That Connect to Your Curriculum by Lara Webb and Margaret Berry Wilson. 2013. (Includes correlation guides to the Next Generation Science Standards and A Framework for K–12 Science Education, the basis for the standards.)

Doing Language Arts in Morning Meeting: 150 Quick Activities That Connect to Your Curriculum by Jodie Luongo, Joan Riordan, and Kate Umstatter. 2015. (Includes a Common Core State Standards correlation guide.)

Doing Social Studies in Morning Meeting: 150 Quick Activities That Connect to Your Curriculum by Leah Carson and Jane Cofie. 2017. (Includes correlation guides to the National Curriculum Standards for Social Studies—*The Themes of Social Studies, the College, Career, & Civic Life C3 Framework for Social Studies State Standards*, and the Common Core State Standards for English Language Arts.)

Positive Teacher Language: Use words and tone as a tool to promote students' active learning, sense of community, and self-discipline.

The Power of Our Words: Teacher Language That Helps Children Learn, 2nd ed., by Paula Denton, EdD. 2014.

Teacher Language for Engaged Learning: 4 Video Study Sessions. 2013.

Engaging Academics: Learn tools for effective teaching and making lessons lively, appropriately challenging, and purposeful to help students develop higher levels of motivation, persistence, and mastery of skills and content.

The Joyful Classroom: Practical Ways to Engage and Challenge Elementary Students. From *Responsive Classroom* with Lynn Bechtel and Kristen Vincent. 2016.

The Language of Learning: Teaching Students Core Thinking, Speaking, and Listening Skills by Margaret Berry Wilson. 2014.

Make Learning Meaningful: How to Leverage the Brain's Natural Learning Cycle in K–8 Classrooms by Kristen Vincent. 2021.

Teaching Discipline: Use practical strategies, such as rule creation and positive responses to misbehavior, to promote self-discipline in students and build a safe, calm, and respectful school climate.

Teasing, Tattling, Defiance and More: Positive Approaches to 10 Common Classroom Behaviors by Margaret Berry Wilson. 2013.

Teaching Self-Discipline: The Responsive Classroom Guide to Helping Students Dream, Behave, and Achieve in Elementary School. From *Responsive Classroom* with Laurie Badge, Suzy Ghosh, Earl Hunter II, Caitie Meehan, and Cory Wade. 2018.

Responsive School Discipline: Essentials for Elementary School Leaders by Chip Wood and Babs Freeman-Loftis. 2011.

Foundation-Setting During the First Weeks of School: Take time in the critical first weeks of school to establish expectations, routines, a sense of community, and a positive classroom tone.

The First Six Weeks of School, 2nd ed. From *Responsive Classroom*. 2015.

Movement, Games, Songs, and Chants: Sprinkle quick, lively activities throughout the school day to keep students energized, engaged, and alert.

Closing Circles: 50 Activities for Ending the Day in a Positive Way by Dana Januszka and Kristen Vincent. 2012.

Energizers! 88 Quick Movement Activities That Refresh and Refocus by Susan Lattanzi Roser. 2009.

99 Activities and Greetings: Great for Morning Meeting . . . and Other Meetings, Too! by Melissa Correa-Connolly. 2004.

Preventing Bullying at School: Use practical strategies throughout the day to create a safe, kind environment in which bullying is far less likely to take root.

How to Bullyproof Your Classroom by Caltha Crowe. 2012. (Includes bullying prevention lessons.)

Solving Behavior Problems With Children: Engage students in solving their behavior problems so they feel safe, challenged, and invested in changing.

> *Sammy and His Behavior Problems: Stories and Strategies from a Teacher's Year* by Caltha Crowe. 2010.

> *Solving Thorny Behavior Problems: How Teachers and Students Can Work Together* by Caltha Crowe. 2009.

Child Development: Understand children's common physical, social-emotional, cognitive, and language characteristics at each age, and adapt teaching to respond to children's developmental needs.

> *Yardsticks: Child and Adolescent Development Ages 4–14*, 4th ed., by Chip Wood. 2017.

> Yardsticks Guide Series: Common Developmental Characteristics in the Classroom and at Home, Grades K–8 (based on *Yardsticks* by Chip Wood). From *Responsive Classroom*. 2018.

School-Home Connection: Learn a variety of resources and strategies to build effective and positive school-home relationships and collaborate confidently with students' families.

> *Strengthening the Parent-Teacher Partnership* by Jane Cofie. 2021.

Special Area Educators: Explore key *Responsive Classroom* practices adapted for a wide variety of special areas.

> *Responsive Classroom for Music, Art, PE, and Other Special Areas.* From *Responsive Classroom*. 2016.

Professional Development/Staff Meetings: Learn easy-to-use structures for getting the most out of your work with colleagues.

> *Energize Your Meetings! 35 Interactive Learning Structures for Educators.* From *Responsive Classroom*. 2014.

Index

About the Publisher

Center for Responsive Schools, Inc., a not-for-profit educational organization, offers professional development, curriculum, and books and resources to support academic, social, and emotional learning.

Center for Responsive Schools (CRS) is the developer of *Responsive Classroom®*, a research-based education approach associated with greater teacher effectiveness, higher student achievement, and improved school climate, and of Fly Five, a comprehensive social-emotional learning curriculum for kindergarten through eighth grade.

CRS Publishing, the independent publishing arm of Center for Responsive Schools, creates inspiring yet practical books for educators and students to support growth, learning, and success in and out of school.

Center for Responsive Schools' vision is to influence and inspire a world-class education for every student in every school, every day, and to bring hope and joy to educators and students alike. Visit us at crslearn.org to learn more: